MECHANICS·
MERCANTILE
LIBRARY.

Arthur F. Mathews '06

TO THE
LIFE OF
THE SILVER
HARBOR

TO THE LIFE OF THE SILVER HARBOR

EDMUND WILSON AND MARY McCARTHY

ON CAPE COD **REUEL K. WILSON**

University
Press of
New England
Hanover and
London

Published by University Press of New England,
One Court Street, Lebanon, NH 03766
www.upne.com
© 2008 by University Press of New England
Printed in the United States of America
5 4 3 2 1

Library of Congress Cataloging-in-Publication Data
Wilson, Reuel K., 1938–
To the life of the silver harbor : Edmund Wilson and Mary McCarthy
on Cape Cod / Reuel K. Wilson.
    p. cm.
Includes bibliographical references and index.
ISBN 978-1-58465-713-2 (alk. paper)
1. Wilson, Edmund, 1895–1972—Homes and haunts—Massachusetts—Cape
Cod. 2. McCarthy, Mary, 1912–1989—Homes and haunts—Massachusetts—
Cape Cod. 3. Authors, American—20th century—Biography. 4. Critics—United
States—Biography. 5. Cape Cod (Mass.)—Intellectual life—20th century. I. Title.
PS3545.16245Z935   2008   818'.5209—dc22
[B]   2008029049

FRONTISPIECE
*The author with his parents Edmund Wilson and Mary McCarthy in Wellfleet,
Massachusetts, 1943. Special Collections, Vassar College Libraries.*

*Illustration on page 108. © Yale Collection of American Literature,
Beinecke Rare Book and Manuscript Library, Yale University.*

ENDPAPER:
*Coulton Waugh's Map of Provincetown, summer 1928, with its full complement of
artists, writers, and musicians.*

Cape Cod is the bare and bended arm of
Massachusetts: the shoulder is at Buzzard's Bay;
the elbow, or crazy-bone, at Cape Mallebranche
[Monomoy Island, Orleans]; the wrist at Truro;
and the sandy fist at Provincetown.
—Henry David Thoreau, *Cape Cod*

CONTENTS

ACKNOWLEDGMENTS

First and foremost, Bowden Broadwater and Michael Macdonald were indispensable sources of in-depth information on my parent's lives and times. The following people, some now unfortunately deceased, have given me substantial help: Richard Bailey, Bing Bingam, Jonathan Bishop, Gail Cohen, Wendy Hackett, Jack and Marty Hall, Ruth Hatch, Betsey J. Patterson, Elizabeth Groom, Penelope Jencks, Alexandra Kimball, Anna Matson-Hamburger, Mary Meigs, Andrea Petersen-Chermayeff, Ken and Jean Rose, Henry Thornton, Peter and Gloria Watts, Adelaide, Charles, and Daniel Walker, Tom Wallace, and Dan Waterman.

I also owe a debt of thanks to Patricia Willis at Yale's Beinecke Rare Book and Manuscript Library and to Ronald Patkus at the Vassar College Archives and Special Collections. They and their accommodating staff did everything possible to facilitate my research.

My daughter, Sophia Wilson, and my wife, Natsuko, have made important contributions: reading or copying the manuscript at various stages, making critical suggestions, and motivating me to persevere.

Finally, I would like to thank Richard Pult, my editor, for bringing this project to fruition.

INTRODUCTION

Both of my parents, Edmund Wilson and Mary Mc-Carthy, present a formidable challenge to biographers and critics. The oeuvre of each encompasses literary criticism, fiction, autobiography, political journalism, the travelogue—and, in Wilson's case, poetry and the theater. Their creative lives in each case span more than half a century. Wilson's impressive formal education went from the Hill School in Pottstown, Pennsylvania, to Princeton, where he acquired a thorough command of Western literature as well as Latin, Greek, French, Italian, and some German. Later he would learn Russian, Hungarian, and enough Hebrew to read the Torah. Over his lifetime he relentlessly pursued developing interests in new countries and cultures. Because of the scope of his erudition and the breadth of his intellectual horizons, few investigators can approach him from a position of equality. Even Leon Edel, the distinguished biographer and editor of Henry James, who edited in accordance with Wilson's own wishes his journals of the twenties, thirties, forties, and fifties, did not do them full justice. Had Edel been younger when he undertook the daunting task of following Wilson's eyes and ears over four decades, he might have more accurately and informatively elucidated the texts, especially the later ones that the author never had a chance to revise.

In McCarthy's case, the investigator faces another kind of obstacle: how to separate the public from the private persona, the writer of fiction from the self-proclaimed truth teller. Both McCarthy and Wilson led complicated and emotionally fraught lives—which dramatically intersected during their seven-year marriage. Both seemed to court public controversy, and neither could, or would, avoid private scandal. Like so many intellectuals of the twenties and thirties, they held leftist views; neither joined the Communist Party. For a while their sympathies lay with the Trotskyites; both would come out against Stalin and his supporters in the United States. Wilson, however, never renounced his admiration for Lenin, which exasperated some of his best friends, among them Vladimir Nabokov, always a worthy intellectual adversary.

Wilson and McCarthy both single-mindedly furthered the cause of sexual freedom, often with little regard for the feelings of others. By the time they reached their thirties each craved bourgeois security (McCarthy fully attained this only after divorcing Wilson). Both took parenthood seriously, and both thought that children needed structure rather than license. Neither of my parents ever completely gave up old habits. Until his last days Wilson continued to imbibe prodigious amounts of alcohol on an almost daily basis. McCarthy, a lifelong smoker of Lucky Strikes and avid quaffer of preprandial martinis, reduced her consumption of both in later years; nonetheless she died of lung cancer and heart failure. Add to two complicated, sometimes tortured psyches a mile-long list of friends, acquaintances, and family members. As the writers' lives progress, many of the names change; horizons are reset as they move from one marital or creative phase to another. The reader of Wilson's seven autobiographical books—six volumes of journals, plus *Upstate*—meets a cast of hundreds of characters set against a myriad of geographical locations. Over their writing careers Wilson and McCarthy often shifted focus: each tended to choose a subject, often very place-specific, work through it, and quickly move on to another.

I have chosen to situate my parents within a single framework—Cape Cod. Because of its great natural beauty, and its odd mixture of locals and self-exiled, or vacationing, writers and artists, the newly married Wilson and McCarthy decided to cast anchor in Wellfleet, just fourteen miles south of Provincetown at Cape's end. Although the couple would divorce five years after Wilson bought the Wellfleet house on Money Hill, adjacent to Route 6, he would maintain a permanent household here with his fourth and last wife, Elena Mumm Thornton. Wilson remarried in 1946 as did McCarthy, to Bowden Broadwater. The Broadwaters would buy a house in Wellfleet in the early fifties only to sell it three years later, after McCarthy had published *A Charmed Life*, a novel that has been widely viewed as a roman à clef about Wellfleet. In chapter 5, I will argue that such a view, while not without foundation, overlooks the novel's far-reaching moral and philosophical implications.

Rather than try to encompass my parents' lives, or work, in any comprehensive manner, I have chosen to shadow their footsteps on Cape Cod. This unique setting gives a handy framework to my narrative, which draws on their writings, including correspondence, my own memory, and my research. As a child and adolescent I spent much time, especially in the summer, in the Money Hill house. I would continue to visit my father there as an adult; in fact I was in Wellfleet on June 12, 1972, the day he died in his New York State house. In chapter 6, "Remembering My Parents and Cape Cod," I plumb my own memories; the main corpus of the book, however, deals with images of Cape Cod as reflected through my parents' optics. Having situated my father within the Cape's spatial and temporal confines (chapter 1), I go on in subsequent chapters to follow him, and later McCarthy. I include some new biographical revelations as well as texts that have not been published. I hope, finally, to impart a sense of the two protagonists' flesh, blood, nerves, and determination to make an artistic synthesis from observation and experience. If they re-create the place, my role has been to re-create them in it.

ABBREVIATIONS

Beinecke
    Edmund Wilson papers, Beinecke Rare Book and
    Manuscript Library, Yale University, New Haven, Conn.
"CCL"
    Reuel K. Wilson, "Edmund Wilson's Cape Cod Landscape"
CL
    Mary McCarthy, *A Charmed Life*
"Growing Up"
    Reuel K. Wilson, "Growing Up with Edmund Wilson
    and Mary McCarthy"
Magician
    Rosalind B. Wilson, *Near the Magician:*
    A Memoir of My Father
Notebooks
    Edmund Wilson, manuscript notebooks of the 1920s
    in Beinecke (most of which were published in Wilson,
    The Twenties: From Notebooks and Diaries of the Period)
NYTBR
    New York Times Book Review
Vassar
    Mary McCarthy papers, Vassar College Archives and
    Special Collections, Poughkeepsie, N.Y.

1 : THE BACKGROUND

With its crystal-clear light and water, its heady salt air, and striking palette of primary colors, Cape Cod has a special mystique that has intrigued many generations of visitors, some of whom became permanent residents. Surrounded by water, and looking toward Europe, the Cape (as it is commonly known) seems remote and exotic, despite its relative proximity to the East Coast urban centers of Boston and New York. During the 1920s Provincetown, at Cape's end, became a destination of choice for many artists, writers, and other assorted bohemians. Anxious to escape the claustrophobia of urban life, they embraced Provincetown's natural setting and laid-back mores. Some, like Eugene O'Neill, divided the year between Greenwich Village and Provincetown; a few, like the writer and labor activist Mary Heaton Vorse (the first urban intellectual to "discover" Provincetown), elected to reside there permanently. Gradually, some of the Provincetown intelligentsia migrated to the nearby communities of Truro and Wellfleet. Edmund Wilson, who had since 1920 been a repeat visitor in Provincetown, settled in Wellfleet in 1941. For him, and the other transplants, the Cape offered lovely scenery, open space, and, until the 1960s, an inexpensive cost of living. To be sure, few of the newly minted Cape dwellers chose to spend the winter on bleak, windswept Cape Cod, but the glorious summers irresistibly beckoned. Caught up in the perennial "August madness," visitors and seasonal residents alike beachcombed and partied, only occasionally to endure the temporary setback of a weeklong rainy spell, or even an early hurricane. We should keep in mind, however, that Cape Cod as we know it, and as it has been for the last hundred and fifty years, offers a very different landscape from the one that gave shelter to the Pilgrims in 1620.

Even before its "discovery" by Bartholomew Gosnold on his way to Virginia in 1602, and Samuel de Champlain in 1605, Cape Cod (as Gosnold named it) was known to Basque and Breton fishermen in the sixteenth century. Its natural resources—forests, land, and waters abundant with fish—would prove to be easy targets for commercial exploitation. Two members of Captain Gosnold's crew, Gabriel Archer and John Brereton, describe the Cape as endowed with fertile land and a generally friendly native population. To be sure, many Europeans saw the New World as a kind of earthly paradise. Their written accounts of it, like those of Archer and Brereton, were often calculated, by minimizing the perils involved, to lure new settlers from their home countries (Finch, 2). The Pilgrims set sail from Holland in 1620, hoping to reach the Hudson River. They sighted landfall near present-day Provincetown on November 19, 1620. William Bradford and most of his followers weighed anchor here and remained for five weeks. In the meantime, some of his men reconnoitered the coast for a less exposed place to spend the winter. They found what they were looking for directly across the bay, and they established the Plymouth Colony there.

In 1622 "G. Mourt" published a fascinating account of the colony's early days. "Mourt" was probably an alias for George Morton, the Pilgrims' agent in London who compiled and published the *Relation* (*A Relation or Journal of the Beginning and Proceedings of the English Plantation Settled at Plimoth in New England*). This was almost certainly a collective effort, one of whose authors was the colony's governor, William Bradford (Finch, 419). Bradford later published a "monumental" history of the Plymouth Colony under his own name (Finch, 412). "Mourt" describes the Cape Cod Indians as tall, handsome people who sustained themselves by hunting the abundant game as well as by growing corn and other vegetables. During an exploratory expedition from their base at Plymouth the Pilgrims helped themselves liberally to Indian supplies of corn. They named one fertile patch of land "Corn Hill," now a bay location in Truro that still bears the same name. Over the next three hundred years the white man's domination gradually reduced the local native population to the two tiny Wampanoag enclaves that remain today: one on Martha's Vineyard, the other near Falmouth. Successive generations of white settlers cut down the hardwood forests and exhausted the once-rich soil. The timber went into shipbuilding and is extant today only in the walls and floors of the old Cape houses. These houses, often built by men of the sea, are endowed with a rugged grace. Basic in design, some have withstood two centuries of biting, salt-drenched wind and water. Easily movable from one locality to another, often over water on barges, many Cape Cod houses have migrated to new locations. Such was the case with the village of Billingsgate, on the bayside land that extends northeast of Wellfleet Harbor. Threatened by encroaching waters, the inhabitants moved their houses to Wellfleet Center; today Billingsgate is merely a spit of sand that becomes an island at high tide.

Henry David Thoreau was the first major author to explore and write about Cape Cod. He left his native Concord, Massachusetts, to undertake four expeditions, in 1849, 1850, 1855, and 1857. His book *Cape Cod*, based on his research and extensive walking tours of the Cape, is a masterpiece of travel literature. In it the intrepid narrator meanders through villages and hikes over woodland, dunes, and beaches. He scrutinizes the inhabitants with an amused Olympian eye. Sensitive to natural beauty, as well as human suffering, he sketches some memorable Dickensian portraits, like that of the Wellfleet oysterman. With a naturalist's precision, he etches the contours of sea and landscape. His descriptions will later find an echo in the Cape Cod entries of Edmund Wilson's diaries.

Thoreau gives ample space to the human victims of the Atlantic's cruel anger—bodies and clothing washed ashore after shipwrecks. He also notes the bloody wholesale massacre of blackfish (a small species of whale) on the Provincetown and Truro beaches. The local inhabitants would drive a school of blackfish close to the shore where they could be easily killed in the shallow water. Having extracted the mammals' blubber, the locals abandoned the corpses to rot on the beach. In the midst of natural beauty malignant forces lurk. Here is Thoreau's description of some blooming wild rosebushes in Eastham, just south of the Wellfleet border:

> When the roses were in bloom, these patches in the midst of the sand displayed such a profusion of blossoms, mingled with the aroma of the bayberry, that no Italian or other artificial rose-garden could equal them. They were perfectly Elysian, and realized my idea of an oasis in the desert. Huckleberry bushes were very abundant, and the next summer they bore a remarkable quantity of that kind of gall called huckleberry-apple, forming quite handsome though monstrous blossoms. But it must be added, that this shrubbery swarmed with wood-ticks, sometimes very troublesome parasites, and which it takes very horny fingers to crack. (Thoreau, 129)

Thoreau's micropicture of a flawed Arcadia seems close to the reality of today's Cape, where a new variety of tick, the bearer of Lyme disease, has become a dangerous threat to forest walkers and berry pickers.

Since Thoreau's time, commercial fishing on Cape Cod, together with that of the entire North Atlantic coastline, has fallen into eclipse. Whaling, the driving force behind the Cape's economy, was no longer viable by the end of the nineteenth century, and the stocks of cod, halibut, tuna, and even mackerel had been depleted to alarming levels by the end of the twentieth century. As recently as the 1980s, boats carrying tourists would, over the summer months, ply back and forth from Provincetown to the Cape Cod Canal for half-day sessions of cod fishing. Today, with the cod almost gone, these same boats, or rather their successors under the same names, *Ranger, Dolphin, Portuguese Princess*, bring tourists out to view the whales in the waters north of Provincetown. Tourism has become the Cape's only viable large-scale industry. Its beginning can probably be traced to the construction of the railway line, which reached its final goal, Provincetown, in 1873. The Cape Cod Canal was finished in 1914, thereby providing a direct, safe link for north-south seaboard navigation. Even for steamships the circumnavigation of the Cape had been a very risky business in times of bad weather. Before the canal's opening, the ocean side, especially the stretch from Chatham to Provincetown, was regularly strewn with the broken pieces of wrecked ships and drowned seamen. Before the canal, death had in fact been a way of life for the Cape Codders, who regularly combed the beaches for the spoils of shipwrecks ("mooncussing"); others to benefit were the men whom the government employed to help rescue the survivors.

Once the Cape's soil had been exposed by woodcutting and then eroded by overgrazing and overfarming, the topography drastically changed. Some areas of the Lower Cape (NB: "Lower" designates the northern part, "Upper" the southern end of Cape Cod) were stabilized by the planting of sea grass and pitch pines. One factor that seems to have remained constant over the centuries is the shifting shoreline: islands disappear underwater or become linked to the mainland; voracious tides gobble up the beach on the Atlantic side, forcing lighthouses and human habitations to retreat inland. Despite and perhaps even because of the battering it has taken from man and nature, the Cape presents a minimalist patchwork of salt marshes, moors, low-lying woods dotted with postglacial hollows, muddy as well as sandy ponds, dunes, and still a few wild cranberry bogs. The Cape's villages, well maintained by their inhabitants, many of whom today are retirees from other locations, seem quaint and inviting to the casual visitor. The surrounding countryside beckons with its vivid, ever-changing shades of blue, green, and ocher. The air, everywhere redolent of salt and seaweed, rewards the tired visitor with a deep sleep, only to arouse his senses upon awakening. Today much of the Lower Cape's natural beauty has been preserved by the Cape Cod National Seashore, an important legacy of John F. Kennedy.

Of all the communities on Cape Cod, Provincetown has been consistently known for its picturesque situation and fiercely independent inhabitants. It has, since its earliest days, enjoyed the reputation of something like a wide-open frontier town. Overlooking a majestic deepwater harbor, the only one on Cape Cod today, and backed by the Atlantic Ocean, it has served as a safe haven for people who would like to live outside the strictures of conventional morality. Since the Pilgrims' landing, Provincetown (named "Cape Cod" until it incorporated itself in 1727) has tenaciously coped with the dangers posed by its precarious geography. It has weathered devastating hurricanes and, more threatening to its physical survival, successive inundations of sand that have almost choked it to death. Today inundations of summer visitors strain the town's frail resources to the utmost. After Labor Day it reverts to its natural contours, as shops and restaurants gradually board up for the winter and the streets fall silent. Like Key West, Florida, its original layout and style of architecture has been preserved. Other Cape towns, such as Hyannis, Dennis, and Falmouth, have largely succumbed to ugly and rampant commercialism.

Settled by Yankees, Nova Scotians, and later a large Portuguese immigration that peaked in 1880 (Egan, 91), Provincetown's ethnically diverse inhabitants got along well. They were for the most part hardworking and passionately committed to the sea, which sustained them. Far from the eyes and ears of state or federal governments, the rough-hewn Provincetonians did more or less as they pleased, showing little regard for the environment or any kind of bureaucratic rules. Visitors in the first decades of the twentieth century complained in one voice of the ubiquitous stink caused by rotting fish. It was common practice for fisherman to abandon the unwanted elements of their daily catch on the beach that lies only a few yards from Commercial Street, the main thoroughfare (Egan, 16–17). Nonetheless, Provincetown had a natural appeal for outsiders who fancied its authenticity (as a then self-sufficient working New England port), its breathtaking views, and its easygoing mores. Beginning around 1915, a steady stream of New York writers, artists, and bohemians made their way to Cape's end. Some came there because World War I had forced them to return home from Europe, while others came because the war prevented them from going to Europe in the first place (Egan, 7–8). Provincetown's history as an art center began in August 1914, with the founding of the Provincetown Art Association. Mostly because of the war, the number of resident artists had drastically increased by the summer of 1916. Charles Hawthorne, originally from Maine, was one of the association's first officers and an enormously popular, and effective, teacher of painting. He would exert a deciding influence on a younger generation of landscapists like Edwin Dickinson and Ross Moffat, who would become first-class artists with firm roots in Provincetown.

As a result of the new trend, many Greenwich Villagers began migrating to Provincetown for the summer. The town's first theater group, the Provincetown Players, was born over 1915 and 1916, inaugurating a new chapter in American literary history. On July 28, 1916, George Cram ("Jig") Cook put on and acted in young Eugene O'Neill's *Bound East for Cardiff* in a former fish [storage] house on the Lewis wharf. The rickety structure's owner was Mary Heaton Vorse (1874–1966), journalist, fiction writer, and labor activist, who had bought a whaling captain's house on Commercial Street in 1907. Vorse's moving autobiographical memoir, *Time and the Town* (1942), gives an affectionate and also highly informative account of the town's history and her participation in it. Up until her death she was its most longstanding resident intellectual. Vorse encouraged other literary people to visit Provincetown; some would decide to live there.

According to firsthand accounts, *Bound East for Cardiff*'s opening performance was spellbinding: one side of the improvised theater where it was performed had been opened out to the moonlit harbor. The setting was highly appropriate for a sea drama portraying the death of a merchant sailor. Susan Glaspell, the talented writer of fiction and plays, whose husband Jig Cook founded and ran the Provincetown Players, attended the first performance. She described that memorable evening in her autobiographical *Road to the Temple* (1927), written after Cook's death mainly to honor his memory:

> I may see it through memories too emotional, but it seems to me I
> have never sat through a more moving production than our *Bound*

East for Cardiff, when Eugene O'Neill was produced for the first time on any stage. Jig was Yank. As he lay in his bunk dying, he talked of life as one who knew he must leave it.

The sea has been good to Eugene O'Neill. It was there for his opening. There was a fog, just as the script demanded, fog bell in the harbor. The tide was in, and it washed under us and around, spraying through the holes in the floor, giving us the rhythm of the sea while the big dying sailor talked to his friend Drisc of the life he had always wanted deep in the land, where you'd never see a ship or smell the sea.

It is not merely figurative language to say the old wharf shook with applause (*Road*, 254).

During the summers of 1915 and 1916 the new theater group included the writers Hutchins Hapgood and his wife Neith Boyce, John ("Jack") Reed, the future author of *Ten Days That Shook the World*, and Louise Bryant, who was then having a love affair with O'Neill but would marry Reed and accompany him to Moscow in 1917, where he bore witness to the Russian Revolution. In addition, Wilbur and Margaret Steele (he was a well-known short-story writer, she was a painter), the self-proclaimed "dunes poet" Harry Kemp, and the sculptor William Zorach and his wife Marguerite (they did costume and set design) made significant contributions to the new theater (Egan, 123–125, 136–137, 168 passim). In the fall of 1916 the nucleus of the group would move back to New York, where Jig Cook would continue the Provincetown Players at 139 Macdougall Street. Eugene O'Neill's plays, originally rejected by other theaters, were performed there so successfully that his future career as a major playwright became assured. Over the years 1916 to 1924 O'Neill would spend the summers in Provincetown. In 1919 his father bought for him the newly decorated former Peaked Hill Life-Saving Station.[1] The vendor was Sam Lewisjohn, a New York businessman. Mabel Dodge, the rich socialite and supporter of leftist causes who had been romantically involved with the apparently irresistible John Reed, had had the house totally renovated for Lewisjohn over the winter of 1914–15. (Among the furnishings she chose were two stuffed couches that had belonged to Isadora Duncan [Egan, 244].) O'Neill received the deed for the house as a wedding present. Edmund Wilson would rent the same house from O'Neill during the summer of 1927. Wilson knew O'Neill, since his first wife, the actress Mary Blair (married Wilson 1923, divorced 1930), acted in O'Neill's plays. The two great writers treated each other with diffidence. (For Wilson's reminiscences of O'Neill see *The Twenties*, 110–112.) By 1926 Wilson and Mary Blair had separated. By 1930 he had remarried—to Margaret Canby, a Californian—and the couple spent the summer of 1930 very happily in the same O'Neill house on the ocean. Wilson's daughter by Mary Blair, Rosalind, was with them, as was Jimmy Canby, Margaret's son by James Canby. The following January, the house, now officially condemned as unsafe because of shoreline erosion, stood precariously on its cliffside perch. O'Neill's friends, among them Dos Passos and Wilson, organized an expedition to rescue some of the furniture and other household effects. Hutchins Hapgood reports that his two daughters extricated the portly Wilson from the cupola of the house, where he had gotten stuck in the window embrasure (Hapgood, 519). A few days later the house, which the Wilsons had once thought of buying, fell into the sea. Seeing it in the surf, "they wore the expression of people who have just missed being run over at a railway crossing" (letter from Katy Dos Passos to Henka Farnsworth, quoted in Carr, 284). After spending the summer of 1931 with Margaret in California, Wilson returned to Provincetown in the summer of 1932, but without Margaret, who lacked the money to bring her son east from California that summer. In September she would fall down some steps while leaving the Santa Barbara Presidio after a party; she subsequently died of a fractured skull. During the 1930s Wilson spent almost every summer, or part thereof, on Cape Cod. In 1941, some three years after his marriage to Mary McCarthy, he would buy a house in Wellfleet, just fourteen miles south of Provincetown. I was two and a half years old at the time.

During the twenties and thirties Wilson did his share of carousing with the Provincetown bohemians. To his credit, he never allowed dissipation to interfere with his demanding work agenda. He did much of the writing of *Axel's Castle*, his brilliant study of modernism, in Provincetown, and would revise the book's manuscript at Peaked Hill in the last months of 1930. (It was published in February 1931.) In the middle 1930s he would begin a secret affair with Elizabeth Waugh, a Provincetown friend. She and her husband, the painter Coulton Waugh, owned and ran a store on Commercial Street that sold rugs and other bric-a-brac to tourists. Her passionate relationship with Wilson finds expression in her correspondence with him from 1933 to 1940. The intimate relationship

The threatened O'Neill house and outbuildings in 1931.

The house undermined on its ocean side.

The house on its way out to sea.

lasted intermittently over four years, until the time Wilson met Mary McCarthy. Elizabeth Waugh had a masochistic side and worshipped Wilson for being "a real old-fashioned man." Although the two first met in Provincetown, they carried on the affair at other locations—as Wilson's published journals, where Elizabeth appears as "D.," suggest. Even after it was over, he seems to have helped her: in the early forties she wrote him a letter (now at the Beinecke Library) thanking him for getting her a job with the "Committee to Defend America by Aiding its Allies." Although, owing to its intensity, the affair may not have been a total secret to Elizabeth's husband Coulton, Rosalind Wilson, who knew the couple well, maintained that "everyone" in Provincetown regarded Elizabeth Waugh as a paragon of domestic virtue.

Wilson's best friend in Provincetown was John Dos Passos. The personally winning "Dos" (as his friends knew him) served as a model for the idealistic Hugo Bauman in Wilson's novel *I Thought of Daisy* (1928). Clearly on the left until 1937, when he became disillusioned with the Communists' ruthlessness during the Spanish Civil War, Dos Passos went on to become a right-wing conservative. The Wilson–Dos Passos friendship just barely weathered their increasing ideological differences. After marrying Katherine (Katy) Smith in 1929, Dos moved into the Arequipa (as the house had been called by its former owner, Mary Heaton Vorse) at 571 Commercial Street, Provincetown. The house, purchased by Katy and her brother Bill Smith from the nearly destitute Vorse the year before, was now also called "Smooley Hall." The name represents a conglomerate of the names of its four occupants: Stella Roof, Edith Foley, Katy and Bill Smith. Bill was the only nonwriter in the group. The Smooley Hall foursome actually had lived at six different locations in Provincetown before moving to the Arequipa (Carr, 256–257). When Edie Foley married Frank Shay, writer, publisher, book dealer, and general literary impresario, in December 1930, Smooley Hall dissolved, although Bill Smith continued to live some of the year at the Arequipa. Dos and Katy would make it their permanent home in the United States. Wilson saw a good deal of them there until 1947, when Katy died in an automobile accident. Dos then sold the house and moved to Virginia, where he had inherited property. During the thirties Wilson rented the Arequipa at least twice.

Another literary friend, John Peale Bishop, came to live on Cape Cod in 1936. He and Wilson had known each other at Princeton, where they worked together on the literary magazine; Bishop, who came from a moneyed West Virginia family, was three years older. Both men had worked for *Vanity Fair* during the early twenties, and both fell simultaneously in love with the poet Edna St. Vincent Millay. Despite the rivalry—Millay had no long-term love interest in either—Wilson and Bishop remained close friends. They published a collaborative volume of stories and poems, *The Undertaker's Garland*, in 1922; later Wilson posthumously edited *The Collected Essays of John Peale Bishop* (1948). Wilson had a high opinion of his friend's poetry, which he praises in *The Shores of Light: A Literary Chronicle of the Twenties and Thirties*. Over the years, the two conducted a voluminous correspondence, most of which deals with literary matters. In 1937 Bishop and his wife Margaret built "Sea Change," an imposing house that faces Nantucket Sound in South Chatham (just twenty miles south of Wellfleet). The architect was another Princetonian. Although Chatham, a rather stuffy community, was hardly Wilson's cup of tea, the Wilsons and the Bishops visited back and forth during the years from 1941 to 1944. The friendship ended only with Bishop's death in 1944 at age fifty-two. Wilson and the poet Allen Tate, another of Bishop's oldest friends, served as his literary executors.

After spending the winter of 1939 and the summer of 1940 in rented houses in Truro and Wellfleet, Wilson decided in 1941 to buy his own, in Wellfleet. The big house on Money Hill cost $4,000 and required considerable renovation. Ever broke, Wilson borrowed $1,500 from his mother to make a down payment and took out a mortgage on the rest (Kiernan, 174–175). At the time the Cape must have seemed an inviting place to cast anchor. By marrying Mary McCarthy, he was hoping to find stability after a very turbulent decade. Throughout his thirties Wilson had followed an exhausting schedule that involved a long stay in the Soviet Union and the writing of four major books: *The American Jitters* (1932), *Travels in Two Democracies* (1936), *The Triple Thinkers* (1938), and *To the Finland Station* (1940), none of which were moneymakers (Meyers, 148). At the same time, he conducted a series of high-powered love affairs that overlapped. He continued these even during his brief marriage to Margaret Canby (1930–1932). He courted, and won, a succession of female adventure seekers, while maintaining a long-standing relationship with Frances, a working-class woman of Ukrainian origin. He spent the last years of the thirties in "Trees," a gloomy house in Stamford, Connecticut, that he had rented from an old friend, Margaret de Silver.

*Money Hill (circa 1920?). Future Wilson house is
in the middle, partly obscured by trees.*

Duly installed in Wellfleet, Wilson continued to write with customary
verve and dedication; but his relationship with McCarthy, his third wife,
had been problematic from the very outset. On the positive side, he encouraged McCarthy in her own writing, especially the writing of fiction.
He defended her against her critics and even called her a "female Stend-
hal" in a letter to his old mentor at Princeton, Christian Gauss (*Letters on
Literature and Politics*, 343). Eben Given, a Truro friend who saw the
Wilsons often, told me that when the couple was "on," their repartee in
company was highly stimulating. Rosalind Wilson in her memoir about
her father notes that "Mary and my father could be very amusing, but
cozy and tranquil were never words that you'd apply to their household"
(*Magician*, 109). She also suggests that they took pleasure in "dismem-
bering people mentally" (*Magician*, 107). Unfortunately for all the women
who chose to marry Wilson, he showed them a dark side of his character
that surfaced with predictable regularity when he drank heavily. Rosalind
correctly remembered him as a "domestic tyrant who never presided
over a household in which the inhabitants were comfortable. It seemed

almost as though if they were comfortable, he was not" (*Magician*, 28). Often driven by a negative instinct, he would arbitrarily denigrate his wife's character. Well aware of this almost pathological trait in himself, he did little to curb it. Add to this his chronic impecuniousness and, at least in the case of his marriage to McCarthy, his refusal to allow his wife to maintain a bank account in her name. Anna Matson Hamburger remembered that, on one occasion, she and her husband Norman met me and my mother at the soda fountain in Wellfleet. My mother had brought me on the back of her bicycle for an ice cream. Since Wilson had given her only five cents for my cone, she asked Norman to buy one for her. Anna notes that Wilson was hardly poor at the time. She adds: "It was one of the ways he had of holding on to her" (Kiernan, 175).

McCarthy, to be sure, was a strong-willed and assertive person, although underneath the surface she was highly insecure. As she relates in *Memories of a Catholic Girlhood*, her childhood was far from happy after she was orphaned at age six. She and three of her brothers were sent to live with an obtuse, stingy aunt and her sadistic husband. Wilson attributed her "hysterical" behavior with him to traumatic childhood experiences with "Uncle Myers." McCarthy's "hysteria" mentioned by my father to me and by Rosalind in her memoir must have been fueled by his own irrational behavior, since after she left him it subsided—only to surface occasionally when subsequent husbands' behavior did not meet her expectations. Possibly McCarthy's fiercely competitive nature arose from a subconscious desire to make up for childhood deprivations. During those Wellfleet years she commuted regularly to New York City, thereby contriving to escape from her husband's overpowering presence. Ostensibly she went to the city for sessions with a psychiatrist; she also used her temporary freedom to meet lovers, one of whom was the art critic Clement Greenberg. Wilson's biographer Jeffrey Meyers speculated that the Wilsons' "good sexual relations . . . as well as their weekly separations and his tolerance of her infidelity, defused their conflicts and enabled their troubled marriage to survive for seven years" (Meyers, 208). I might add that both partners were capable of two-, three-, and four-timing spouses or other lovers. Ample testimony for this can be found in McCarthy's posthumous *Intellectual Memoirs* (a title that was ineptly chosen by the publisher for a book that deals more with sex than intellectual matters), other autobiographical writings and statements, and in her personal letters, now at Vassar College (her alma mater). Wilson's multiple infidelities emerge from his journals and the personal correspondence held at Yale's Beinecke Library.

After her separation from Wilson in 1944 and her divorce from him in 1945, McCarthy returned with me to spend the summer of 1945 in Truro, just a few miles north of her old home in Wellfleet. She would return to Cape Cod, and Wellfleet, in 1952, when she and her third husband, Bowden Broadwater, bought a house on Pamet Point Road, a mile and a half from Money Hill, just across the border from Truro. They would keep the house until 1955. The renewed acquaintance with the Cape, and its bohemian ethos, gave the impetus for McCarthy's fourth novel, *A Charmed Life* (1955).

Wilson married his fourth wife, Elena Mumm Thornton, in 1945. In order to marry him, Elena had to divorce her first husband, James Thornton, who was then living in New York with her and their young son Henry. The newly constituted Wilsons would reside on Money Hill until Wilson's death in 1972; Elena would live on there until her death in 1979. Beginning in 1951, however, Wilson would gradually shift the fulcrum of his life to the tiny hamlet of Talcottville, upper New York State, where he had inherited an ancestral house from his mother. During the months from May to October, he chose to spend as much time as possible in the Talcottville stone house. Elena, an uprooted European who was working at *Town and Country* magazine when she first met Wilson in 1944, became quickly attached to Wellfleet—its beaches, her garden, and the nineteenth-century house that she had reshaped and beautified. Although her father, Heinrich Mumm, was a rich businessman, she never received a formal education. Aside from some private tutoring at home, the only course she ever took was at a cooking school. She told me that she spent a good deal of her childhood accompanying her father on business trips around Europe. In 1930 she married James (Jimmy) Thornton, a Canadian whose father was then the chairman and president of the Canadian National Railway. The newlyweds first lived in Montreal and then moved to the United States. Thornton joined the U.S. Army in 1942; he was assigned to intelligence work in England and, after D-day, in France. During the years of her first marriage she moved frequently from one city or job to another. Her first really stable household was with Wilson, on Money Hill. When he became absorbed in rediscovering his own and his family's past in Talcottville, Elena could not fully accept the burden of creating a new, second household in rural New York. In addition, she resented missing the lovely dog days of summer on Cape Cod. She therefore increasingly resisted going to stay in Talcottville. The resulting friction, which led her husband to threaten her with divorce, did not actually destroy the marriage; the acrimony continued, however, until Wilson's death in the Talcottville house, June 12, 1972. It is ironic that those very characteristics for which Cape Cod is celebrated—unspoiled landscapes, inviting expanses of salt and freshwater, and a lively social life in the summer—would enthrall Elena just as Wilson was tiring of them. Wilson never put the Cape into his essays or fiction, but, as will be shown, it does figure in his poetry and diaries. From the twenties onward, Cape Cod periodically surfaces, a haunting mysterious presence on the pages of his journals. By contrast, the diary entries on Talcottville were to give the framework for an ambitious large work, *Upstate*, the chronicle of a unique place, its history, and its open spaces.

When my parents divorced, the court ordered that I spend the school year with my mother and summer vacations with my father. This arrangement worked well until I left home for boarding school at age thirteen. The transition from my mother's fairly easygoing authority to my father's authoritarianism was, however, initially difficult. Each successive summer I had to make the necessary adjustments to Wellfleet, but I had in Elena a loving, indulgent stepmother, plus two faithful dogs, unparalleled bathing in pond and ocean, and three close friends, Eben Given Jr., Charles Jencks, and Michael Macdonald. My father, the "minotaur" as my mother referred to him outside my hearing, would not brook interruptions, such as the sound of childish voices near his study windows, during working hours; in midafternoon, however, he would benignly emerge from his den for a family excursion to the beach. Having never learned to drive, he had relied on my mother to take us to the beach in her car. When she left, he relied on taxis for all short and long-distance travel. Our town taxi man, Bill Peck, did yeoman service for many years, but he retired in the late fifties. At this point Elena took driving lessons, passed the test in Hyannis, and became her husband's new chauffeur.

I would continue to return to Wellfleet through adolescence and my four years at Harvard. The bracing salt air, the surf, swimming in the nude, the clam digging, the parties, romantic and sensual nights and days in the company of girlfriends, all melt in retrospect into a heady blur. For those who drink too deeply of intoxicating libations on the Atlantic shore, a word of warning: the hangover cuts deep the next morning. For very different reasons and under different circumstances, Mary McCarthy and Edmund Wilson came to find a bitter aftertaste in the Cape experience, turned from exhilarating to dully familiar. I now propose to examine their lives there.

2 : EDMUND WILSON'S PROVINCETOWN IN THE TWENTIES AND THIRTIES

Wilson's first documented visit to Cape Cod took place in the summer of 1920, when he visited Edna St. Vincent Millay and her family in Truro. He had met the poet earlier that year in New York. Already a devoted admirer of her work, he was instantly smitten by her persona. They became friends and soon lovers. The friendship way outlasted the physical relationship, which was brief, but the latter was enormously important at the time and in retrospect to Wilson. It was his first love affair. Later he would write about his first love in an essay, "Edna St. Vincent Millay," published in *The Shores of Light* (1952). In the essay he recalls his visit to the Millays in Truro. Edna was summering there with her mother and sisters. They were living spartanly in a cottage lent to them by Jig Cook and Susan Glaspell. It stood in a hollow just behind the Longnook Ocean Beach. The sisters sang humorous songs to entertain their houseguest; Edna sang him a "merry and poignant tune from Estonia." They all listened to Beethoven's Fifth Symphony on the phonograph. The music, heard under the circumstances, made a strong impression on Wilson: "She [Edna] was committing the whole thing to memory, as she liked to do with music and poems; and, raspy and blurred though it sounded, the power of its bold or mysterious motifs came through to me—surcharged with her power—as it never had done before." The previous day Wilson and Millay had sat on a swing on the open porch outside and, while they were being devoured by mosquitoes, Wilson had proposed marriage to her. Her answer was noncommittal. A later weekend that same summer, Millay invited another admirer, the poet John Bishop, to visit as well. The rivalry over the same woman did not compromise the Bishop-Wilson friendship; each knew that he was hardly the only rival for her favors.

Wilson would remember the Truro episode with Millay when he was in Provincetown in 1927. (See chapter 4 for a discussion of "Provincetown," the poem he wrote that year in her memory.) Years later, in a chapter in *The Forties* titled "Katy Dos Passos," he would again return to his 1920 visit to Millay in Truro. In the entry dated September 17, 1947, he reports that he has had a chance to enter the former Cook-Glaspell cottage where the Millays had been living on his visit twenty-seven years earlier. The house is now a "middle-class cottage" with modern conveniences. Its occupants, Dr. Mandel Cohen and his family, invited him in. (Cohen was a well-respected "non-Freudian" psychiatrist who liked to summer in Truro or Provincetown: he had a nodding acquaintance with Wilson and a social friendship with Mary McCarthy.) Having inspected the house, Wilson records in his diary the resurgent memories of his earlier visit. He remembers Edna's mother's pronouncement: "I was a slut myself; so no wonder my daughters are." He also recalls his attempts to make love to Edna on "some kind of swing" that stood on the mosquito-infested porch. The article in *Shores of Light* mentions only a marriage proposal under the same circumstances. The journal entry written five years earlier also recalls a kiss exchanged behind a bush on their way back from the beach; later, returning from the post office, he has breezily asserted to his companion: "By the time we're fifty years old, we'll be two of the most interesting people in the United States." She has replied: "You behave as if you were fifty already" (*Forties*, 223–224). All in all, Katy Dos Passos' untimely death conjured up a series of nostalgic Cape memories in Wilson's mind, the oldest of which centered on Millay. Experience that he recorded simultaneously in his diaries shows satirical rather than idealizing tendencies. The diary reveals a significant contrast between the world of nature and the puerile antics of the Provincetown bohemians.

Wilson seems to have visited Cape Cod twice in 1922. His journal records his arrival in Provincetown. His eye first captures the harbor with its omnipresent seagulls and its "yellow rim of sand that seems to lock the town in a world of its own." We also encounter the notion of Provincetown as a self-contained "world of its own" in the writings of its other chroniclers. The atmosphere of a magic circle was reinforced by its geographical position, the "otherness" (to outsiders) of its natives, and its evocative rendering by such artists as Charles Demuth, Bruce McCain, Edwin Dickinson, Ross Moffett, and W. H. W. Bicknell. In his 1922 word painting of Provincetown, Wilson describes "the water all buff and blue and lavender and green in the shallows when the tide is out and the yellow islands of sand on bleaker, less vivid days; the great unshadowable dunes like enormous snowdrifts or tinily crow's-footed by the sprouting lips of moss, which in time puts forth little yellow flowers as if it had sucked from the arid sand its last drops of vital pigment . . . the great sea unfurrowed and bright blue, frothing whitely over the bright yellow beach, which it chews and spits out and chews again like a dog worrying a bird." In its tints and contours nature is beautiful, but Wilson's person-ifications are hardly idealizing: the "crow's-footed" dunes, the sprouting and sucking lips of moss, the frothing sea that chews and spits. The mix-ture of agreeable and disagreeable elements often lends pungency to Wilson's descriptions, which move well beyond realism. The 1922 jour-nal entry goes on to describe the tastefully decorated interior of the house on the dunes (that he would rent a few years later):

> O'Neill's house with its wide square rooms decorated in the colors of the landscape—the light but vivid yellows of the sand and the sky and in the living room, with its set of big plates each one pictured with a different kind of fish: droll conventionalized flounders and butterfish—the mottled white and brown cat which had come in on the wreck of a barge that was smashed at their very door and which produced a snow-white kitten. . . . (*Twenties*, 125)

The same diary entry now moves out into the town streets with the Portuguese inhabitants "dark, beady-eyed and squat-nosed." Wilson notes the houses "close and thick along either side of the street, with their single row of windows . . . enormous box-like buildings to store fish; a high square chocolate-colored house—as if the chocolate were moldy and melting . . . a white horse grazes on the unkempt weeds of the lawn." This is the house that has belonged to "a miser, recently dead . . . his sis-ter used to be seen picking up driftwood on the shore; blue-silver sheets of water that lay like broken mirrors in the sand" (*Twenties*, 125–126). The signs of Cape Cod neglect and decay, the cubistic architectural forms, the white horse and the cats, the broken-mirror water, all convey the eerie surreal reflection of a flawed and hollow world.

The next Cape Cod entry, which begins on the following page of the published journals, is captioned "Boston-Truro." It sketches a landscape as seen from the window of a moving train. Wilson observes the train's slow progress as it crept along the South Shore toward the Cape. It seemed "as if one were making one's way slowly and with difficulty into a foreign country: sea marshes tufted thickly with marsh grass: little low rootless houses strewn about the mapless downs that did not admit of being turned into villages or even netted into a cage of roads; the country tousled with scrub pine or broken out in a green rash of bay: desolate churches looked like boxes on the highest eminences; the great hummocks of the dunes, scarred and bald; the green grass that draws its color from the pale gravelly sand; the sudden infinity of the gray level sea streaked with faint violet and green and scarcely fringed with white where it touches the shore" (*Twenties*, 128). As in the previous description, figurative language underscores the desolation of a flawed but painterly world, animated only by the tints and contour of the sea.

On February 14, 1923, Wilson married the actress Mary Blair. She was two months pregnant at the time and would bear their daughter Rosalind on September 19 of the same year. The couple separated in 1925. They were not well matched: Wilson probably resented his wife's commitment to a full-time career in the theater and the fact that she earned more than he did; she, on the other hand, criticized his heavy drinking and interest in other women. The breakup seemed friendly enough, and they would stay in regular contact until her death from tuberculosis in 1947 (Meyers, 85–90). Mary Blair remarried after retiring from the theater to her house in Pennsylvania, but she saw her daughter only during occasional visits; Rosalind would remain her father's responsibility, growing up mostly with his mother, Helen M. K. Wilson, at her house in Red Bank, New Jersey.

Wilson would return to Provincetown in 1927. The previous summer the artist Magda Johann, whom Wilson was pursuing, spent some time there on her own. Writing to Wilson, who had remained in New York City, on July 18, 1926, she states that the people whom she has met in Provincetown are "stupid," while even those who work are "socially useless." She has, on the other hand, enjoyed her landlady's garden and painted two pictures. She has been physically active, walking and swimming; she also declares that she has no intention of returning to New York in the near future. This witty, attractive, and independent-minded woman seems to have been amused by Wilson's attentions, without being much attracted to him. Her caution contrasts with the impetuous behavior of Louise Connor, Elizabeth Waugh, and Wilson's cousin Helen Augur, all of whom had searing relationships with him during this same period. Some years later Magda Johann, now Tarleton, sent Wilson an invitation to an exhibition she had in New York. He carefully saved for posterity the invitation, a large professionally taken photograph of her, and a few of her letters.

As Wilson points out in his short, bracketed introduction (written in the 1960s) to the long 1927 Provincetown entry in *The Twenties*, he arrived on the Cape at the beginning of the summer and looked for a place to rent. He would be joined by Rosalind and her nurse, Stella. Through John Francis, the local real estate agent, he learned that the prospective tenants for the O'Neill house on the dunes had just canceled. Wilson took the house. That summer proved to be an eventful one for him, although somewhat less so for his four-year-old daughter and her nurse.

Just after arrival, Wilson describes Provincetown thus: "exquisite delicacy of mother-of-pearl sea thinning to a fragile shelly blade along the shallow shore—a sort of iridescence of violet, blue and green—a few gulls." With his usual attention to salient detail, he goes on to note the food he has eaten, bits of overheard conversation, two churches, houses, gardens, and "the painted wooden figurehead of woman with head thrown up and one hand clasping wreath across breast over doorstep shelter of yellow house, sunk like an old water-logged ship in a dooryard of long uncut grass, with an old woman sitting at the window" (*Twenties*, 381–382). The statue in question was one of a half dozen sailing-ship figureheads that had gone on to adorn Provincetown houses. From the street scene rendered in feuilleton style, the narrative quickly shifts to a conversation with a real woman. The passage begins: "*Florence.* Her voice on the telephone—'people who hear me say that it's the most terrible thing they ever heard.' 'Ted hates dirty stories you know'" (*Twenties*, 382). Florence O'Neill, a chorus girl and the model for Daisy in Wilson's novel *I Thought of Daisy* (1929), was the lover of Ted Paramore, an old friend of Wilson's. The latter saw a good deal of Florence, it appears, during Paramore's absences from New York. Wilson and Florence made an excursion to Coney Island together, which he incorporated into his novel. The journal entry now under discussion, consisting of fragmentary bits of past conversations with her, alludes to the Coney Island trip. The notebook version continues beyond the sentence "I don't know what it's all about" that concludes the published version of the entry. The notebook text continues: "When she arrived in Provincetown . . . ," and goes on to describe Florence's bedraggled appearance and sagging spirits (Notebooks of Twenties [hereafter Notebooks] VIII, 37). It is clear from the unpublished text that the two are staying in the same rooming house. She reappears in the published version a couple of pages later in another entry captioned "Florence." It begins with references to the Coney Island episode but quickly moves to the present: "high-keyed and gala the day she arrived in Provincetown—we're all high-keyed and you're quiet and sober—her rompers—her color began to come back the next day." The truncated fragments of conversation end with a distraught and probably drunk Florence bewailing her fate and the sexual crudity of men. "I hate 'em [men] anyway—just ogling and pinching and pawing—grasping and pushing!" (*Twenties*, 387). In the notebook this is followed by Florence's leading remark: "You old sheik . . ." (a reference to Wilson's performance as a would-be Valentino). In the light of the above citations, one might fairly speculate that the relationship between these two was hardly as platonic as Wilson suggested years later when he was editing *The Twenties* for publication. In a bracketed insertion he states that although Florence was "the original of Daisy in my novel . . . the story is itself invented—we were never lovers" (*Twenties*, 240). Whatever the case, Florence visited Wilson in Provincetown before he had secured the O'Neill house and summoned Rosalind and Stella to live there with him.

In his journals Wilson consistently merges overheard conversations, remarks made by friends, jokes, anecdotes, songs, quickly jotted landscape sketches, and graphic sexual episodes (often more developed than any of the foregoing). In the section just quoted he introduces a whole cast of Provincetown characters. We meet the bombastic poet Harry Kemp, vagabond king of the bohemians; Susan Glaspell, already an established playwright and novelist; and Wilson's neighbor on the dunes, the aspiring writer Hazel Hawthorne, currently married to a Protestant minister. Like so many other visitors to Provincetown, Wilson had a special affection for John Francis, a real estate agent and the proprietor of a grocery store his father had acquired. Half-Irish and half-Portuguese, Francis was well liked in the community, and he gave generous credit in his store to impecunious bohemians like Harry Kemp (who returned the favor by penning an affectionate recreation of Francis in his novel *Love among the Cape Enders*). Wilson observes that the unmaterialistic Francis "discouraged clients from taking any of the houses he showed them" (*Twenties*, 379); in addition Francis was something of an intellectual, having read Thomas Mann, Hemingway, *The Dial*, and having "voted the Communist ticket (the only person in town who did)" (*Twenties*, 387). Francis expressed outrage at the death sentence recently passed on Sacco and Vanzetti, the two Italian anarchists convicted of the murder of two guards in an attack on a payroll delivery in Braintree, Massachusetts,

April 15, 1920. The case had become extremely politicized, with conservatives and "patriots" clamoring for the Italians' execution, while liberals and leftists (such as Wilson and Francis) denounced the guilty verdict as a miscarriage of justice. The two immigrants' absolute guilt or absolute innocence has never been conclusively proven. There is no doubt, however, that they were mistreated by the judicial system because of their radical activities. They were executed in Boston on August 23, 1927.

It is at this point in Wilson's journal, and real life, that he decided to spend a few days in Boston, where many writers and intellectuals, as well as ordinary people, had gathered to demonstrate against the impending execution. Among the demonstrators were many of Wilson's friends: Edna St. Vincent Millay, Dorothy Parker, and John Dos Passos; a Provincetown contingent included Susan Glaspell, Mary Heaton Vorse, and Frank Shay. Dos Passos, who was active in the "Citizens' National Committee for Sacco and Vanzetti," did everything he could to bring prominent people to Boston for demonstrations (Carr, 227). On August 19, 1927, Dos Passos telegraphed Wilson in Provincetown the following message: "Need picketers and speakers for last Saczetti protest staying here Dos Passos" (Beinecke). Dos Passos subsequently got a wire from Wilson inviting him to a party at the Peaked Hill house. On September 19, Dos Passos replied: "Jesus X. Columbus, man, didn't you realize that we were all virtually mad up in Boston? You try battering your head against a stone wall sometime" (Carr, 228). Wilson's apparent indifference to the Sacco-Vanzetti cause is not easy to explain. His biographer Jeffrey Meyers (Meyers, 118–119) and Leon Edel, the editor of his journals, both sidestep it, while citing Wilson's letter to John Peale Bishop (October 22, 1928). Writing to his old friend, who was then residing in France, Wilson commented on the way the case affected all classes of American society and "raised almost every fundamental question of our political and social system." Wilson went on to paraphrase Dos Passos' view that "during the last days before the executions, as if, by some fairy-tale spell, all the different kinds of Americans, eminent and obscure, had suddenly, in a short burst of intensified life, been compelled to reveal their true characters in a heightened exaggerated form" (cited by Edel, *Twenties*, 389). These Olympian pronouncements do not express Wilson's own feelings about the execution, which had taken place more than a year earlier. His diary entries for August 1927 do reveal something about his mind-set, and actual activities, at that critical historical moment. His short story "The Men from Rumplemayer's," dated September 28, 1927, and based on his trip to Boston one month earlier, contains similar revelations. (The story first appeared under the title "Lobsters for Dinner" in *The New Republic*; it was republished under its present title in *The American Earthquake*, 1958.)

Wilson sailed from Provincetown to Boston, probably on August 16, 1927. His goal was not to attend the demonstrations but to visit two sisters, Louise and Henrietta Fort. (Louise was married to Peter Connor, a lawyer; they lived in Chicago with their young son, also Peter. Some six years later, in 1933, Wilson would begin an ardent love affair with the eccentric Louise; he also remained close to Henrietta, and may have had some responsibility for the breakup of *her* marriage.) In his journal Wilson notes his impressions of Provincetown, and Boston, as seen from the water during the trip. According to the time frame he gives for his stay in Boston, August 16–18, he returned to Provincetown the day before the big demonstration for Sacco and Vanzetti (during which Dos Passos, Millay, and others were arrested); nonetheless, the doomed men's shadow loomed over the city. The entry detailing his visit with the Fort sisters, who seem to have been staying at a country club where they put him up, is preceded by a dense passage titled "Boston Harbor." In this impressionistic description he seems to be shifting between a nineteenth-century picture of Boston Harbor with which he is familiar and the scene he is observing at first hand.

> Boston before us under a setting sun of industrial red copper, metal edging a bulk of rain cloud filling the sky to the left and overcoming the still limpid blue of earliest fall, the old-fashioned looking boats— but the gloom on the waters was of Sacco and Vanzetti, not the nineteenth century upholstery obscuration of a landscape which somehow made it profounder and richer, but merely dulling, the further denuding of a level and uniform metallic surface, pricked and spiked by the buoys and ship masts—the dumb immobile unthundering storm, like some great blank immovable menace, the blank menace not merely of some disaster to humanity, but of the negation of humanity itself.—I shouldn't have thought of the Boston Harbor of the picture—hardblowing, but unsultry wind. (*Twenties*, 389)

Aware of the "blank menace . . . of some future disaster to humanity . . . the negation of humanity itself," Wilson reproaches himself for thinking of something else, the picture of Boston Harbor. Drawing on the journals and the above-mentioned short story, I will argue that although he understood the terrible injustice of Sacco and Vanzetti's imminent execution, he could or would not get personally involved.

His sojourn in Boston with the Forts and a friend of theirs, the jejune former Harvardian Percy Wendell, involved an alcohol-soaked ramble through the city streets, with stops at the Ritz Hotel, Revere Beach, Swampscott, Wendell's apartment, and the country club where they were staying. The narrative collage, made up of disconnected pieces of conversation and the narrator's own disjointed commentary, mimics the inebriated condition of the participants. Much of the focus is gastronomic. At the Ritz rathskeller a bedazed Wilson tries to order a second chicken sandwich, while an untouched one remains on his plate—at which point one of the sisters asks: "did I want to drive by the prison where Sacco and Vanzetti were?" Later in the day, someone asks rhetorically: "Have the men from Rumplemayer's come?" This refers to a famous London catering firm; the quote comes directly from the first page of Virginia Woolf's novel *Mrs. Dalloway*. A later reference to Sacco and Vanzetti's unsuccessful appeal to the Supreme Court is juxtaposed with a description of carrying lobsters in a paper bag to Wendell's apartment, where he cooks them. Finally Wilson ends up by himself, waiting in South Station for his train back to Cape Cod, in "that awful upstairs restaurant" where he orders "an all-white-meat chicken sandwich with giblet gravy and three poor inch-long banana fritters" from some "repulsive, touching, bespeckled, pale-haired and -eyed Irish waitresses." While eating, Wilson, "daze-minded and -eyed with alcohol," reads about Sacco and Vanzetti in the newspaper, and he remembers Vanzetti's words: "I am innocent of these two harms." Once on the train, Wilson gradually sobers up and muses about the time spent with the Forts and "the close of the American summer." Then he becomes absorbed in the landscape. Returning to Peaked Hill, "I found the sea turned cold and sheeted with iron-blue tinsel of fall" (*Twenties*, 395–396). The next notation is: "Wire from the girls: 'Come at once. Rumplemayer's men are draining the old oaken bucket. Forsaken.'"(The bucket belonged to Percy Wendell; it held a copious supply of bootleg alcohol.)

The short story "The Men from Rumplemayer's" follows the same general narrative line as the journal entry. The story, however, is more overtly political. It includes a lucid discussion of the reasons that the convicted anarchists would not get a new trial. The four characters drive out to Revere Beach, where they smell a rotten odor of condemned clams. Sighting two clam diggers, one of the women comments: "Two condemned people digging for condemned clams" (*Earthquake*, 156). Despite "Julia's" squeamishness at boiling the lobsters alive, "Ralph" cooks them at his mother's Beacon Hill apartment (clearly a veiled allusion to the condemned men's imminent fate in the electric chair). Ralph has nixed the suggestion that they dine at the Squamscott Club, thereby, opines the narrator, saving himself the potential embarrassment of the narrator making "a speech [there] about Sacco and Vanzetti." At the end of the story the narrator returns to his rural "camp" to find two telegrams awaiting him. The first is the same Rumplemayer's message quoted in the journals; the second, from "a friend connected with the Sacco-Vanzetti Defense Committee," reads like the real Dos Passos telegram: "Picketers and speakers needed for last protest." Having used up all of his extra money, however, the narrator "couldn't answer either summons" (*Earthquake*, 160).

Leon Edel states that Wilson saw the story as an example of the "high ironic" (*Twenties*, 388). David Castronovo develops this idea through perceptive textual analysis. He points out, for example, that when the story's characters sing "Flamin' Mamie" and "Forsaken," they are ironically unaware that the titles apply to the two men who have exhausted every legal recourse and are awaiting execution. Overall, Castronovo reads the story as a protest against the well-meaning, well-off characters' isolation and insularity. He calls it "a microcosmic presentation of American guilt and American awkwardness" (Castronovo, 54–55).

Clearly the journal entry and the story are ironic in their juxtaposition of the public and the private spheres. When dealing with the question of moral responsibility, we must however distance the politically conscious narrator from his three naïve friends. The irony is probably intended to underscore the narrator's sense of impotence (which has led to indifference?) in the face of the impending victory of right-wing forces. A clear alternative to such a defeatist attitude would, to be sure, have been an active participation in the protests.

The rest of the 1927 Provincetown entries show the sea, ugly and smelly in bad weather, and transcendently beautiful at dawn or on a good day: "the sea so smooth, such faint and tender blue and, in the light-blue sky above, a few clouds tinting delicately pink like shells—the faint surf fringing the silk of the sea with a light swish and a little silver" (*Twenties*, 396–398). Little Johnny Ufford, Hazel Hawthorne-Ufford's son, also catches Wilson's attention, as does his own little daughter Rosalind. The following passage, which he deleted from *The Twenties*—probably in deference to the adult Rosalind's feelings—when he edited his diaries for future publication, shows Wilson to have been a loving parent. Here is his description of a game he played with Rosalind at Peaked Hill; the passage ends with a reference to a story he told her at bedtime.

> I was a grasshopper faint from shipwreck—Rosalind brought me doll, things to eat, books to read—"some water with sugar in it"— would bring some purple water tomorrow. I was chirp-chirping— "stop chirping: you're going to have a tea-party."—Little Jane Ufford complained that Rosalind was always promising them things and never made good—had promised each a little green bird—my story of old man with three little green birds—kept chattering all night— acting it out, she as little birds danced and sang to keep me awake. (Notebooks VIII, 53)

It is clear from these Provincetown entries that Wilson led a lively social life that summer of 1927. Although he doesn't mention it in the diary, he must have given his legendary nonparty that August—probably the same one to which he so untactfully invited Dos Passos, who was then organizing the Sacco-Vanzetti protests in Boston. According to Hazel Hawthorne, Wilson's neighbor at Peaked Hill, Wilson invited his friends to a cocktail party at the O'Neill house. That afternoon he walked into town to buy a block of ice for the drinks. Hawthorne watched him returning over the dunes, "his robust form struggling in the sliding sand, buttons loosened at the knees of his flapping golf pants, and the ice dripping from a gunny sack he was carrying. . . . Looking at his bouncing, rolling form," Hawthorne observed: "'I knew then why they called him Bunny.' What little was left of the ice was placed in a galvanized box. But Wilson forgot to close the lid. By the time the guests had arrived, the ice had melted and Wilson had locked himself in the former mess room and fallen asleep. The early guests helped themselves to Wilson's Prohibition-era bathtub gin. When they left to telephone the other guests to ask them to bring ice, Wilson locked them out" (Hawthorne paraphrased by Egan, 247). The story exists in several variants, but it is clear that Wilson had liberally imbibed immediately upon arriving home—he never had much inclination to postpone gratification, especially in matters relating to alcohol. As legend, the story had a very long life. During a short stay in Provincetown in 1939, Fred Dupee, an editor at *Partisan Review*, to which Mary McCarthy regularly contributed, heard the tale and mentioned it in a letter to McCarthy, now Wilson's wife. I myself heard it from a Wellfleet old-timer in the 1980s.

During that summer Wilson fraternized with Harry Kemp (1883–1960), a Greenwich Village bohemian who first came to Provincetown in 1916, in time to join the Provincetown Players that summer. He would root himself in the Cape's shifting sands and live on the dunes. Originally from the Midwest, he had traveled the country as a hobo and once contrived to reach England for free—as a stowaway on an ocean liner. Hard-drinking and rambunctious, Kemp managed to write quite a lot of highly rhetorical traditional verse. He also wrote plays and several autobiographical novels.[1] He was erudite. Although he had no university degree, he read ancient Greek, Latin, French, German, Italian, and Russian. When in his thirties he married a vivacious younger woman, the actress Mary Pyne, whom he treated badly. (She left him.) Rosalind Wilson's mother, the actress Mary Blair, remembered that Kemp "had locked up his first wife, a beautiful redhead, for long periods of time with nothing to eat but bananas" (*Magician*, 75). Wilson himself tells some amusing stories about Kemp in 1927. He reports that Harry "conjured away" a thunderstorm that had interrupted an absinthe party. (This must have been unusual, since during Prohibition Provincetonians were more or less condemned to drinking "alky," a lethal home brew flavored with orange peel.) According to Wilson, Kemp was an ineffectual promoter of his dramatic works: "He used to go around to restaurants with a cowbell to get people to come to his show" (*Twenties*, 400). After his wife left him, Kemp wanted to abandon or drown the household cat: "Harry Kemp would just get ready to put his cat in a bag and drop him in the water, when the cat would come and put her paw on his arm and he'd say, 'No, by God, you darn old bugger—I'll stick by ye!'" (*Twenties*, 399). Wilson describes Kemp as a "mountebank" but found him a droll raconteur. These two oddly matched writers would continue to see each other during the thirties. Norman Mailer remembered meeting Wilson in the sixties in Provincetown; the venue was Hazel Hawthorne's house on Bradford Street, which was next to the shack where Harry lived in his last years. Mailer, who was meeting Wilson for the first or second time, found him aloof—the great critic became animated only in order to re-count Harry Kemp stories (interview with Norman Mailer, February 15, 2002). Unfortunately, as an old man Kemp became a sad, burnt-out relic of his former self. I remember him wandering the streets of Province-town, talking to himself and haranguing passersby. In 1927, Wilson thought of writing a play with a Harry Kemp character in it. The note-books for *The Twenties* show the following notation: "Harry Kemp, in last act of play, borrowing stamps, reciting poetry, complacently exploit-ing his own weaknesses." In a later note to his handwritten diaries Wil-son wrote: "I finally used him (H.K.) for Fred Burroughs in *This Room and This Gin and These Sandwiches.*" The play was published in 1937. In it, Burroughs/Kemp, a believer in the spirit world, promotes his "reli-gion," cadges drinks, and eloquently recites a Keats sonnet.

Wilson spent most of the year 1928 in New York City. There he re-connected with Margaret Canby (née Waterman), a divorcée and a for-mer girlfriend of Wilson's college pal Ted Paramore. (Wilson had first met her in San Francisco in 1924.) He then visited Margaret in her native California, where they spent the last three months of 1928. All this to the discomfort of Paramore, who was courting her anew after her failed marriage to the oft-abusive James Canby. Wilson would marry Margaret in 1930. Nonetheless, during 1928, 1929, and then, sporadically, until 1937, he continued a serious affair with Frances, a working-class girl of Ukrainian origin whom he had first met in a dance hall. He would also continue other dalliances in times of geographical separation from Mar-garet. In the summer of 1929, he returned to Cape Cod, to Dennis, some thirty-five miles south of Provincetown, with Rosalind and Stella. (Their stay probably lasted three weeks.) They took rooms at the Hotel Nob-scusset (named after a local Indian chief) facing the waters of Nantucket Sound. The "Dennis, Cape Cod" entries are in the last section of *The Twenties*, titled "New York." We know from the unpublished text that fa-ther and daughter went to see the Uffords in Provincetown. Overall they seem to have had a pleasant vacation in Dennis. Wilson's diary predom-inantly focuses on seascapes: the varied forms of marine life and the sen-suous figures of adolescents frolicking on the beach.

After Wilson and Margaret Canby were married, they spent the sum-mer of 1930 in the O'Neill house on Peaked Hill. The newly married couple was accompanied by Rosalind, age seven, and Margaret's son Jimmy Canby, age twelve. The children had a wonderful time that summer.

Rosalind Wilson, age 5, while vacationing with her father in Dennis, Cape Cod.

(Rosalind would remember it affectionately in her memoirs and in a moving short piece titled "The Condemned Coast Guard Station at Peaked Hill Bars.") Rosalind's nurse Stella, originally from Jamaica, did household chores and served as a live-in babysitter. Her life was far from easy—she did not know how to swim, the only easily available recreation—and she was more or less at the mercy of her demanding employer's vagaries. Rosalind reports that her father once demanded that Stella make him a fried egg sandwich in the middle of the night. When Stella demurred, "he bellowed at her" (*Magician*, 75). In her memoir, Rosalind remembers the long walk, lasting an hour and a half, over the dunes into the town, "with mosquito nets wrung out in citronella over our heads"; then they would return to Peaked Hill with the groceries in knapsacks. By this time the house was partly immersed in sand, which had rendered the bathroom inoperative, except for the bathtub, now turned to the manufacture of home brew. (There was an outhouse.) Ros-

Edmund Wilson reading a newspaper at the O'Neill house at Peaked Hill, off Provincetown, 1930. Daughter Rosalind is partly visible.

alind noticed that guests, like the Dos Passoses, who used the bathroom to change into their swimming suits emerged "much more talkative and animated." The two children explored the beach and found shipwrecks by the new coast guard station, just half a mile south of the O'Neill house. They fraternized with the kindhearted coastguardsmen, as did their parents, who welcomed them at their well-irrigated beach picnics. Rosalind also remembers the neighbors, Hazel Hawthorne and Harry Kemp, who lived in nearby shacks. Harry put on some séances for the Wilsons at their house. During one of these Jimmy and Rosalind, standing on the roof, lowered a log, suspended from a rope, into the fireplace. They were hoping that Harry would take this as a "message from a ghost," but the adults paid no attention (*Magician*, 75). Wilson seems to have enjoyed the children's company. He read to them in the evenings and procured a pony named "Betsy" to board with them over the summer. The children remained blissfully unaware that their parents were pursuing a vigorous and inventive daytime sex life on the beach and the dunes; at night, the couple resorted to a white chaise longue in the sitting room, where "naked—she [Margaret] looked in the moonlight which gave her the pale bluish whiteness of a statue, like a little short plumpish Venus— a sort of Leda-and-the-Swan effect astride the chair" (*Thirties*, 21).

On August 12, 1930, Wilson records going out with fishermen to empty their traps in the bay. The voyage began in Truro and ended at the Provincetown pier. Against the predawn setting, the five fishermen, seen first on the wharf as "dark-faced shapeless figures," silently "rowed out toward the traps with regular heavy and funereal rhythm of oars." As the fish are hauled into the boat, the scene is orchestrated by "the butterfish, great flapping silver flakes, making a smacking crepitation of fireworks when they were thrown onto the floor of the boat." Then we see the helpless squid, which squeak in contrast to the slapping of the other fish—"they seemed so futile, so unpleasantly uncannily incomplete flimsy forms of life, with their round expressionless eyes, like eyes painted—a white iris with a black spot—on some naïve toy, their plumes like the ostrich feathers of some Renaissance woman of the court in an engraving by Callot." Having "squirted their last squirt" in a vain attempt to escape, the squid "expire indistinguishably in a mixed bluish and amberish carpet of slime." Wilson goes on to note the "mackerel, with their little clean-clipped tails like neat little efficient propellers: everything the squid were not—iridescent mother-of-pearl along the bellies and striped distinctly black and green along their backs." The mackerel are followed by a big, ugly goosefish (thrown overboard) and "dogfish with their mean smug sharks' mouths on the white underside and their ugly absurd sharks' eyes with a gray cat-pupil on a whitish lozenge of iris." The last comers are "a few whiting and codheaded hake" and "rather prettily mottled sand dabs." When they returned to port after sunrise, "The blue shirts and the dirty yellow oilcloth of the five fishermen matched the sky and the sea and the unseen presence of sand" (*Thirties*, 27–28). Epic passages, like this one, in the journals almost always refer to Cape Cod. Perhaps the predominating sea motif is the reason for this.

Although Wilson records marine life, just as he does landscape and architecture, with an eye for minute detail, most of his human subjects are lacking in sharp contours. Only Margaret, who reminds him of a "pony," is accorded careful description in these entries, but her image comes through slightly blurred: "Brown V of the flesh of her neck, so rich without rosiness against the white skin of her breast—little feet with their bony toes in New York, when she would take them out of her shoes—more rounded, more cunning, with more sex appeal below her rounded cunning brown woman's thighs" (*Thirties*, 22). In his journals, Wilson tends to characterize people through their spoken words rather than their physical appearance.

Toward the end of this memorable summer of 1930 E. E. Cummings and his second wife (Anne Barton) came to stay with the Wilsons at Peaked Hill. Their arrival coincided with some very stormy weather. In his journal Wilson notes that the sea "devoured" the dune on which the house stood, "spray or rain blew in through the windows at night," while a strong undertow made swimming impossible; after the storm flotsam and jetsam and dead marine life littered the shore. His friend Bruce Rogers (1870–1957, the well-known book designer) found an old musket; Wanda Lyon, "a friend of Margaret's, once a musical-comedy actress," pronounced the washed-up "crystal-looking things" to be "sea anemones, like the ones she had seen in Japan"; her boyfriend, "the San Francisco playboy Stan Gwynn," found "a giant cochineal-red starfish." Wilson also notes "the biting man-eating flies on the beach [that] also waked you up in the morning" (*Thirties*, 34–35). The weather cleared and, judging by the photographs that Wilson later gave his daughter Rosalind, everyone seems to have spent time on the beach. (According to Rosalind, her nanny was the photographer.) The two snapshots of the Cummingses are quite comical: the poet, visibly inebriated, seems unaware of his wife's statuesque presence at his side. The Cummingses must have done a lot of drinking together. In *The Twenties* Wilson reports that E.E. and Anne were so drunk before their 1927 wedding in New York that the best man, Dos Passos, had had to take desperate measures to sober them up (*Twenties*, 429). There is no doubt that the Cummingses enjoyed their sojourn in Provincetown. In a conversation with me at Harvard, where he had come to give a public reading, the poet recalled the former coast guard station where he and Anne stayed with my father and Margaret. More to the point is his bread and butter letter to the Wilsons, written September 2, 1930, from their farm in New Hampshire. In accordance with the convention to which it belongs, it recreates, with Rabelaisian gusto, some of the pleasurable moments spent on the seacoast of Bohemia.

JOYBARN, nh
Eyedz of Kaylenz,* '30
Gentle Denizens of Thalassaville:
Hail:
We, the undersigned
do hereby proffer our benignities and do very much trust that
you survived the Dreadful and Terrible Scene Over the Cut of Pig;

*Herman Kahle was a Provincetown artist.

whereof consequences still echo in our surfsmit hearts. Nor shall
years (neither time with his scythechariot) ever so much as begin to
obliterate—let alone erase—your generosities; to whom ourselves
are most fain if all too willing debtors: nonetheless it is our purblind
aspiration that you'll give us a whack at evening things up without
benefit of underto and allowing for the difference in density between
aqua fresh and saline. As for True Row,* 'tis a mere paddle by comparison with Dune City—but for god's sake watch those O. Jene
U.Kneelites and keep 1 weathereye peeled for the bishopy cook John
Silver[†] alias Heartofgold. In the name of Harry the Hamlet, Harry
the Kemp, and Harry the Rogers Bruce

> Dingaling A BAS LES BARRELPIPPILS VIVE LA VIE
> Shantyshantyshantyshantyshantyshantyshanty
> Hovelhutcabinhouseaboderesidencedemesnemanorcastlepalace-
> farmshack
> ah,
> (wo)
> Men.

Under Cummings' typescript is a short handwritten note from Anne:

> Dear Margaret and Bunny—
> How about this weekend? There will be a general exodus New
> York wards on the 12 leaving only the Lardners.
> Give our best to those best beloved of children
> affectionately
> Anne

With the above letter at Yale are three drawings by Cummings inspired
by his stay in Provincetown. One of these has been partly eaten by mice;
the other two show, according to Wilson's later inscriptions on them,
"probably Cummings himself, after drinking out P-town alcohol," and

---

*Truro, the community fourteen miles south of Provincetown. Dos Passos and
some Provincetonians had cottages there.

[†]Seems to be a reference to Wilson's and Cummings' friend, the poet John Peale
Bishop, although he was residing in France at the time. Perhaps he came to
Provincetown for a visit. Harl Cook, the son of the writer George Cram Cook and
something of a ne'er-do-well, was then living in Provincetown. The reference to
Robert Louis Stevenson's *Treasure Island*, also titled *The Sea-Cook*, is obvious.

E. E. Cummings and his wife Anne (Barton) during
their stay with the Wilsons at Peaked Hill, 1930.

"Cummings, EW, Margaret, Jimmy and Rosalind—O'Neill house on dune." Both sketches are caricatures. The first shows a grotesquely sinuous Cummings-figure with an outsize head. He is holding his stomach and grimacing; next to him is a table with bottles and a glass, and behind him a stern policeman is doing a little caper. The other is a beach scene with Cummings holding his stomach while a diminutive and portly Wilson is draining a bottle to the last drop; a sultry Margaret is sunbathing while the two children frolic in the water.

The Wilsons left Provincetown in mid-September. They spent a few weeks in New York. In October Margaret went back to the West Coast and Wilson returned to the Peaked Hill house, which he now shared with an artist called "Blazy," the current boyfriend of Hazel Hawthorne who lived in a neighboring shack. "Blazy" did all the cooking—his repertoire consisted mostly of applesauce and clam chowder. In January 1931, Margaret came east again and the couple spent some time with the Dos Passoses in Provincetown. It was then that the Hapgoods, Dos Passoses, Wilsons, and others undertook the salvage expedition to the now moribund O'Neill house.

Cummings' sketches from his sojourn with the Wilsons on Peaked Hill, 1930. Yale Collection of American Literature, Beinecke Rare Book and Manuscript Library, Yale University.

Edmund Wilson has written beneath:
"Probably Cummings himself, after drinking out P-town alcohol."

Cumming, EW, May and, Jimmy & Rosalind
O'Neil house on dune

These sketches by Cummings — now partly eaten by
mice — were all done, I think, at the time of his
visit to us at Peaked Hill

Under the sketch Edmund Wilson has written: "Cummings, EW, Margaret,
Jimmy, and Rosalind . . . O'Neill house on dune. . . . These sketches by Cummings—
now partly eaten by mice—were all done, I think, at the time of his visit to us
at Peaked Hill." Note that Rosalind has superimposed her own initials, RBW
(Rosalind Baker Wilson), over the middle.

From the right side, the Peaked Hill house gives access (see ladder) only via the roof and turret. Figure on roof is possibly Hazel Hawthorne.

The doomed house with Phyllis Duganne, Susan Glaspell, and Norman Matson below. Note the new coast guard station in the background.

It might now be useful to recapitulate exactly who Wilson's Provincetown and Truro friends were, since most of them would remain on the Cape and Wilson would continue to see them, if only in some cases intermittently, until they, or he, died. Of the artists, he saw a good deal of Niles Spencer and his wife Betty; Charles (Charley) Kaselau; Frederick Waugh, a successful marine painter called "the Wizard" by his admirers; his son Coulton, a modernist; Edwin Dickinson (who would later move to Wellfleet); Eben Given, a portraitist who suffered from a neurotic block over the last forty years of his life; Bill and Lucy L'Engle (pronounced "Longle"); and Helen Sawyer Farnsworth (Henkaberry). Wilson's circle of literary friends included John and Katy Dos Passos; Frank Shay, editor, bookseller, and minor writer and his wife Edie (née Foley); Susan Glaspell; Mary Heaton Vorse; Harry Kemp; Hazel Hawthorne (a niece of the artist Charles Hawthorne); and Phyllis Duganne, who married Eben Given in 1930. Phyllis, the only native Cape Codder in this literary-artistic circle, lived in Truro with her mother, Maud Emma, whom I remember as a taciturn old lady with the chiseled features indicative of her Native American ancestry. Eben's sister Thelma had been a violin prodigy as a child. In her later career, while on tour in Russia in 1917, she had to flee across the ice to Finland after the outbreak of the Revolution. In 1920 Thelma, a widow, and her parents were living in the family house overlooking the harbor on Commercial Street, Provincetown. She later married Mint Verde, a rich lawyer who housed his two Aston-Martins in the Given garage. Phyllis Duganne Given wrote mostly short fiction, which she sold to *Collier's*, the *Saturday Evening Post*, and other commercial magazines. In Provincetown, Wilson saw a good deal of Chauncey and Mary (Bubbs) Hackett. Chauncey was a former lawyer who had been a partner with Mint Verde in Washington; he wrote some fiction, which he had little or no success publishing. Bubbs was a "naïve" painter whose haunting portrayals of Provincetown and other locations achieved significant recognition only in the decade before her death. Erudite and politically savvy, Chauncey had been forced into retirement from his profession. Like another former lawyer, Charles (Bud) Boyden from Chicago, who belonged to the same circle, Chauncey had independent means. Bud and Polly Boyden (a writer) lived in Truro—highly sociable, their lives revolved around alcohol. Inconstant, and yet unable to live apart, they remarried each other for a total of three marriages.

Katy Dos Passos and Edie Shay were both talented writers, although they were overshadowed by their more famous husbands. As already mentioned, before their marriages they had shared "Smooley Hall" with Bill Smith (Katy's brother) and Stella Roof (another writer). Katy and Edie collaborated in 1936 on *Down the Cape: The Complete Guidebook to Cape Cod*. While Dos was struggling in New York to finish *The Big Money*, Katy and Edie were working in Provincetown to meet the publisher's deadline for the guidebook. According to Dos Passos' biographer Virginia Carr it was only thanks to Edie's organizational and editing skills that they met it (Carr, 346). In 1944 Katy and Edie wrote a best-selling novel together, *The Private Adventures of Captain Shaw*. The notoriety and much-needed money it earned for the authors surprised the husbands and friends of both.

In 1951 Frank and Edie Shay published what is arguably the best omnibus of Cape history, lore, nature, and culture. Their anthology, *Sand in Their Shoes: A Cape Cod Reader*, includes passages on Cape Cod geology and architecture by Katy Dos Passos, an article, "Cape Cod Bird Life," by Oliver Austin Jr., then director of the Ornithological Research Station in South Wellfleet (now a bird sanctuary), "The Captain's Table," a chapter on Cape Cod cuisine, "Esteemed Girl" by Phyllis Duganne about the Brewster courtship of two of her nineteenth-century forebears, with the couple's original correspondence, and much, much more. The component parts, mostly documentary or semidocumentary in nature, give a tangible, grainy picture of Cape Cod's rough-hewn inhabitants and their sea-dominated past. This anthology has recently been complemented but not surpassed by Robert Finch's *A Place Apart: A Cape Cod Reader* (1993). The texts in both books, penned mostly by minor hands, show that the major professional writers who came to Cape Cod wrote little about it. Dos Passos didn't write about it at all. Norman Mailer used Provincetown as the setting for a roman noir, *Tough Guys Don't Dance* (1984). Wilson's case is special: the Cape has a very important place in his occasional writing, the diaries and the poetry, but it is absent from his essays and fiction. The visual artists, especially those who came to live and work in Provincetown, have, on the other hand, rendered the land and seascape in many styles and tonalities. For many painters, the Cape was compelling and indispensable in their work. Some minor novelists, among them Harry Kemp, Susan Glaspell,[2] Hazel Hawthorne,[3] and Robert Nathan,[4] have scrutinized the Cape with flashes of insight. Perhaps the Cape's social pattern has been too small-scale, and seasonal, to inspire a major novel. When we turn to consider Mary McCarthy's *A Charmed Life*, her most dramatic novel, we shall notice that, although the flora and fauna resemble those of a Cape-style bohemian enclave, the delineation of the geography is intentionally vague. Clearly she felt that the inclusion of overly specific *couleur locale* would only detract from the universal moral issues that she wished to confront.

In February 1931 Wilson went to see the Pennsylvania steelworks; from there he stopped in Detroit, where he worked up the automobile industry. He moved on to the coalfields of Kentucky, West Virginia, and Tennessee (to investigate the Scottsboro case, which he would profile in "The Scottsboro Freight Car Case"). After spending some time in the Midwest and Colorado, he met up with Margaret and Jimmy in New Mexico. They were joined by Rosalind and Stella, and they all went on to Southern California, where they spent the summer. Wilson returned to the East Coast with Rosalind in September. He reestablished contact with Frances in New York and then in late October went to Lawrence, Massachusetts, to cover a textile workers' strike. On October 31 he went to Provincetown, where he lived in Susan Glaspell's house while she and her partner Norman Matson were away. Margaret joined him there in November. Wilson later remembered that they shared a hillside rental (*Thirties*, 147). In early November he recorded a long evening walk with Katy Dos Passos. Dos must have been away, and Margaret still in California. The diary entry reads:

> Walk with Katy in Provincetown in early November—Hawthorne's hilltop lawn [the reference is to the painter Charles Hawthorne], the [Pilgrim] monument—queer, strong, but mild and almost warm wind blowing—white square steeples down below in the darkness—a night of plain rumpled beauty, shadows dark and white.
>
> Milky, milk stains.
>
> —winter—big white square churches and white high-keeled houses built like ships.
>
> —Katy said it was like something in a book.
> Katy's little green socks and untied gray leather moccasins (*Thirties*, 153–154)

Sensitive, as ever, to gradations of light and architectural contours when describing the inanimate world, Wilson's glance finally zeros in on his companion's footwear. Like Alexander Pushkin, the Russian poet whom he so admired, he was susceptible to the charms of women's feet. Under his lasting attachment to Katy Dos Passos there doubtless ran a current of physical attraction. Katy had striking features, a ready wit, and a kind of languid grace that appealed to men, among them Ernest Hemingway, who pursued her before her marriage to Dos. She valued Wilson's friendship highly and would later find her dear "Antichrist" an inseparable companion in Provincetown when Dos was covering the war in the Pacific in 1945 (Reuel Wilson, "Cape Cod Landscape" [hereafter "CCL"], 106–107). Wilson himself had assumed the persona of "Hiram K. Antichrist" in his correspondence with the Dos Passoses, and they began their letters to him "Dear Antichrist," or "Dear AntiX." (In May 1938 Wilson wrote the Dos Passoses: "Marxism is the opium of the intellectuals. . . . All Hollywood corrupts; and absolute Hollywood corrupts absolutely.—Old Antichrist's sayings" [*Letters on Literature and Politics*, 302]). After Katy's death in 1947 Wilson recalls in his journal that he had once glimpsed her naked when she was changing into a bathing suit with other women in the Peaked Hill bathroom.

By the end of the twenties and with the advent of the Depression Wilson moved further to the political left. His journalistic writings, published in *The American Jitters* (1932), later republished in *The American Earthquake* (1958), reflect his interest in social justice. In the collection, he explores the deplorable plight of impoverished farmers, exploited miners, and factory workers whose efforts to organize and strike consistently met with brutal repression. In February 1932 Wilson joined a concerted attempt on the part of left-wing intellectuals and activists to bring food, clothing, and moral support to striking coal miners in Pineville, Kentucky. Among his companions were the critic Malcolm Cowley; Allen Taub, a famous International Labor Defense lawyer; Mary Heaton Vorse, whose journalistic pen often served labor causes; Waldo Frank, novelist, critic, Marxist, and mystic; and Polly Boyden. (Wilson already knew Vorse from Provincetown; he would later rent Boyden's house in Truro; Frank would become a regular summer resident of Truro.) Wilson emerged physically unscathed from the terrifying ordeal in Pineville—Taub and Frank were badly beaten by the police. Ultimately the group was run out of town by the local authorities. It seemed to Wilson that the Communists were using him and the other "fellow travelers" for their own political ends: therefore he came away from the experience with a severe dislike for "the comrades." He would later write Dos Passos: "The whole thing was very interesting for us—though I don't know that it did much for the miners" (cited by Edel, *Thirties*, 179; for Wilson's account of the episode see *Thirties*, 160–186).

The Wilsons spent most of the winter of 1932 in New York together; in the early summer Margaret returned to California, hoping to come back east with Jimmy for another two-family summer in Provincetown (*Thirties*, 192–193). Unfortunately, however, Margaret's former husband had just lost a lot of money and could not contribute to his son's summer expenses; therefore Margaret felt obliged to remain with Jimmy in Santa Barbara, while Wilson and Rosalind summered in Provincetown as planned. In the late summer Wilson again resumed his liaison with Frances in New York. It should be mentioned that he contributed to the support of her daughter throughout the time he was married to Margaret.

Wilson's 1932 diary entries from Provincetown show him bicycling around town, drinking with his friends, reporting their anecdotes and telling his own about them, going to the beach, and writing a political play, *Beppo and Beth*. It was at this time that he wrote a personal manifesto guardedly avowing his faith in communism as the panacea for America's woes. On September 30 Wilson, who had just arrived in New York, was informed, possibly by his former wife Mary Blair (Dabney, 180), of Margaret's accidental death in Santa Barbara. This shocking news hit him very hard. He must have felt guilty for leaving her to fend for herself over the summer, and he deeply regretted losing a woman whom he deeply cared for. The diary entries that follow the news of her death recreate his memories of her, including some new scenes of their lovemaking on the Peaked Hill dunes. He also records his mistreatment of her: "When I hurt her once or twice she was stunned and simply nodded with her head, as if it were going to drop. . . . Perhaps I had gotten more like her father: extravagance, drinking, arrogance, and tyranny" (*Thirties*, 248). He would subsequently dream of Margaret often, and continue to evoke her on the pages of his diary. Unfortunately these passages strike a maudlin note, as though only irretrievable absence could have made his heart grow fonder. Wilson returned to Provincetown in the winter of 1932–33. He noted that Susan Glaspell had been drinking heavily in the company of a female companion called "Knobby" (Stella Roof) who had been stay-

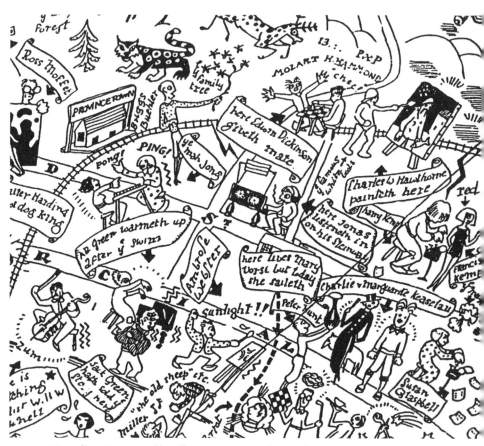

Map of Provincetown (detail), summer 1928. The map's creator, Coulton Waugh, a modernist painter, had a beautiful wife, Elizabeth, who would later become Wilson's clandestine lover.

ing with her (*Thirties*, 307). Glaspell had just been jilted by her much younger companion of eight years, Norman Matson. Matson, an aspiring writer whose career, slight as it was, had gained from his association with Glaspell, had become smitten with a beautiful eighteen-year-old, Anna Walling, whom they had met in Paris. (Anna's parents were the well-known socialists William English Walling and Anna Strunsky, whose family had emigrated from Russia.) Matson and Walling married and bought a house in Wellfleet.[5] The Glaspell-Matson breakup was acrimonious and hurtful for Glaspell, as Wilson and some of her other friends noted in their memoirs. Glaspell consoled herself with another younger man,

The author viewing Susan Glaspell's house in Provincetown.

an alcoholic journalist called Langston Moffett. Moffett, who was married, was visiting his sister Mary Hackett.

In 1933 Wilson and Rosalind rented Susan Glaspell's house in Provincetown. That summer he spent time visiting back and forth with the Fort sisters in Topsfield, Massachusetts. He was now carrying on an affair with Louise (who appears as "K" in his journals). He began the summer of 1934 renting Frank Shay's house in Provincetown. Without mentioning her by name he recorded a tryst with the married Louise there (*Thirties*, 474–475). According to the 1934 Provincetown entries, Wilson often visited with the Hackett and (Coulton) Waugh families. Around this time he became the secret lover of Elizabeth Waugh, a beautiful redhead. (She appears as "D" in the erotic journal entries.)

Wilson spent the summer of 1935 in Europe, mostly in the Soviet Union. In 1936 he rented the Dos Passos house at 571 Commercial Street, Provincetown. During this time Katy and Dos retreated to her property in nearby Truro. Here Dos cultivated a garden and enjoyed the solitude. From the house they had a sweeping view of Truro's rolling moorlands and the bay—the same landscape that Edward Hopper painted. Katy

later sold the Truro house to the Australian-American writer Joan Colebrook. (An indomitable women, who seems to have been born the quin-
tessential Cape Cod bohemian, Colebrook supplemented her meager
writer's income by renting the house out in the summer. Although they
never were close friends, Wilson gave her valuable advice about her writing and helped her to publish it.)

Here is Katy Dos Passos' letter to Wilson, dated July 23, 1936, about
his forthcoming rental of their house:

> Dear Antichrist
>
> Oh we are so pleased that you are coming—your villa will be in
> order and fully equipped for gentry with blankets and towels, elec-
> tric stove trimmed tastefully with chromium and Westinghouse
> ruffles, complete with sea garden and oil paintings.
>
> If you can bring table silver please do as I do not have any. Also
> sheets and pillowslips, although if this is difficult can furnish them.
>
> Provincetown has collapsed intellectually and is now turning into
> a mild country honky tonk with all the Café Azuls and second hand
> tourist traps filled with fishermen A & P boys and girls and the last
> thin line of Bohemia drinking harmless whiskeys and ale in the
> evening up till ten [Prohibition had been repealed the year before].
> The movie house is done over in plush. The weather is wonderful,
> Provincetown seems to be the promised land this summer—rainy,
> sunny and green—only threatened by the Japanese beetle. . . . Dos
> and I have gone aquatic and sail and boat all the time we are having
> a dandy time.
>
> (Beinecke)

Katy concludes with some practical questions and expresses the earnest
hope that Wilson will enjoy their house. Curiously enough, Helen Augur,
Wilson's second cousin, a journalist, and author of historical novels, spent
time in Provincetown earlier that summer. While staying just down the
street from the Dos Passoses, she wrote Wilson (rather flirtatiously) on
July 8, 1936: "Dear Bunny, The tide goes up and down, and the sun shines
like mad and they are still swishing in Parisian counterpanes down Commercial [Street], and the Dos's transplant more and more pinks and pop-
pies, talking like two children on their play, now we'll do this, now we'll
do that, and rye highballs and still lowballs at the Beach Club, and Susan

Glaspell's ankle is better and she has read your book [*Travels in Two Democracies*] and sends her love, and the other day there was a Calliope but I missed the circus which they say was nothing much." Augur goes on to urge Wilson to come up to Provincetown before August to see the Dos Passos house, which Katy is working so hard to make a "pluperfect paradise for you" (Beinecke). Augur had departed by the time Wilson arrived on August 1. By January 1937 Wilson and Augur were involved in a torrid, though short-lived, love affair (Meyers, 182–184).

In order to get to Provincetown, Wilson enlisted Betty Huling, a New York editor, who was an old friend and former lover. She drove him in a thirdhand Stutz Bearcat that he had purchased for the occasion. (Huling returned to New York after a couple of days.) He describes the trip with his usual sensitivity for landscape as well as the excrescences of modern civilization. Also aboard were the black housekeeper Hattie (Stella's replacement) and her granddaughter "baby." Wilson consistently speaks of Hattie with affection in *The Thirties*. She was a good soldier who kept his household going and provided for his guests. Hattie and "baby" would live in with him when he moved to a rented house in Stamford, Connecticut, in the fall of 1936; they would stay with him until he married Mary McCarthy in 1938.

That August Wilson and Rosalind (who came on late) took the Dos Passos' rowboat out into Provincetown Harbor, but they "had a terrible time with it: I asked Dos what the mysterious force was which, no matter how you rowed kept bringing the boat back to shore—in spite of the fact that the current was going in the other direction. He said 'you don't think it could be Trotsky, do you?'" (*Thirties*, 657). That same August, Wilson attended the wedding of Bill and Lucy ("Brownie") L'Engles' daughter.[6] The L'Engles were exceptional among the Provincetown bohemians because they had money. Brownie was a stupid, self-assertive woman who seems to have been everyone's bête noire. Both she and her husband were competent artists. In order to economize, the L'Engles staged a two-tiered wedding reception: the first tier was for their Long Island friends who had arrived "in morning coats and striped trousers": it took place in the studio, complete with caviar and French champagne. The second tier offered the impecunious Provincetown friends "a few bottles of California champagne which was poured into a freezerful of orange sherbert." The hoi polloi feasted on "big thick locally made sandwiches, crusts on, filled with mouse-trap cheese and pink jelly" (*Thirties*, 646). During an earlier time,

Wilson remembers in the same diary entry, Brownie L'Engle had been so stingy that she made her guests write their names on their paper cups so that they could be recycled on the next visit.

Wilson doesn't seem to have spent much time in Provincetown in 1937, but the Dos Passoses kept him au courant of happenings there. Here is Katy's amusing letter (dated November 8, 1937) to him in Stamford, Connecticut:

Dear Antix,

You would not imagine how often our thoughts turn to you in your arboreal solitude. [The house Wilson was renting in Stamford from his friend Margaret De Silver was called "Trees."] The sea here is eating out the bulkhead and gradually pushing us back to Commercial Street where we certainly will be run over. I wish you could come down for Thanksgiving dinner and we could have it in a raft in the basement and it would be just like China. Do you think Archie MacLeish is really going to China to make a picture with Joris Ivans.[7] Pauline Hemingway was here for a few days and she says Joris is a member of the Secret Council and gets his orders from Moscow and has Ernest in his web. I had a letter from Bill [Smith, Katy's brother]: he did not mention anything but war and fascism. Sometimes I wish the New Masses had never been born.

Provincetown is lovely now, but very empty. We have flowers and lettuce still in the back yard. Eben and Lady Given are here. Eben looks very handsome and dramatic, and Lady Given looks ten years younger, full of life and fire, goes all over town. Her hair's bright red, eyes flashing through the mascara, diamonds on her fingers—a veil. She drinks cocktails and predicts war and fascism, the victory of France, the stock market real estate values, and automobile smash-ups, has dreams and visions and is simply wonderful. [It almost seems as though Phyllis was here predicting Katy's later death in an automobile accident.] The other night Dos and I were having a drink with them and Mrs. Given spoke of Tom Blakeman's[8] appearance— he does have a rather withered look. "Do you know what that man needs?" said Mrs. Given. "Skin food! Rich oils. My grandfather used it every night of his life." Eben bore this out, saying he remembered his grandmother chasing his grandfather all over the house with the coldcream rubbing it into his face—the old man spitting it through his whiskers.

The Spencers[9] have had the flu but better now. Hutchins and Neith Hapgood are here and Robert Lovett,[10] Frank and Edie Shay very cosy at Truro. We have yellow curtains in the living room and I asked Austin Dunbar [a sculptor?] how he liked them and he said they are bright. Austin looks very pale and wears glasses and acts very old and nervous. He has only a few iron spiders and a book on flagellation in his kitchen now. No stuffed mice or dead hands or skulls or even a dummy in the bed. But the spiders are really terrible. They are tarantula-size, made of spidery iron and are pinned to the walls and door. I screamed when I saw them and that was the only time Austin smiled.

The weather is incomparable but I wish I could get out of the low income brackets. M. Fish [her nickname for Dos; he called her "Possum"] complains all the time there is only 24 hours in a day. I wish I had five beautiful children all Morgan partners. Dear Antix we enjoyed seeing you. Don't go for to forget the old faces. Love to Rosalind. Remember us to Hattie.

Cape Cod love from
Katy

In an undated letter, probably written in the fall of 1937, Dos writes Wilson the following:

Dear Bunny—New England's Riviera is elegant this fall—I'm starting on a new enterprise in the narrative line [probably the future *Adventures of a Young Man*]—we garden and mooch around the moors and dunes—we complain a good deal about your being so excessively scarce around these parts. In fact Antix Wilsonis is now definitely the scarcest of the local wild fowl. Next time we go down to the Big City we'll try to flush one out in the woods round Stamford."

(Beinecke)

From 1937 on, Wilson would no longer spend much time in Provincetown. A new phase of his life would begin in October of that year when he met Mary McCarthy, who was then working for Covici Friede Publishers in New York. For better and worse, their casually initiated liaison was cemented by marriage in early 1938. In August 1938, the Wilsons paid a short visit to Provincetown. Wilson notes in his diary that they stayed a few days in the unoccupied Dos Passos house. It all seemed a bit déjà vu to him. He wrote: "It has been a bad summer for the honky-tonk tourist trade, so that the town looked both sordid and dead. But we had one lively evening of conversation at the Walkers with Manny Gomez, a relapsed Communist whose real name was Charley Phillips, and a local evidently well-to-do young composer—a regular college conversation about whether each art can be judged by whether it works—writing music, building bridges, etc" (*Thirties*, 708). Charles and Adelaide Walker, fervent Trotskyites at the time, had a house in Wellfleet. During the same trip in the fall of 1938, the Wilsons visited the Bishops in South Chatham. The poet John Peale Bishop, his wife Margaret, and their three children had finally settled on Cape Cod after selling their château in France. Bishop loved Cape Cod, and it inspired some of his best poetry.[11] Wilson liked neither his friend's newly built house, which he deemed pretentious, nor the social set in Chatham. As also noted in his journal, beginning with the entries from 1934 Wilson took a decidedly jaundiced view of Margaret Bishop. Over the years, he notes her odd caprices and what he saw as her ruthless domination of a dependent husband. Nonetheless, he stood by Margaret, by actively helping her and the children, after John's death.

At the end of September 1938, the Wilsons went for a picnic and swim at Gull Pond in Wellfleet. Wilson had already been to Gull Pond earlier in the thirties. He would become attached to its (then) unfrequented sandy shores, and he would write about it in various ways. In the next chapter we shall examine the 1942 journal entry (deleted from the published version) that details, with lyrical sensuality, an afternoon he and McCarthy spent at Gull Pond.

After I was born on December 25, 1938, my parents went to Chicago for the summer. My father taught some courses at the University of Chicago summer school; in early August my mother took me on the train out to Seattle to visit her grandmother and other relatives. In letters to Wilson from Seattle she persistently asked him for the money to buy a fur coat. He responded by pleading dire poverty. By the end of August, Wilson was preparing to go to Provincetown—it would have been a well-deserved vacation after the academic grind (teaching did not come easily to him)—and he was counting on McCarthy's joining him there (*Man in Letters*, 119–121). The couple doubtless reunited in Provincetown, although Wilson didn't mention it in his journal. In September they were back in Stamford. Wilson still hadn't finished his book on the Russian Revolution, *To the Finland Station*. He decided to rent Polly Boyden's house in Truro for the winter and get on with his work—which he did successfully. The Boyden house was set on the hill that dominates Truro Center, and it had a tennis court, a rare sign of affluence in what was then a poor community. The Givens' house was just on the other side of a low fence; both families shared the Givens' ample parking lot.

On March 23, 1940, Wilson noted a full moon seen through the window on a very stormy night. He and Mary looked at the "inky clouds driven rapidly across it [the moon], showing their silver hems as they passed, and then the bright complete white (blinding) moon showing through the dark gauze fringe and swimming clear, complete and bright again. . . . The moon remained fixed and supreme. Mary said she always thought it was moving—I always thought it was standing still" (*Thirties*, 724–725). Although their disagreement was here amicable, after they moved to Wellfleet the following year the relationship became increasingly discordant. Probably because of the troubled nature of the marriage, Wilson kept a very sparse diary from 1941 to 1945 (the year they separated). The unpublished "Wellfleet Poetry," however, throws some insight into this chaotic period in his life, as will be shown in chapter 4.

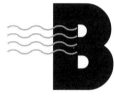

y 1939 Wilson had decided to buy a house on Cape Cod, and he enlisted his old friends Charles (Charley) and Adelaide Walker to help him find one. Charley and Wilson had known each other since college, when the former worked on the *Yale Literary Magazine* and the latter wrote for the *Nassau Literary Magazine* at Princeton. They both joined the army in 1916 and were assigned to the same training camp at Plattsburgh, New York, in the summer of that year. Charley was an expert in labor relations, a writer, and a translator of Greek drama. During the twenties he and Adelaide ran the Theatre Union in New York. They staged plays by proletarian writers like Clifford Odets. Both Walkers were fervent leftists, although their political ideas didn't prevent them from living comfortably. Adelaide in her youth was an impetuous sultry beauty, with real dramatic élan in her voice and carriage. After their two children Charles (Chuck) and Daniel (Danny) were born, they bought a house on Coles Neck Road in Wellfleet. The year was 1938. The agent who sold it was Elizabeth Freeman, a rawhide-tough local character who had inherited a large property between Route 6 and the ocean. On January 17, 1939, Adelaide Walker wrote my father to congratulate him on my birth (December 25, 1938) and on his brilliant parody "The Omelet of A. MacLeish," which had just appeared in the *New Yorker*. She also mentioned a house for sale near Wellfleet Center belonging to a "very good Baltimore architect." She commented persuasively: "It's in Wellfleet which is infinitely superior as residence to Provincetown or even Truro. People can't drop in on you continuously (just the last weekend last summer was exceptional). The few extra-native inhabitants are extremely nice, there are no Stalinists and the tradesmen love to give credit in practically unlimited amounts" (Beinecke). The Wilsons rented a house, close to the Walkers, for the summer of 1940, and in March 1941 my father bought the three-story nineteenth-century house on Money Hill from Miss Freeman.

Wilson had married Mary McCarthy for her fine, combative mind, her literary and political sophistication, and her physical beauty. Seventeen years older than his bride, he was embarking on a third marriage; it was her second. More than anything, he yearned for a stable domestic life that would assure his comfort, while allowing him to pursue his writing. In addition, his daughter by the actress Mary Blair, who had been named Rosalind after his great aunt—the Shakespearean association had doubtless appealed to Blair—was now fourteen years old and also stood to gain from his remarriage. She had been living most of the year with her grandmother Wilson in Red Bank, New Jersey; now she would have a new home in Wellfleet. McCarthy, for her part, seems to have fallen for Wilson's commanding literary profile. He was broader in his interests and more productive than the *Partisan Review* (Wilson called it "Partizansky Review") "boys" with whom she had been working. Philip Rahv, the editor of *PR*, was McCarthy's live-in partner when she first met Wilson. She quickly made the decision to leave Philip, but they remained lifelong friends (with a short hiatus that occurred when he took offense at the portrait-caricature of Will Taub in her satiric novel *The Oasis*). In pursuing his courtship of McCarthy, Wilson spoke with authority about their future "quiet settled life together and the rearing of a large family" (Gelderman, 90).

They married in February 1938. Unfortunately, neither partner could peacefully coexist with the other under the same roof. Their differences over the years 1940–1945 have been amply covered by their biographers. Suffice it to say that Wilson, goaded by inner demons, was capable of boorish, cruel, and even violent behavior. McCarthy, who carried the stigma of childhood trauma—as a young orphan she was cruelly used by her guardians—reacted emotionally to her husband's frequent needling and criticism. Very early in the marriage, McCarthy, at her husband's urging, went into psychoanalysis; she herself thought that she needed it. Her treatment began in early summer 1938 after a sojourn, from June 8 to June 29, 1938, in the Payne Whitney Clinic in New York. Having struck his wife in the course of a late-night confrontation, Wilson called a physician the next day. She was then, by mutual agreement, admitted to Payne Whitney, the psychiatric clinic at New York Hospital. She agreed to stay in the outpatient unit there, while her husband carried out the move from one rental house to another in nearby Stamford, Connecticut. (Later she would accuse him of committing her against her will.) This was hardly an auspicious beginning for a marriage. During the Wellfleet years, 1941–1944, McCarthy would regularly commute to the city for sessions with a psychotherapist; there would be three. One of them was Sandor Rado, a Provincetown summer resident who was an acquaintance of the Wilsons. In the summer of 1942 McCarthy, then pregnant, and Adelaide Walker drove to Provincetown to pay a social call on Rado. (Wilson was away at the time.) McCarthy felt unwell and took refuge at the Dos Passoses', just across Commercial Street from Rado. Adelaide went home. During that night, which McCarthy spent at the Dos Passos house, she miscarried, much to her hosts' chagrin. Rosalind drove her back to Wellfleet the next day, but they were delayed when the car's brakes failed. By that night Wilson had returned, and he took her to the hospital in Hyannis. According to Rosalind Wilson, the Dos Passoses thought McCarthy had somehow planned to have the miscarriage at their house (*Magician*, 111); Adelaide Walker told biographer Kiernan that Wilson accused his wife of aborting herself, with Adelaide's help (Kiernan, 191), while McCarthy told biographer Brightman that Wilson blamed Dr. Rado for causing the miscarriage. She also told Brightman that it may have been precipitated by some window washing she did the day before (Brightman, 236–237).

While in New York, McCarthy usually stayed at the New Weston Hotel. Sometimes she would go to the city just to escape an unpleasant situation at home in Wellfleet. It could hardly have been a secret from Wilson that she was having casual liaisons with other men. One of these happened after a beach picnic in Wellfleet (which she must have attended solo). Her partner was Ralph Manheim, a charming and erudite translator of French and German literature. The result was a pregnancy that McCarthy ended with an abortion (interview with Bowden Broadwater, July 25, 2004). The abortion took place in New York, in the middle of January 1942. Wilson saw her through it and the ensuing complications. On Valentine's Day, a month later, he gave her a handmade valentine heart with a little poem urging her to respond to his warm love in this chilly season (Dabney, 282–283).

The Wilsons also lived together in New York. They spent part of the winter of 1942 in an apartment rented from Polly Boyden. Probably at that time, my mother had a most unusual encounter with my father. As she told it to me, Wilson had one day sighted an attractive woman walking on the sidewalk ahead of him. Having accelerated his pace he overtook her, doubtless ready to pronounce the old line "Haven't we met before?" when he recoiled in consternation. He had just tried to pick up his own wife! He apologized. She seems to have been more amused than angered by the incident.

When they were getting on well, they found each other mutually stimulating and, in the company of friends, they excelled at repartee, not argument. Although McCarthy had little good to say, either in interviews or in her own memoirs, about Wilson as a husband, she clearly benefited as a writer of fiction from his sustained encouragement and support. It seems that the couple agreed for the most part on political and literary matters, but were often at odds over things mundane (Kiernan, 169). Wilson, by his own admission, tended to misbehave at precisely those times when they were getting along well. Considering their marital difficulties, it is not surprising that Wilson made fewer entries in his journal during the years the marriage lasted. The passages dealing with Cape Cod nature are, however, of great interest to us, especially the one captioned "Gull Pond 1942." Because it shows McCarthy against a natural backdrop, the portrait is unique; unfortunately it displeased its still-living subject and was cut at her request from the published version of *The Forties*. She reacted indignantly to Wilson's portrayal of her as a sex object (although the journals describe the other women with whom he had been intimate in much the same way). She also had the publisher cut another sexual scene between them, this one at the Little Hotel in New York, as well as a one-sentence entry that refers to "Mary's derangement." The text "Gull Pond 1942" shows Wilson's considerable talent for evoking wild nature, and McCarthy, with meticulous precision and sensual verve. Therefore I shall include it in its entirety.

GULL POND 1942
Gull Pond May 21, 1942—The ladyslippers were out, sprinkled so sparsely around the brink of their solitary flowers—deepening in a couple of days from flimsy stooping ghosts as pale as Indian-pipe to a fleshy veined purplish pink swollen between pigtails and curling top-knot that also suggested Indians; and along the white sand of one side, where the bowl of the pond shelved so gradually, the little white violets with their lower lips finely lined as if with beards in purplish indelible ink, their long slim rhubarb-purplish stalks and their faint slightly acrid pansy smell, grew with thready roots in the

damp sand; they were yellowish like ivory here, but on the opposite more marshy bank (with its round stones, its patches of red irony water, its shooting-box with a flock of square black and white decoys, its steeper banks, its dead gulls and fishes) their effect was not quite so dry and they showed a vivid white like trillium where they bloomed against the deeper and the more luxuriant green. As one walked in the water one encountered pines putting out their soft straw-colored (?) bunches of cones and smelling with a special almost sweet-fern fragrance. The baby cones seemed almost embarrassingly soft, almost like a woman's nipples.—When we got to the shallow channel between Gull Pond and the next one, I found a mother herring trying to get through from the latter by gliding and flapping on her side. She was silvery with purple-silver along the upper part of her length. At the mouth of the channel there were several of them splashing and when I came close I saw that the water was all dark with a whole crowd of them—from above they are just roundish muddy streaks under water. The sand here, flat and more marshy and grown with green rushes, was all tracked with the trefoil (?) of gulls' feet, where they had come to get the fish.

On the other side of the pond, the stretch where there was a screen of tall pines, a new and grander note, almost theatrical— and then the little screen of scent-pines that left a little strip of sand between it and the thick tangled jungle of bushes and shrubs and briars that covered the hill behind. In there we used to make love while all kinds of little birds rustled and twitched and sang behind. Today we cleared a place under the low branches of the pines so that we could get a little shade, and the light openwork shadows rippled on Mary's white skin;—her waist and abdomen where she lay naked—as the breeze stirred the branches; also fish splashing. Afterwards, Mary put her feet up and grabbed a branch with her long square-tipped prehensile toes—and she giggled and grinned about it, enjoying the idea of being able to do it, one thing she wasn't sensitive about—stretched up further and seized the branch and, rather to my astonishment, pulled her whole body up till only her shoulders rested on the ground. She said that I couldn't do that— I replied that I was in a little more advanced stage. She said that her ancestors had been kings of Ireland—I said, Yes: in the trees.

—When I was trying to keep my mind off it, in order not to come before she did, leaning on my hands, I was able to look out on the lake and the afternoon landscape, where only the cries of the gulls were heard.

—For lunch we had had from the brown picnic basket the classical boiled eggs, bean salad in glass jars, cucumber sandwiches, and sandwiches filled with some mixture of green chopped herbs and white cottage cheese (and there were bananas, tomatoes and sliced sweetish, green cucumber pickles which we didn't get around to eating); and had iced lemonade out of the thermos bottle and white California wine out of a glass jar that had been cooled in the refrigerator and that we tried to keep from getting tepid by standing it in the water.—Before lunch we had gone in for a dip: not too cold to be uncomfortable. Mary had gone in naked, I had put on my old brown trunks. Mary looked very pretty and white. But she was ripened by the summer sun where her face and neck and arms had been exposed while working on her garden, and the tan of her forearms and the reddening tints brought out in her rather pale skin were in harmony with her blue suit of overalls and made her seem almost luscious. When I kissed her after we'd eaten as she was lying in her new rather shiny pink latex bathing-suit, with its skirt chopped smartly off just at the base of her buttocks (it was when she was standing up, though, that you noticed this)—the shoulder-straps down and rather amiable mouth, which had character, while she shaded her eyes from the sun with her hand, it (her mouth) seemed to me naked and made me think of the lips below. At this point we finished the yellow wine and went on to the screen of the scrub-pine.

—I had a sense of adventure in exploring the other bank of the pond and walking all the way around. At one point, the bottom was stony; in one place, there were little fish; at another, there were water-bugs featherily and (elusively) flawing (scrawling?) the surface. (Shooting box, etc.) Further on, a light and slow ripple gave the illusion, as you walked in the water, that it was the sand of the bottom, with its rare stones and sticks, that was rippling like some thin and light sheet slowly and lightly shaken out as one might shake out a long carpet.

—When we had first come between one and two the lake had not looked so attractive—a little roughened and opaque from a distance, (in the foreground along the water were forts and walls and moated castles built by and for Reuel from several days before); but when we came back from our walk around it, there were dark and soft-looking clouds, which did not look as if they were really going to rain, hanging over the pond from the opposite bank, and yet leaving above us, among white (shreds? more like bits of cotton pulled out from the roll) of cloud, a fresh and bright and (rarified not dense) blue; and the water had a leaden look that was at the same time perfectly limpid—and lovely.

—When I went back to get the towels, on which Mary had been lying, I saw a little orange and black bird, like a finch, hopping around in those scrub-pines just where we had been.

—The little yellow buds of the pines are not the cones, neither these nor "the candles," with bristly conelike scales, that rise from the middle of the cluster. The cones are little round green cones that grow underneath on the branch. When you shake the soft things, they give out a lemon-yellow dust that looks like (lemon-colored) smoke.

—The deer dung and sharp divided hoof-prints just opposite where we lay—the yellow and black butterfly (monarch?) that was flying out over the pond.

[EW's marginal note] All to be followed by violent quarrel the next morning and her running away to New York.

The entry is not presented in chronological order, and it is framed at the beginning and the end with views of the landscape. By way of explanation, Gull Pond is the only large pond in Wellfleet to be almost perfectly circular; it is attached by a narrow sluiceway to smaller Higgins Pond, which links to tiny, dark Williams Pond. Here is the chronological sequence of events: Between one and two in the afternoon, the couple arrives on the side of Gull Pond adjacent to Gull Pond Road (where my mother usually parked the car); they establish themselves in the shade of the scrub pine trees, have a picnic lunch, swim, make love, and play. Then they walk around the pond; before they depart Wilson picks up the towels. The passage begins with a description of his favorite wildflower, the lady slipper. "Flimsy stooping ghosts as pale as Indian pipe" a few days earlier, the lady slippers have now turned to a "fleshy veined purplish pink swollen between pigtails and curling top-knot that also suggested Indians." This erotically suggestive description of the flowers and the personification of them as Indians ushers us into a sublimely natural world where he and McCarthy, modern versions of Adam and Eve, will be the only human presence. Nothing escapes the narrator's watchful eye as they circumambulate the pond (NB: the same walk is described in two separate passages). He notes the shoreline, alternating between mud and sand, the white violets, the migratory herring, the gulls' footprints in the sand, the sandy bottom rippling underwater with its "rare stones and sticks," the sand castles made by me (age four) just days earlier, the cottonlike clouds, and, the most dominant presence of all, the fragrant pine trees covered with blooming baby cones "almost like a woman's nipples." After the picnic and the swim, their lovemaking takes place behind the shelter of the pines, at a site that they have used before for the same purpose. In order to postpone his orgasm, Wilson looks "out on the lake and the afternoon landscape, where only the cries of the gulls were heard." The harmonious outcome shows the contiguity of "wild" and human nature.

When he returns to the beach to retrieve "the towels where Mary had been lying," Wilson observes a little orange and black bird, like a finch, in the scrub pine. Now, for the reader's benefit, he delivers a short lecture (the same one, doubtless, that he had in real life given McCarthy) on the nature of a pine tree's reproductive apparatus. The multiple pine flowers respond to his touch with an orgasmic cloud of pollen.

The above-quoted journal entry not only shows Wilson's deftness at rendering nature but also reflects his view of a female partner as an intriguing toy, to be studied and manipulated. The woman emerges as a lesser kind of vessel. In the text he remarks: "I kissed her red fleshy and rather amiable mouth, which had character, while she shaded her eyes from the sun with her hand, it (her mouth) seemed to be naked and made me think of the lips below." While imbibing the woman's sexuality, he simultaneously dehumanizes her. After their lovemaking, a supine McCarthy has playfully grasped a branch with her "prehensile toes" and triumphantly hoisted herself off the ground. Wilson parenthetically remarks that this was "one thing she wasn't sensitive about." True enough, McCarthy took offense easily and resented any criticism, but Wilson's own tendency to find fault in his wives could only have exacerbated her "sensitivity." In the marginal note fixed at the end of the entry, Wilson writes:

*The author with his mother Mary McCarthy and family dog Rex,
by front door of the Wellfleet house, 1943. Photo by Sylvia Salmi.
Special Collections, Vassar College Libraries.*

"All to be followed by violent quarrel the next morning and her running away to New York." He seems to suggest that the quarrelsome McCarthy was only too happy to find an excuse to leave him. Much later, his daughter Rosalind would write: "What he did when he set about destroying a woman was almost incommunicable because it combined the conscious and unconscious to such an extent on his part and constant criticizing from morning until night" (*Magician*, 133).

When traveling in Italy in 1945, Wilson remembered Gull Pond and McCarthy in his journal. This memory finds expression in a single sentence also deleted from the published version at McCarthy's request. It is part of a series of freely associated images at the end of the section titled "Return to Italy," and reads: "Morning, dawn at Gull Pond—threat of darkness at Mary's derangement—which hung over things and sometimes seemed to have some connection with what was going on abroad." Wilson firmly believed in McCarthy's "hysteria" if not her actual insanity. He did not admit that his behavior could trigger her outbursts and that his excesses qualitatively exceeded hers.

On June 21, just one month after he made the long "Gull Pond" entry cited above, Wilson wrote a moving poem on the occasion of McCarthy's thirtieth birthday. In it he seeks to convince her of his ongoing love and admiration; he also pleads for her sympathy. His tone is didactic, for his role in the marriage has consistently been that of a mentor as well as a lover. Here is the poem, typed on three sheets of paper with the letterhead EDMUND WILSON, WELLFLEET, MASSACHUSETTS

Darling do not weep with tears
My four years of your thirty years:
I too once felt the scene turn thin,
The sky come down, the road close in;
The faces that I had thought my own
Dull dolts that left me all alone;
The places where I breathed and fed
A dismal dump to lie down dead—
And if today you were to go,
Were gone, again I should feel so.

Between two seas a strip not wide
Splits ocean side from harbor side,
And keeps apart, with beaten knees,

The blank unbuilt unplanted seas;
Or, better, between pond and pond
The streak of water makes a bond,
A limpid stream in white sand.
—And if you say a turtle stalks
This stream, debating as he walks
Where best to burrow in the slime,
To wait the proper snapping time;
Remember that I say the snails
That leave their little hollow trails
Along the bottom that stays white
Are tiny beasts that do not bite.

- Mary, this morning when sunrise
First met your green and lighting eyes
In debt and dèche the way I live,
I have no other gift to give –
Nothing to guard our flickering foyer
Against Judge Otis, paranoia,
Tovarishch Stalin's dark apostles,
The envious reviews of hostiles,
Against the rank and shallow weeds
That rise to wreck our ripest seeds;
That ring the bell and spring the door,
But never yet have to split the floor—
Nothing to give today but these,
Across the ponds, between the seas,
Between the tadpoles and sweet peas:
Lined words to one who can align 'em
Till weaklings cry out, "Quem ad finem
Sese iactabit—what a gal!—
Audacia?—the animal!"*

But failing better coin, my dear,
Please take these for your thirtieth year;
And disregard the thinning scene,
But read the love that lies between.

*The Latin means: "To what end will he/she vaunt him/herself . . . Audacity?"
Above "the animal!" Wilson has penned a possible substitution: "but what a pal!"

In the first stanza the poet urges her not to despair over their four years together; he too has faced desperation and despair (possibly a reference to his nervous breakdown in 1929). Using the surrounding landscape as a unifying motif, he speaks to her as one writer to another. Paying homage to her literary skills and bravura, he solicits her help in his struggle with penury and a hostile outside world. We can surmise that he duly gave the poem to its addressee; in fact he makes it clear that it is the only birthday present he can afford to give her. Whether she kept it, however, remains in doubt—the Beinecke copy is clearly the original, and no copy is among McCarthy's papers at Vassar. Six years later he would address a long elegy, "The White Sands" (published in *Night Thoughts*, 1953), to his fourth wife Elena. In this tribute, he portrays her as an elegant and graceful European against a background of Cape Cod sand and water.

In October 1943 my father got a permanent job as a book reviewer with the *New Yorker*. This ongoing relationship with the *New Yorker* would last until his death and help his always shaky finances. By 1944 my parents' marriage was pretty well on the rocks, with my mother ensconced in New York and my father holding the fort with me in Wellfleet. Being a temporarily single parent led to some bizarre complications in my father's routine over the summer of 1944. Writing to my mother from Wellfleet on August 6, he comments ruefully on the logistical difficulties posed by having my Scottish nanny, Miss Forbes, living with us. By the way, I loved Miss Forbes, a hearty and affectionate caregiver, who was on the corpulent side, with huge breasts that intrigued me. At that stage, I had managed to conflate the female mammaries with another less visible part of the human anatomy, the tonsils. (My mother had tried not to show amusement when I asked why Miss Forbes' tonsils were so big.) When she was a teenager, Miss Forbes' parents had warned her that, in pursuing her chosen calling as a nanny, she should never spend the night alone under the same roof with a man. This caused my father problems, since he was living alone with me in the Wellfleet house that August. Luckily the Nabokovs (Vladimir and Véra), as well as Herbert Solow and his wife Sylvia Salmi, were staying in Wellfleet; the Walkers also offered to serve as chaperones. The upshot was that my father either had to spend the night with friends or have friends sleep over at his house.

My father's letters to my mother during this period seem contrite, as he pleads with her to return to Wellfleet. They did reunite in New York that fall. Interestingly enough, he was well aware of his "faults and misdeeds"; the journals occasionally record pricks of conscience over his mistreatment of his women. Nonetheless, he lacked the will, or desire, to change or moderate the dark side of his nature. By the end of 1944, my mother and I took final leave of the house my father was renting on Henderson Place in uptown Manhatten, just off East End Avenue. All that remained was for them to haggle over the terms of a divorce.

On April 4, 1944, Wilson lost one of his oldest friends, John Peale Bishop (born 1892). He died in Hyannis Hospital on Cape Cod, leaving a widow and three children. It is probable that as his executor Wilson destroyed some of the poet's ludic erotic drawings that came into his hands after Bishop's death. After living in France for seven years in the thirties, Bishop had sold their château near Paris, eventually to settle in South Chatham, Cape Cod, where he built the rather grand house named "Sea Change." Bishop maintained a high-powered correspondence on literary subjects with both Wilson and Allen Tate. Tate, the "Fugitive" poet, critic, and editor, highly valued Bishop's opinions and advice. Their correspondence, published as *The Republic of Letters* (1981), contains intelligent and creative mutual evaluations of each others' ongoing work. Amusingly, it also shows their affectionate attitude to "Dr. Wilson," a close friend of both, whose stubbornly maintained pro-communist views caused them both serious misgivings. Bishop and Wilson (Tate occasionally visited with both) saw each other sporadically on the Cape, where, however, they belonged to two separate and even mutually exclusive worlds. Chatham, dominated by the country club and sailing set, had nothing in common with the sparse landscape and bohemian mores of the Provincetown-Truro-Wellfleet axis.

Both of my parents remarried in 1946. My mother's new husband was Bowden Broadwater, a dapper aesthete, and recent Harvard graduate, some nine years her junior. While on assignment in Europe for the *New Yorker* magazine in 1945, Wilson had assiduously courted Mamaine Paget, a wellborn, well-educated Englishwoman whose company he much enjoyed. Mamaine would, however, refuse his proposal of marriage and go on to marry Arthur Koestler, with whom she had been close since their first meeting in January 1944. A loyal soldier, Mamaine would play a similarly nurturing role with the cantankerous Koestler as Elena would with Wilson. Once back in the United States and in Wellfleet, Wilson met Elena Thornton (née Mumm, of Mumm's Champagne) at the house of mutual friends, Paul and Nina Chavchavadze, the only Russian royals living in Wellfleet. (Nina was the grandniece of Emperor Nicholas II, the last tsar.) Before he had formally met her, Wilson had glimpsed Elena swimming in Gull Pond. She would have to divorce her current husband, James (Jimmy) Thornton; Wilson, hitherto uncooperative with my mother's demands for a divorce, would now expedite it. There is no doubt that he and Elena were deeply in love—their correspondence shows it—they were married in Nevada in December 1946. At this point, Wilson felt a sense of optimism at the prospect of a new life with a beautiful yet practical-minded companion. The road would not be easy, however, especially for Elena in the later years. In the early fifties Wilson would inherit the house in New York State from his mother. He would come to spend a good part of each year there, far from his wife and Wellfleet.

Before the trip to Nevada, which facilitated their remarriages, Wilson conducted a passionate long-distance correspondence with Elena, who was still living in New York City with Jimmy Thornton and their young son Henry. I was with my father in Wellfleet at the time, the summer of 1946. My mother had gone to Europe to meet Bowden Broadwater. After returning from a trip down south, Wilson wrote Elena on May 10, 1946. He speaks of his emotional reunion with our dog Rex (Reckie), whose temporary keepers had neglected him. The weather was glorious: "The shadbush and beach plum bushes are out with their white blossoms all over. My white lilacs are just coming out, but the purple and Persian ones are way behind—I wish all the time you were with me. If you were we might try swimming in Gull Pond where I met you first. I haven't the heart to go there by myself."

Back in Wellfleet, the love-struck Wilson encountered formidable obstacles in trying to run a household on his own. He could not cook or drive, had little time or inclination for household chores, and was even lacking a telephone, since he refused to pay the deposit required by the telephone company. He hired a succession of housekeepers, including a "morose" couple of East European DPs (displaced persons, uprooted by war in their home countries), all of whom proved unsatisfactory. For transportation he used a custom-made Cadillac limousine that he had acquired at second or third hand. It was driven by Gus, a black handyman who doubled as chauffeur. The car kept breaking down and soon found its way to the junkyard after Gus forgot to refill the oil. Despite his initial hard work, both inside and out, Gus lost interest in the job and was dismissed.

That summer, a live-in sitter named Chris looked after me. She had difficulty coping and left after a few weeks. On June 8, my father writes to Elena: "They have all gone to Gull Pond. Chris gave us her first dinner. Has been majoring in dietetics, but put salt instead of sugar in the gingerbread." This has proved "a rude surprise." Nonetheless, she is a "nice little girl, Boston-Irish—very serious indeed." Ultimately she was driven away by the rats, regular visitors in the kitchen. (Wilson was fond of rats and took only halfhearted measures to exterminate them.) I seem to have been acting up, all through the month of June. My father complains to Elena that I have been recalcitrant, as well as rude to the hired help. In addition Phyllis Given has written him a nasty letter about my misbehavior at their house when playing with their son, Eben Jr. We have attempted to peer under Maude Emma's (Phyllis's elderly mother, who lived with them) skirts and spoken of castrating Phyllis's two-year-old grandson Stephen. By the way, the previous summer (1945), when my mother and I were living next door to the Givens, my mother speaks in a letter to Bowden Broadwater of our spraying Maude Emma with a flit gun. Writing of all this to Elena, my father wonders whether I have inherited my mother's "méchant disposition" and "learned her point of view of being an outlaw." He worries that "I have inherited Mary's bad qualities. . . . There is something awfully bad about the Irish side of her family." In any case he has "disciplined" (i.e., spanked) me, and I am more "subdued." As punishment for our antics in Truro, Eben Given Jr. and I were forbidden any and all association for the next two summers. In the background, and beyond my ken, my father had just published a sensational best seller, *Memoirs of Hecate County*, a novelistic collection of six stories. Because of the sexually explicit content it was targeted by the Catholic Church and the "New York Society for the Suppression of Vice." The book would be banned in New York, but until that happened Wilson enjoyed windfall profits from its sales.

As the summer progressed, my father and I gradually got along better; we bicycled and took walks together. In addition I was treated well by Ruth and Gardner Jencks, whose children Charlie and Penny were close to my age. To reciprocate for their hospitality to me, my father offered to take their children and me to a visiting circus in Hyannis. We all got into the Cadillac limo, with Gus at the wheel, and headed south toward Hyannis (some thirty miles away). According to Penny's recollection, we never reached our destination. As night fell, we got totally lost and stopped repeatedly to ask for directions, but in vain; hours later we ended up where we had begun, at the Wilson house on Route 6 in Wellfleet. Nonetheless, in a letter written on June 29, 1946, Wilson informed Elena that he had taken me and the "Jencks kids" to the circus in Hyannis. Possibly we were successful at finding it on a subsequent day. Elena spent July with us in Wellfleet and then returned to New York. August went fairly smoothly. My father, at least temporarily humanized by his domestic responsibilities, enjoyed being alone with me. In August, he wrote Elena that he was planning to take me, Charlie Jencks, and Mike Macdonald (the writer Dwight Macdonald's son) to the movie *Anna and the King of Siam*, which was showing in Orleans. By September things started to fall apart. My father fell off a chair in the downstairs living room while trying to swat mosquitoes; I was going about the house spraying DDT indiscriminately—which earned me "a little spanking"— and the new black houseman (who came with wife) went on a binge of alcohol and marijuana consumption during which the couple fought constantly. And then the hot-water heater broke down. While all this was happening, my father managed to read Henry James' *American Scene* as well as Harriet Beecher Stowe's *Uncle Tom's Cabin*, the latter aloud to me in the evenings. That September I joined my mother and Bowden Broadwater in New York, where I attended Saint Bernard's School. In October 1946 my father and Elena went to Reno, Nevada, for their divorces and subsequent remarriage, that December. My older half sister Rosalind was now living in the Wellfleet house. Until the new Wilsons' return, Nina Chavchavadze (née Romanov) came to stay with her. Nina's husband Paul was away working for the Red Cross. That winter Rosalind met in Provincetown the half-Greek grandson of George Cram Cook, Susan Glaspell's husband who died in 1924. Glaspell was attached to Sirius Proestopoulis, known to everyone as "Topie," the son of her stepdaughter Nilla Cook. He came to stay with her in August 1946, prior to entering Harvard (Ben-Zvi, 392). Topie told Rosalind, and others, that during the war in Greece he had been drafted into an anticommunist partisan unit at the age of thirteen or fourteen. Presumably this happened during the war when rival Greek political groups were fighting against the Italian and, later, German occupation. He would go on to graduate from Harvard College in 1949, and then Harvard Law School in 1952. As Sirius Cook, he practiced law in New York City. During the summer of 1947 he and the fun-loving Rosalind spent much time together on Cape Cod. One day, while he and Rosalind were at the ocean beach in Wellfleet, a school of dogfish (or sand sharks) were observed swimming close to shore. To impress his companion, the macho Greek waded into the water to battle the two-foot-long denizens. He managed to subdue a few of them, wounding his forearms in the process. He put his dead trophies in our refrigerator. Later, in the early morning hours, my father, as was his wont, opened the refrigerator looking for a snack. Nonplussed, he retreated to his sleeping lair above the study. Early the next day Elena, now pregnant, had a very disagreeable surprise when she came eyeball-to-eyeball with the ugly fish; they were soon relegated to the town dump. Rosalind and Topie spoke of marriage, but the relationship abruptly ended in late 1948; neither, it seems, was ready to undertake such a long-term commitment. Another contributing factor to the breakup: Topie had met Valentina Azarova, an attractive Russian émigré who was teaching at Harvard while doing her M.A. in Russian. Later the two would marry.

In her memoirs Rosalind writes that after her father and Elena returned from Nevada he went to Boston for a few days on business. In his absence, Elena and Nina Chavchavadze redecorated the drably arranged front living room. Upon his return, Wilson reacted violently to the change and "told Elena she could leave" (*Magician*, 130). This rage was an early warning to his new wife that the going might get rough, and it did. The next year Dwight Macdonald, summering in Wellfleet, wrote the following to the Broadwaters after a social meeting with the Wilsons: "Had my annual encounter with Edmund at Joan Colebrook's; asked me heartily how *Politics* [the journal Dwight founded and edited] was doing and did not stay for an answer. Geismar [Max Geismar, who was writing a book on Scott Fitzgerald] was with him, most attentive. Rosalind tense and harried as ever; I like her. Ilyeana [Elena] shows effects of years in the ring: she's stooped, bent-necked, roundshouldered, as though covering up against a right hook. She's sweet and intelligent, but Edmund's boorishness forces her into hypocrisy too much" (letter dated July 17, 1948, Vassar).

On September 12, 1947, Katy Dos Passos died in a tragic accident, just off the Cape in Wareham, Massachusetts. She and Dos were on their way to Virginia to visit the farm that he had inherited. They left Provincetown around noon, then stopped to say good-bye to the Walkers and Shays in Wellfleet. They were planning to spend the night in Old Saybrook, Connecticut. Blinded by the late afternoon sun, Dos crashed into a cranberry truck parked with its back end jutting into the road. Katy was instantly decapitated; Dos lost an eye (Carr, 454–455). He would still be a patient at Massachusetts General Hospital on September 15, the day of his wife's funeral at the Truro Cemetery. She was buried on a plot donated by the Givens from their lot. Recalling the funeral in his diary, Wilson wishes that Katy could have attended the gathering the Shays gave that night in her honor—she would have later described it with characteristic dry humor. Edie Shay was Katy's best friend, but she was a heavy drinker; Wilson mentions Edie's histrionics at the gathering. During the hillside funeral ceremony, Wilson remembered the earlier days on Cape Cod when there was a shared sense of community; now he had the sense of "something ending" (*Forties*, 222). Later that day he took a walk behind his house, while contemplating the early fall landscape and nostalgically recalling fragments of his Cape Cod past, including the visit to the Millays in Truro in 1920. That night he was awakened from sleep by a fox's barking: "I felt then, as I sometimes did when listening to the whippoorwills in spring, that the place was really wild and alien, that I had no part in its life" (*Forties*, 225). The next morning he got a telegram informing him that Mary Blair, his first wife, had died.

Wilson would attend the funeral of another old friend, Susan Glaspell, the following year (June 28, 1948). He writes about it to Elena from Lenox, Massachusetts, on July 30, 1948: "Susan Glaspell's dismal funeral, with everybody stifling in that room while odd fragments of the conventional service were read, depressed me with the thought of how little there was left of the original idealism and enthusiasm of the old P-town group. I approve of the idea of having her ashes scattered at Truro, and I think seriously of having mine, if possible, scattered between the Spectacle Ponds, where they might lie among the roots of the little wild orchids. This would be less of a nuisance than throwing them out to sea" (Beinecke). The Spectacle Ponds, accessible only by dirt road, are located in the woods west of Newcomb Hollow ocean beach. Their haunting dark waters and exquisite flora and fauna exercised a particular spell over Wilson. He once had the chance to buy them, but in the end he wisely refrained from an investment that would have strained his already meager resources to the breaking point.

In September 1948 Elena went to Europe to attend to family business. My father remained in Wellfleet with me, Rosalind, our infant half sister

Helen Miranda, and the live-in nurse, Miss Carver. In his letters to Elena he mentions having acquired a Parcheesi set and that everyone is playing. He loved the board games checkers and Chinese checkers, as well as anagrams; however, he had little interest in chess, the game favored by Elena, her son Henry Thornton, Rosalind, and me. He played games for relaxation only—perhaps chess required too much intellectual concentration. He also reports to Elena that the morning poetry sessions with me have ended with my successfully passing the "exam" that he has set; in the evenings he has been reading me Poe and Conan Doyle's Sherlock Holmes stories. During times of insomnia, he has been worrying about what will happen to me and Rosalind. Rosalind seems to be going nowhere with her boyfriend, Topie; her creative writing is unpublishable because of the sloppy redaction; and she doesn't want to go to Boston and start a job with the *Boston Globe*. He has been so angry that he "has roared at her like a bull." Rosalind's relationship with Topie ended soon; she did end up publishing two short stories, and she did take the job at the *Globe*. Once established in Boston, she found a steady editorial job with the publisher Houghton Mifflin.

Because of Elena's moderating presence, my summers in Wellfleet unfolded for the most part pleasantly enough; however, it was not easy to adjust to my father's authoritarian ways, especially at the beginning of each summer. In June 1946 Charlie Jencks came to spend the night at our house while the rest of his family was away in New Hampshire. Having been separated all winter, Charlie and I were noisy, even boisterous, inside and out of the house. Charlie woke my father up at five thirty in the morning stomping on the floor above his head. Since our loud playing hampered his work, he angrily forbade us any kind of vocal expression. Charlie described him to his mother as "the meanest man in the world" (letter from Ruth Jencks to Mary McCarthy, early July 1948). Two years later, on June 2, 1950, I wrote my mother about another ugly situation involving me and C. Jencks: "Charlie came over yesterday and spent the night here, we went to Gull Pond today, and we went in Rosalind's jeep. Rosalind borrowed a jeep from Paul Chav [Chavchavadze]. My father is in a bad mood ["bad mood" underlined three times] right now and was yelling last night at Charlie and I for nothing, and took my gun away from me today, he is very disagreable [*sic*] right now. Please help me on that. We have got the turtle fixed up in the big aquarium. The baby Helen has grown and sits in the baby carrage [*sic*] on the porch on sunny days."

The author with his father Edmund Wilson in front of the Wellfleet house, 1949.
Photo by Henri Cartier-Bresson. Courtesy of Magnum Photos.

*The author in front of the Wellfleet house with half sister
Helen Miranda, Rex, and Bamby, circa 1952.*

My father's friendship with the rambunctious Charlie's parents seems
not to have mitigated his impatience with our activities. He better toler-
ated my other two constant companions during this period: Mike Macdonald and Christy Avery. There was no friendship lost between Dwight
Macdonald and my father. After my parents' divorce my mother sold
Dwight her Chevrolet sedan for one dollar. My father took violent ob-
jection, because he had made some or all of the installment payments on
it. On several occasions he publicly accused Dwight of having stolen it.
Christy Avery's father, Bill, worked for the U.S. government in aeronau-
tics in Washington; his mother, Helen (née Palmer), had inherited an
eighteenth-century house overlooking Gull Pond. It sits on a hill near the
sluice between Gull and Higgins Ponds. The Averys were not bohemians,

although they did take a nude swim every morning in the pond. Their son Christy was a very likable "square," with a southern drawl and a strong interest in science. I got to know him about the time of my parents' divorce, and I found a welcome haven of tranquillity in his household. A few years later, in October 1952, my mother and Bowden were staying at the Macdonald cottage on Slough Pond. She writes me, now in my first year as a boarder at Brooks School: "This afternoon, we walked from here all around five ponds to the Averys' through the pine woods. They really have a wonderful house; it used to belong, years ago, to a minister, and it's exactly the house you imagine a quiet old pastor living in. Have you seen the Latin inscription over the fireplace? 'Murus aureus coscientia sana' [A clean conscience is a golden wall]—can you translate this?" (Vassar).

~~~~~

From the time of Wilson's remarriage in 1946 to the early 1950s he led a relatively stable life. Elena quickly developed a strong attachment for the Wellfleet house and her life there. A letter she wrote him in New Mexico, where he was studying the Zuñi Indians, gives eloquent testimony to that attachment. The letter, dated "Wellfleet, December 14, 1947, Tuesday morning 10:35," relates that the Chavchavadzes had driven her to Provincetown the day before: "It was such a wonderful evening and P-town looked prettier than I have ever seen it with all the shops lit up and yet dark enough for all the tinsel and tawdry things to look attractive. Dr. Ferry [doubtless the veterinarian who will board the dogs in Elena's impending absence] came in the morning, both dogs, especially Bamby [the cocker spaniel] rubbed themselves against me, but he was gentle with them and should take care of them well. The house is empty without them. It is like the children who sometimes aggravate you when they are there and yet it is perfectly awful when they leave. Mr. Dayon [a handyman?] got a fat little pine tree and lots of green stuff from Miss Freeman's sandpit and everything looks nice. It is a bright wonderful day and I was thinking as I stood on the road and looked at the house—which certainly needs a coat of paint—that I just adore this place" (Beinecke).

Wilson became a father for the third time in February 1948 when Elena gave birth to a daughter, Helen Miranda. By now his finances had improved with the publication of the best-selling *Memoirs of Hecate County* (in my blissful ignorance I pronounced the title's key word as

"He-cat"). Trouble was brewing, however, for during the period spanning 1946–1955 Wilson would not file a single federal income tax return. (Wilson's exact thinking on this matter is unclear—if he thought about it at all during those nine years. In retrospect, he justified it on moral and political grounds. He voiced his anti-government views later, in an extended pamphlet "The Cold War and the Income Tax," 1963.) In 1950, when he first realized that he would have to come to terms with the IRS, he engaged an old friend, the lawyer John Amen, to advise him. Amen, once a crime-busting federal prosecutor, had no experience with tax law, and he was a chronic alcoholic. He proved totally ineffective in dealing with Wilson's delinquency problem. By the time he had reached a settlement with the IRS, in 1963, Wilson had suffered humiliation and penury; over subsequent years he would pay off his whopping debt to the government out of ongoing royalties.

In 1949 the *Reporter* magazine sent Wilson to Haiti, where he enthusiastically tackled a new culture and literature. In Port-au-Prince he stayed at the Olaffson, an old-fashioned hotel much frequented by foreign writers—Graham Greene put it in his novel *The Comedians*. While there, Wilson met up with his old pals John Dos Passos, Dawn Powell, and the Givens, who had chosen to leave Truro and winter in Haiti that year. In 1950 he published *Classics and Commercials*, a collection of reissued essays; the results of his Haitian research would come out in *Red, Black, Blonde and Olive: Studies in Four Civilizations: Zuñi, Haiti, Soviet Russia, Israel* (1956).

By the end of the forties Wilson had become disenchanted with Cape Cod's intellectual community, nor did he see himself any longer an integral part of it. In June 1950 he decided to visit his family's house in Talcottville, New York. As a child his parents had taken him there in the summer, and he had many fond memories of nature walks, bathing in the river, and family dinners made with local produce. During these summers he spent time with his favorite cousin Sandy (Reuel B. Kimball), who would later become incurably insane. After his father's death in 1923, his mother continued to summer in Talcottville until the middle thirties. Since then the house had been closed, and he had not seen it since a brief visit in 1933, which had inspired him to write "The Old Stone House," a brilliant reflective essay on the place, its original white settlers, and the American pioneer spirit. In June 1950, shortly before his mother's death, my father, together with Elena, Rosalind, and me, made the memorable trip to Talcottville that was to signal a crucial turning point in his life. We traveled in Bill Peck's taxi. Bill, a dapper and imperturbable New Englander, drove a large, unmarked, well-appointed Buick, which for some years served as Wellfleet's only taxi. He provided my father with an indispensable, albeit costly, link with destinations both near and far. On the way to Upstate New York we stayed at the Hotel Vendome in Boston, whence I wrote a long, newsy letter to my mother in Portsmouth, Rhode Island (June 14, 1950). In it I mention the various practical jokes I have been acquiring from Johnson Smith & Co., a mail-order purveyor of whoopee cushions (an inflatable bag that "breaks wind" when an unsuspecting victim sits down upon it—this item disappointingly failed when placed on my father's chair at the dinner table), fake dog messes, auto scare bombs, and the like. I also comment on my father's bad disposition that year and Rosalind's garrulousness. I have recently broken a crutch. (My lower right leg was in a plaster cast after I had fractured a toe in a bicycle accident on my way from home to Wellfleet Center.) I mention my new Wellfleet living quarters, in the cottage bought and renovated by Elena for her son Henry Thornton and me. Once the wing of a nineteenth-century house slated for demolition because of the Route 6 expansion, Elena's "little house" was set up across the driveway from the family residence. There Henry and I would be well insulated from my father's late-night vagaries.

After Boston, Bill Peck drove us up to Concord, New Hampshire, where we attended Henry's graduation from Saint Paul's School. The next stop, and our final destination, was Talcottville, New York. The old stone house was fusty, dusty, and cold. Rosalind and I shared a large bed together—there must have been a shortage of usable mattresses. Rosalind's nerves were acting up, and no wonder; the atmosphere was creepy. We noticed, with some trepidation, that the lock on our bedroom door was placed on the outside rather than the inside. As I later learned from my father, one of the room's previous occupants had been Sophronia Talcott, who was mentally ill and prone to nighttime wandering in her later years. A portrait of Sophronia hung in the vestibule. It had probably been painted with the figure and background already in place, with only the subject's head done from life. In any case Sophronia's eyes followed the spectator, no matter what his observation point in the rectangular vestibule. The house, whose solid interior with its finely crafted artifacts evoked past generations of self-sufficient Americans, overlooked and dominated a tiny hamlet that had once housed the Talcott estate's dependent farmers and workmen. Today, as in 1950, Talcottville has fewer than one hundred inhabitants, served by a run-down general store. Aside from the stone house, the only building of note is a well-maintained white wooden grange on the other side of the street. To my father, the house, with its massive understated elegance, represented the saga of two families: the Talcotts and the Bakers, his mother's family, one of whom, Thomas Baker, acquired it through marriage to Sophronia Talcott. In *Upstate*, my father would lovingly re-create his own and his family's stories against the background of this unchanging and unspoiled landscape.

Having rediscovered the stone house, my father hastened to take possession of it after his mother's death in Red Bank, New Jersey, in January 1951. From then on, until his own death in 1972, he would spend a good part of every year, ideally from May to October, in Talcottville (with one or two short forays back to Wellfleet). In Upstate New York he joyfully embraced what seemed to him a natural, unspoiled world where people really "belonged." Far from the astringent Atlantic and its arid sand he found inspiration in fields dotted with cows, dark rushing rivers, waterfalls, and the breathtaking view of the Adirondacks visible from the porch of his house. Here was freedom, as open as the landscape! The Cape, in contrast, seemed stagnant and rootless. The autobiographical *Upstate* (1971) projects a brilliant synthesis of local and family history, philosophical musing, and lovingly evoked nature. His residency in New York State also led him to the Iroquois Indians, its original inhabitants. In *Apologies to the Iroquois* (1960), he championed them and their struggle against the government's latest efforts to appropriate their land. Unfortunately, his wife Elena did not share his enthusiasm for Talcottville, and in the end she refused to be his summertime companion in the old stone house. She could not bear to leave Wellfleet, where her life revolved around the beach, her garden, and easy conversation with friends, many of them young people, around the kitchen table. Although the marriage suffered as the result of their annual separation, Elena stood by her husband until the bitter end. By 1960 their relations had become so strained that Wilson threatened Elena with divorce. When, in the summer of 1959, she had arrived for her annual visit in Talcottville, with Dan Aaron (a professor of American literature and friend of Wilson's), Wilson was so drunk that he failed to recognize her; he subsequently kept her awake all night telling her "to go to hell." During the first ten years of their marriage Elena had refrained from criticizing her often abusive, always demanding husband; now she fought back by refusing to run an alternative summer household in Talcottville. Having led a nomadic existence when she was young, Elena had become passionately attached to Cape Cod and the house that she had worked so hard to improve. Wellfleet was the anchor of her universe, and she hardly wanted to risk losing it in a divorce. In addition, she genuinely admired her famous husband and enjoyed being the great writer's wife, confidante, and amanuensis. She once remarked to me that all the discipline my father had at his disposal went into his work, with little left to temper his dealings with family members. Elena had a good point, although Wilson responded well to critical situations—sickness, accidents, and such—among family members and close friends. At those moments he thought clearly and acted humanely. In any case it is hardly surprising that, despite his many faults (including late-life sexual antics with other women in Talcottville and New York City), Elena chose to keep the marriage together ("CCL," 112–117).

Although he had now chosen Upstate New York as his primary geographical locus, Wilson continued to explore the Cape Cod landscape. From Gull Pond's sweeping contours, now marred by an ugly public beach and new summerhouses, he gravitated toward the smaller, remoter ponds. He still experienced sexual arousal at pond- and bayside where, under favorable conditions, he and Elena would make love upon the fine warm sand. Since the late forties, the mysterious Spectacle Ponds had cast a spell on him. He reports in his diary that he first visited them in my company:

> *Spectacle Ponds, early July '48:* I went there for the first time with Reuel, then with Elena, not long afterward. I expected to find them interesting from what I had heard, and they enchanted me when I found them, after several futile expeditions, and had on me an emotional effect.
>
> One sees the big one first, coming down the sandy road: its dark blue hill-and-tree-locked water. At the bottom of the road, on the left, are the gray boards of some old shack, of unrecognizable shape and purpose, and in the little clearing that leads to it, the white shriveled-up splinters of turtle eggs that lay about the holes for the nests—Reuel took them for the bones of crabs. . . .

There is a flat stretch of ground between the two ponds, a sort of wild cranberry bog covered with little cranberry blossoms and with marvelous pogonia and adder's mouth, larger than at Higgins Pond, and intensified to vivider tinges. The colors vary in proportion to whether they have sprung up in places where they got more or little sun—the adder's mouth from a fainter to a flamelike mauve, startling as it rises against the green of cranberry shoots and bog grass—with the fine little wings of its flowers and its bearded crazy flap that, in this exceptional orchid, rises at the top like a crest instead of hanging down like a tongue. There is something snakelike about these pogonia blossoms while the adder's mouth, with its colubrine name, is shyer and less defiant.

On the left is the smaller and muddy pond, with both the white bowl-like and the yellow ball-like water lilies. If you wade in, you sink through a layer of goo but find firm ground underneath. The clay is absolutely red, as if the soil had a lot of iron.

On the other side, the larger pond lies, half enclosed by a hilly bank, solitary, deep, wild, mysterious. A zone of some water plant with tiny white flowers runs all the way around a little out from the shore. Between the shore and this is white sand, where great polly-wogs lie; but the stems of the waterweeds make a forest where it is black below. On the other side, the bottom drops steeply, and the middle is deep and dark. But inshore it is limpid and still, a contrast, full of dignity and distinction, to its muddy probably shallow neighbor. Jack Phillips once saw under the water what he thought was a fabulous monster but turned out to be an enormous snapping turtle wrestling with an enormous eel. We found a painted turtle's shell, with the red markings very bright, completely cleaned out. The bull-frogs had the finest voices that I ever remember to have heard: they were really musical, tuneful. I felt about the place a wildness unlike anything one finds at the ponds we frequent. It was as if it existed for itself, as if the frogs and orchids flourished and perfected themselves, had their lives, for their own satisfaction. Nobody came to see them. They did not have to be on their guard against being picked or caught (the frogs were not troubled by our presence but, after a moment, went on with their singing). There it was, walled in, complete in itself, absorbing its summer days, lying open from sun to sun, with the ponds bending water lilies and water grass, frogs and turtles, pickerel and perch, in their unplumbed unfished-in depths.

The emotional effect of the spot was due, I suppose, to some affinity that I felt between it and my life, at this time—and a darkness into which I sink and a clear round single lens, well guarded and hidden away. Many things nourished and lurking at the bottom that have not yet been brought to light.

Elena, when she swam across it, said that it was a little stagnant. (*Forties*, 271–273)

Paradisiacal and yet elusive nature here hides monsters—the giant turtle and eel—in its depths, only to surface in a few moments of mortal combat. Overall, the pond's water nurtures its vegetation and living dependents, while reflecting and refracting them in its light. For Wilson the Spectacle Ponds are emblematic of the Cape's most profound natural essence; he also sees in them a reflection of his own inner darkness, a darkness that can, however, be penetrated by the lens of consciousness or self-exploration. In point of fact, when Wilson trained his fine-tuned "lens" on the world of nature the results were compellingly evocative verbal sketches; he was less successful at plumbing his own inner depths, nor did he attempt often to do so. He would return to the Spectacle Ponds the following year (1949) and briefly record his impressions in his diary. The entry concludes: "Satisfaction while looking at the pond . . . of feeling that one remained with the things of the Cape and saw them as vacationers never did" (*Forties*, 295).

During the fifties he would survey the Cape, if at all, with an increasing sense of déjà vu and weariness. In a journal entry from 1958 he compares living in Wellfleet in February and March with "being on a long ocean voyage with Elena . . . strong winds are blowing against the ship and make it difficult for me to go on deck. Everybody we know is away . . . and it is for me as if there were, outside the house, nothing but the sea" (*Fifties*, 521). During the last two decades of Wilson's life, he and Elena (to a lesser extent) were beset by assorted health-related problems. He had long suffered from chronic gout and, when he reached his middle fifties, he developed angina pectoris. He was also plagued with failing teeth, most of which had to be extracted and replaced with shaky prostheses. Although Elena had a strong constitution, she went to see Dr.

Burke in Orleans for a number of minor ailments; he gave her regular vitamin injections, which she thought increased her resistance to sickness. In addition she was accident-prone: on one occasion she almost cut through her big toe while using a new electrical lawnmower; on another she walked into a glass door in a New York store, sustaining multiple lacerations on her face (with a lawyer's help she gained financial compensation for the accident). During the fifties and sixties my father's and Elena's affectionate letters to me from Wellfleet deal with mundane things: their health, the weather and beach conditions, my well-being and vacation plans. Here is a sample of a letter from my father. It was written in Wellfleet on October 2, 1953.

> Dear Reuel:
> We are coming over to see you at Brooks School [North Andover, Massachusetts], on Sunday the 11th. The Jenckses are going to drive us and think we shall get there around 11. Please arrange to get off for lunch and the afternoon.
> The big news here is that Rosalind is engaged to be married to Frank Rounds,[1] but she doesn't want to make it public yet, so you mustn't mention it to your mother or to the Jenckses (including Charlie). Rosalind seems very happy, and I am pleased. Frank is going to Moscow as correspondent for the *Herald Tribune* and will presumably take Rosalind with him. We don't yet know when they are going to get married.
> We have missed you and look forward to seeing you.
> Walter Mumm [Elena's uncle] stayed till last Monday. He continued to be quite ill, but finally got off by plane. I expect we'll be having him back during the holidays.
> I have had the gout, and, just as I was recovering, bumped my knee-cap against a chair in the hall, so have been mildly crippled all this week.
> We discovered that the people had gone from Duck Pond, so have been going there in the afternoons. One day we found a water-scorpion, a weird kind of underwater insect that looks like a small mantis—I had never seen one before.
> I hope things are going well. Elena, Rosalind, and Helen send love.
> Love,
> Father

During the sixties my father found some solace from the now-gloomy Cape scene in his burgeoning relationship with the artist Mary Meigs and, to a lesser degree, with her companion, the writer and civil rights crusader Barbara Deming. He referred to the couple as "The Meigs." Mary, who came from a prosperous Philadelphia family, had been the Broadwaters' next-door neighbor on Pamet Point Road in Wellfleet. Meigs was already friendly with the Broadwaters when she bought the yellow house next to their red one. She would get to know them better over the next three summers. (One by-product of their intimacy was the portrait of Dolly Lamb in McCarthy's novel *A Charmed Life*.) The property with the two houses, sharing a common well, had been put up for sale as a package. Mary Meigs was delighted to acquire the smaller house, with studio; she would now be close to her best friends the Poors, who had a summerhouse in Truro. Henry Varnam Poor was a famous and successful artist; his daughter Anne was also an artist, while his wife Bessie Breuer wrote novels. When the Broadwaters decided to leave Wellfleet for good in late 1955, Mary Meigs bought their house immediately and moved in.

Wilson made no secret of his romantic attachment to Mary Meigs, a late-blooming lesbian. He admired her fine sensibility, quick intelligence, and demure beauty. Flattered by his attentions, and overwhelmed by his intellect and erudition, she had no inclination for anything more than a platonic relationship. She quickly realized, moreover, that his interest in her as a human being waned once he knew that he had gained her loyal attachment. Although he may have been patronizing toward Mary, he did respect her. Her companionship and very material generosity in lending him money when he was in dire financial straits gave him support at a time when his relations with Elena were becoming increasingly strained. Meigs describes her relationship with Wilson, and the Broadwaters, in her autobiographical memoir *Lily Briscoe* (1981). Because of Meigs' sexual orientation, Elena showed her no jealousy, while she actively befriended Barbara Deming and later Barbara's replacement, Marie-Claire Blais. In the summer of 1963 Wilson introduced Meigs to his young protégée, the French-Canadian writer Marie-Claire Blais. He had praised the latter in *O Canada*, his opus on Canadian literature, and, at his urging, his publisher, Farrar Straus and Giroux, had begun to publish her novels in English. Blais would write about Cape Cod in the sixties in *American Notebooks: A Writer's Journey* (U.S. version, 1996). Although she uses the names of real people—Mary Meigs and Barbara Deming, Edmund, Elena, and Reuel Wilson, among others—most of the material in the book is invented. The real Elena, however, in an idealized version, serves as the narrator's moral touchstone. That summer of 1963, while Deming was down south marching for desegregation and peace, in the course of which she was jailed for twenty-seven days, Blais moved into Mary's house on Pamet Point Road. Here is the background. During a walk in the woods with Marie-Claire, Mary Meigs, who was in the lead, had pulled aside a branch and then, without thinking, had released it, so that it struck her companion in the eye. Marie-Claire's injury required medical attention, although it was not serious. Mary's resultant guilt was a factor motivating her to ask Marie-Claire to move in. Barbara, on her return, became part of an uneasy ménage à trois, from which she would often absent herself to pursue her activist goals; eventually she moved out entirely, to resettle in Florida. Mary gave Blais the yellow house next door, which she had lived in earlier. Meigs and Blais, who were never totally accepted as a couple by Nina Chavchavadze, a crucial pillar of the Wellfleet social order, took definitive leave of the Cape in 1971, when Mary sold the house on Pamet Point Road. (Nina referred to Blais as "that Canuck.") They moved to France, where Meigs bought a house in Brittany. Soon they were mired in another ménage à trois, with a French feminist who cruelly manipulated them both. Meigs describes the grim relationship in an autobiographical book, *The Medusa's Head* (1983). Mary and Marie-Claire finally extricated themselves from the situation and retreated to Quebec, where they settled permanently, although they ended up living separately.

~~~~~~

From the beginning of the sixties, Wellfleet attracted a new kind of summer visitor—successful professionals and intellectuals who belonged to the East Coast establishment. The critic Alfred Kazin was one of them. In an article titled "The Great Anachronism [a metonymy for Wilson himself]: A View from the Sixties," later included in his autobiographical *New York Jew* (1978), Kazin remembers those heady days in Wellfleet, when his mentor Edmund Wilson held forth on the ocean beach surrounded by the Harvard historians Arthur Schlesinger Jr. and Stuart Hughes, Daniel Aaron (then professor of American literature at

Smith, later at Harvard), the novelist Edwin O'Connor,[2] and other major and minor luminaries. Just down the shoreline from the spot Wilson occupied was the beach used by Wellfleet bohemians for nude bathing and socializing. Although some of the newcomers joined the old-timers in this practice, Wilson himself never participated. If he had exhibitionist tendencies, they were limited to his mental, not physical, endowments. Kazin's piece begins with a description of Wilson's beach attire: he wore "a stained panama hat" and "a long white dress shirt," "brown Bermuda shorts that bulged with his capacious middle"; he carried "a handsome straight gold-topped cane that had long been in his family." Elena drove Wilson to the parking lot above the beach, and he hobbled down the dune. Kazin notes that once Wilson had finished his working day, "he was now ready to look at nature and have a talk." Kazin continues: "The beach was full of television producers, government and U.N. 'advisors'— social scientists, psychohistorians, professors by the dozen—people all definitely 'in'" (EW *Celebration*, 11). As Kazin correctly remembers, Wilson hated the Cape summer whirl and referred to the scene as "the fucking Riviera." He complained bitterly that whereas the others, including some of his good friends, came to Wellfleet for a vacation, he only wanted to get on with his work. In a journal entry from the summer of 1962 he gives a numbing enumeration of summer personalities and social events:

Wellfleet, summer, '62. La plage des intellectuals, as Stuart Hughes calls it. After not having been here at this time of year for years, I find the elite now congregate, away from the Newcomb's Hollow crowds, on the beach below the little summerhouses that perch on top of the cliff: the Kazins, the Schlesingers, the Hofstadters, the Aarons, Ed O'Connor and his fiancée, sometimes the Walkers and the Jenckses. . . . Elena and I either went out to dinner or had people here almost without interruption: Schlesingers here one night, Kazins another, Hughes and Hofstadters the night after that; dinner at the Francis Biddles' with the Schlesingers, dinner at the Kazins' with the Schlesingers, the Aarons, and a man named Goodwin from the State Department, who is visiting the Schlesingers with his wife, dinner at the Jenckses' with the Newmans, Arthur Berger, two other young musicians and the wife of the Richman in Washington who manipulated the Malraux luncheon, with her nine-year-old daughter, a Lolita, who had a pack of cards and was going to play solitaire as I used to do, in childhood, at parties and for whom I did a few card tricks, finding her an interested audience—earlier, dinner at the Chavchavadzes' with the George Biddles, and dinner at our house or their house with Barbara [Deming] and Mary [Meigs] and others, etc., etc.

Since Barbara and Mary have gone to Maine, the heavy business of the summer has begun, and it makes a striking contrast with the old Jig Cook Provincetown or the Dos Passos–Waugh Province-town. They were all writers and painters who were working and freely exchanging ideas; but these people are mostly attached to the government or some university, or at least they do part-time teach-ing. Jim Newman is the editor of the *Scientific American*. They are accountable to some institution, and you are likely—especially with the Schlesingers—to run into some subject as to which they have to be dumb, so that you feel it is tactless to talk about it. . . .

I have become timid, perhaps too timid, on account of my heart, about going into the cold water or struggling with the surf, and it bores and irritates me to go to the ocean without being able to swim and now that the Sharps are there, I am beginning to get nostalgic for Talcottville. . . .

I stayed in Wellfleet longer than I otherwise should have on ac-count of Reuel's coming on, and I found it rather demoralizing. I thought that, except for Reuel, I should be better off in Talcottville, now that the Sharps were there. (*Sixties*, 105–108)

On August 1 of that summer I drove my father to his beloved Tal-cottville in my car. It is not difficult to understand, and even sympathize with, his impatience with the summer whirl in Wellfleet. I myself en-joyed those Wellfleet dog days in the early sixties. Life seemed to revolve around the ocean, which offered not just bracing surf but a chance to drink martinis in the company of witty older women during the day; at night there were beach picnics with a bonfire, singing, midnight swims, and occasionally spontaneous attractions that turned into one-night stands. None of this would or could have appealed to my father at this point in his life. Interestingly enough, the urban intellectuals who didn't have long-standing roots in the Cape's sandy soil had, by the early sev-enties, gravitated to other vacation places. What then ensued was the

Two photos taken in Cummington, Massachusetts, while on the way from Wellfleet to Talcottville, New York. Edmund Wilson often stopped over at the house of his old friend Helen Muchnic, a professor at nearby Smith College. Helen's companion Dorothy Walsh, also a Smith professor, can be seen in the background of one photo; the author is on Wilson's right in the other. EW is in high spirits, having taken leave of Wellfleet for the bulk of the summer.

"richification" of our part of the Cape, with Mercedes Benzes and new luxurious houses replacing the jalopies and modest shacks of the now almost-extinct bohemians.

Even Wilson's oldest Wellfleet friends came to grate on his nerves. In May 1964 he returned from a trip to Europe, during which he explored Budapest as part of his ongoing interest in Hungary. After a dinner at the Walkers', with the Chavchavadzes, he writes in his journal: "After the quietness of the Hungarians and the English, the conversation seemed to me all blatt blatt. A lot of talk about the Kennedy assassination, about which they all had positive opinions, though none of them except Paul Chavchavadze had read Buchanan's book. . . . This evening made me feel what a lot of loud nonsense is talked in the U.S. about important matters that people want to avoid considering by gregariously shooting off their faces about them. This goes on at Wellfleet all summer" (*Sixties*, 390).

During the summer of 1965, the year he turned seventy, Wilson returned to Wellfleet from Talcottville for an extended family reunion with me and my wife, Marcia; Rosalind; Elena's son, Henry Thornton, and his family; and assorted European relatives of Elena's. Just before Labor Day Rosalind was arrested for drunken driving on Route 6, after leaving an evening party at the Chavchavadzes' in South Wellfleet. Having inheriting a large sum of money that had been held in trust for her by her grandmother Wilson's estate, Rosalind had quit her job at Houghton Mifflin in 1958. After spending most of the money, she had gone back to her old job in 1962. Things were not going well for her. She had had a serious nervous breakdown in the fall of 1963, just at the time when her father and Elena were preparing to leave for Europe. Elena departed as scheduled, but Wilson remained behind to attend to Rosalind. After spending ten days in hospital Rosalind joined her father in Wellfleet for a few weeks before her father finally departed for Europe; she later joined him and Elena in Rome for a few weeks that spring. She would not go back to publishing and found herself at loose ends; ultimately she would regain her equilibrium when she moved definitively to Talcottville in 1969.

That late August night in 1963 Rosalind was taken to the Provincetown jail after her detention on the highway. With the help of a lawyer her father made bail for her and took her home from Provincetown in the early morning hours. Subsequently, while waiting in the magistrate's court for Rosalind's case to be heard, Wilson glumly noted the seamy side of present-day Provincetown: "young bums arrested for speeding, pansies caught in the act. . . . One boy suing another boy for $18 rent. . . ." That fall Wilson went to a party at the Hacketts' in Provincetown. Chauncey had died, but his wife Mary (Bubbs) remained in the little family house on Nickerson Street, diagonally across from Hans Hoffmann's (formerly Frederick Waugh's) palatial compound. There Wilson encountered old friends, much the worse for wear: "I was feeling rather low that day, and it seemed a gathering of ghosts and I seemed a ghost myself" (*Sixties*, 479).

By 1967 Wilson had put his income tax trouble behind him and, while in Wellfleet, he had a relaxed schedule. Elena was there to minister to his wants and act as a live-in chauffeur; she had bravely learned to drive while in her fifties. In addition to writing, as per his usual routine, from about ten thirty to three in the afternoon, he read, listened to the phono-graph in his study, and later played solitaire with the red Persian cat Lulu for company. In two stages, one before, the other after dinner, he usually accounted for a "fifth" of Johnny Walker Red Label Scotch. He retired early after taking a sleeping pill.

On January 12, 1967, he attended Waldo Frank's funeral. Frank (1889–1967), a prolific writer of novels, plays, and essays, was a politically com-mitted leftist with mystic and visionary tendencies. Later in life he wrote extensively on Latin American history and politics. Much appreciated in South America, he saw himself as a prophet without honor in his own country. Since the early 1930s he had summered in Truro, where he eventually bought a secluded house near the bayside. Wilson's descrip-tion of Waldo's funeral beautifully evokes the sad circumstances—the landscape, the moving religious ceremony, and the failings of the writer himself.

Waldo Frank's funeral, January 12: In the South Truro cemetery, full of old gravestones. The day was terribly cold, and Nina [Chavchavadze] and Phyllis [Duganne-Given] looked dreadful. I thought that the Wellfleet undertaker looked at some of us with a lecherous eye. The sky was gray, the sun a mere brighter blur. The wind froze us on that bleak hill. The ceremony was performed by a rabbi from Providence, a friend of Waldo's, a scholar who has just, he told me, translated the whole of the Midrash for the Yale Hebrew series. He read partly in Hebrew, partly in English, and the Hebrew sounded very fine. He made a little speech about Waldo, how he had come to know him through a book of Waldo's about the Jews, how he had presided at Waldo's daughter's wedding; said that Waldo's imagination would go winging away into the future. Simple and austere on the winter hill. I thought it was the most impressive funeral service at which I had ever been present. . . .

I had been asked to speak, but I declined. Besides being no good at making speeches, I couldn't say what I honestly thought about Waldo and his work. The most depressing thing about his death was the unsatisfactoriness of his writing and career. He said to me lately that he had been "rejected." I am sure he never knew why. He seemed to be incapable of self-criticism. Conscious of in some ways brilliant abilities and an unusually wide intellectual range, he could not understand that his practice nowhere near came up to his pretensions. I used to think about him years ago that he had no humility before his medium, never in fact taught himself to write. (*Sixties*, 564–565)

Over the last decade of his life Wilson continued relentlessly to pursue his intellectual, social, and erotic goals; nor did he neglect his children, whose well-being preoccupied him and whose interests he tried to encourage. Despite failing health—a bad heart, angina, acute gout, loss of hearing, attacks of nausea, a painful back injury, shingles, and finally two strokes—he bravely soldiered on. The last volume of his journals, spanning 1960 to 1972, reveals a passionate and ongoing engagement with the world around him. He even manages to describe with equanimity the sorry consequences of his physical deterioration. Writing in Wellfleet at the end of the summer of 1967, he reports that Gilbert and Marian Seldes,[3] Arthur and Marian Schlesinger, and four of the Schlesinger children, one with her husband, came in for drinks, which he dispensed from the parlor sofa. Taking leave of the Seldeses at the front door, he felt an incontrollable urge to urinate. Bolting to his study bathroom at the back of the house, he was unable to restrain a spurt of urine that partly wetted his pants. Once in the bathroom he discovered a mouse swimming desperately around in the toilet bowl. An inveterate animal lover, he extracted the mouse by its tail and set it free. He then returned to the company of the remaining guests, unaware, as Elena later pointed out, that his fly was still open (*Sixties*, 660–661).

This last volume of Wilson's journals is the longest; often partly incapacitated, he had more leisure time to record day-to-day life. During the last decade, he nonetheless traveled to Canada, and Hungary, bringing as was his wont a keen reporter's eye and ear to the chosen subject. From Wellfleet or Talcottville he went frequently for short stays in New York and Boston, with single trips to Virginia and Chicago. He had lectured at the University of Chicago in the summer of 1939 when I was just seven months old; now I was doing graduate work there and had a five-month-old son. He spent the fall and winter of 1963–64 in Western Europe; in the winter of 1969 he and Elena spent a few months in Jamaica (on the Walkers' recommendation). He spent two months of the last year of his life in Naples, Florida. Not a lover of southern climes in general, he found both Jamaica and Florida depressing. Jamaica had the sole advantage of offering him, at least when he was in Kingston, the company of some writers and intellectuals.

During the last twelve years of his life, Wilson published *Apologies to the Iroquois* (1960); *Patriotic Gore* (1962), his wide-ranging study of the American Civil War and its literature; *The Cold War and the Income Tax* (1963); *O Canada: An American's Notes on Canadian Culture* (1965); "Notes from a European Diary: 1963–1964" (including a long piece on Hungary and Hungarian culture); *A Prelude* (1967), the first volume of his diaries; "The Fruits of the MLA" (1968), a polemic against academe and its pedantic approach to editing the classics; a revised edition of *The Scrolls from the Dead Sea* (1968); *The Duke of Palermo* (1968), a witty play spoofing academics, one of whom forges an Elizabethan tragedy; and *Upstate* (1971). Owing to his enormous productivity, Wilson resolved his main financial problems over the last years, but he continued to run a large ongoing debt with Farrar Straus. He notes in the diary, with some disdain for the awarding organizations, his reception of two prestigious literary awards in 1966—one carrying a prize of $6,000, the other netting him $30,000. There would be others. In 1968 he sold all his papers to Yale. He used some of the proceeds to remodel and enlarge his study in Wellfleet.

Some of the late journal entries sound like Chekhov's alienated narrator in his novella *A Boring Story* (Skuchnaya Istoria). The narrator, a doctor and professor of medicine with an international reputation, now deprived of libido and suffering from a terminal disease, sadly and helplessly observes the shallow and mediocre world that surrounds him: friends, family members, students, and his favorite Katya, a young woman to whom he has been a surrogate father while she was growing up and who has gone on to fail in her personal and professional aspirations. Wilson was able to overcome the sense of monotony and ennui by engaging with people whom he singled out as original and interesting. Svetlana "Alleluyeva," Stalin's daughter, was one of these. Wilson fell under the spell of her forceful personality and championed her writing, which was translated by Paul Chavchavadze, the person who introduced them. Wilson was also drawn to the comedy duo of Mike Nichols and Elaine May. An avid fan of their recordings, he attended their live performances in New York and established friendships with both. He became intrigued, if not infatuated, with Penelope Gilliatt, the British writer who had been married to the playwright John Osborne and romantically involved with the theater critic and playwright Kenneth Tynan; she had then taken up with Mike Nichols after he and May parted company. Wilson showed less enthusiasm for Gilliatt's fiction or her movie reviews in the *New Yorker* than he did for her flaming red hair and independent personality. As his journal reveals, she made no secret of her sexual availability—which seems to have put him to an arduous test. The relationship caused him a serious misadventure: having taken Gilliatt, her young daughter Nolan, and the daughter's nanny to a circus performance in New York (Elena was absent at the time), he and Penelope repaired to his lodgings at the Princeton Club. After some martinis there, he attempted to sit down on the bed, but instead landed heavily on the floor. According to Elena, Gilliatt departed at this juncture, although Wilson maintains in his journal that she had already left when the accident happened. The next morning Wilson awoke in excruciating pain and would later learn that he had fractured his coccyx (a small triangular bone forming the lowest extreme of the spinal column) (*Sixties*, 870). Gilliatt was also Wilson's houseguest in Wellfleet on several occasions. While Elena was preparing dinner, he would closet himself with Penelope in his study. Elena took it all with outward equanimity.

Over the last decade Wilson records the death of old Cape friends: Waldo Frank, Edwin O'Connor, Chauncey Hackett, and Paul Chavchavadze. (By attrition the Hacketts had become Wilson's last Provincetown friends.) He also notes the Schlesingers' divorce in 1969. Arthur and Marian jointly shared with Peter and Vita Petersen ownership of a cottage on Slough Pond. The Schlesinger children took over their parents' half interest in the cottage after their parents relocated elsewhere. Another academic couple, Harry and Elena Levin, would settle permanently in Wellfleet for the summers. During the sixties they bought a charming traditional house in a lush, green corner of the predominantly barren Bound Brook Island. Harry was a distinguished professor of comparative literature at Harvard, where he taught his trademark Proust, Joyce and Mann course over many decades. His wife, Elena, was a Russian émigré who had grown up in Harbin, China. Although they saw each other socially, Wilson and Levin had a prickly relationship—each felt superior to the other. Harry took the academic high ground in their recurring wrangles (one of which centered on Wilson's low opinion of *Don Quixote*), while Wilson looked down on Levin not just for his Harvardian self-importance but also, I suspect, for having produced only a modest output of writing over his long career.

Over the winter of 1965–66 Wilson read Goethe's *Faust*, parts 1 and 2, with Elena's help. During the summers of 1965 and 1967 they entertained her Paris White Russian relatives in the Wellfleet house. Wilson was on his best behavior when receiving visitors from Europe. He much enjoyed playing and conversing with the daughters of Elena's cousin Marina Shuvalov. Marina worked in the fur department at Dior's; her husband Ivan was a little-published writer who had written a novel about a condom salesman. Thanksgiving 1967, in Wellfleet, turned out a thoroughly depressing affair—climaxed by Elena's drinking a bottle of calamine lotion in the mistaken belief that it was a bottle of prescription internal medicine. In June 1968 Rosalind gave her father a puppy, which he identified as a "coon hound." "Brown," as he named it, replaced "Button," the little part-beagle (Rex's replacement) who had recently died.

Wilson continued to incorporate elements of the Cape Cod landscape into his late diaries. One of the best examples of his late Cape Cod prose is the short entry from summer's end 1966 (*Sixties*, 543). It evokes a "ghastly and tragic sight," a gigantic finback whale expiring on the Wellfleet bay beach. The passage bears comparison to "The Wellfleet Whale," a longish poem by Stanley Kunitz based on the same real event. Both writers humanize the helpless leviathan; both see it as the victim of Nature's whim, aggravated by a horde of children who tear its skin while their elders gawk. While Kunitz takes an Olympian, romanticizing view of the subject, Wilson paints it succinctly and in tellingly observed detail.

Reading Wilson's diaries of the fifties and sixties, one is struck by the absolute duality of his life, polarized as it was between New York State and Massachusetts. When on Cape Cod he continued his roles as a husband and as father to my younger half sister Helen Miranda, who was growing up during those two decades. He socialized with the same old friends (like him, increasingly succumbing to old age) as well as with the summertime latecomers. In Talcottville, where he lived mostly by himself, he saw concentric circles of people, often strangers to one another, who shared a common friendship with him. Some of these Upstate friends were professionals; none were intellectuals, but they all shared ties to the region and its history. Over the sixties he courted Mary Pcolar, his attractive Hungarian teacher who in Elena's absence served as hostess when he entertained in the stone house. (Elena called her "the Madame Bovary of Boonville," the nearby town where she worked in the drugstore.) For a while Mary (Mariska) chauffeured Wilson around in her car, just as Elena did in Wellfleet. He paid her tuition when she decided to enroll in night courses at the community college in Utica, and he entertained her children with puppet shows given in a little theater that duplicated the one he had in Wellfleet. He also kept an alternate library in Talcottville, with duplicate sets of Pushkin, Chekhov, Henry James, and other favorite writers. Mary Pcolar, who would later perish in a trailer fire in Florida, was not the only woman Wilson desired in the last Talcottville period of his life. At the very end he had a steamy liaison with his dentist's wife (whom Rosalind called "Ms. Groupie" in her book). Some of his very explicit descriptions of their encounters were excised from the published version of *The Sixties*.

Wilson maintained, then, two separate households over a twenty-year span. In the case of Talcottville, he needed considerable domestic help. All this did not come cheaply. The frequent transitions from one locality to the other caused him temporary difficulties in readjusting; but the Talcottville half of his life caused Elena far more serious existential problems. Unwilling to part with her beloved Wellfleet in the summer months, she had no leverage over her husband's Upstate behavior. Fully aware of this, he deflected her recriminations about Talcottville with threats of divorce.

Over the last years my father often felt that he wanted to do things—projects for books, new travels—but then came the momentary realization of his physical incapacity. He was, moreover, depressed by events, trends, and people in the world around him: the Kennedy assassination, Lyndon Johnson, the Vietnam War, the hippies, the ugly commercialism that was sweeping America (mercifully sparing his beloved Lewis County, New York). He declined the option of a pacemaker implant that would almost certainly have prolonged his life, as it had President Dwight Eisenhower's. He spoke of some of these matters to me, without self-pity, during our periodic meetings in his Wellfleet study. Mostly, however, our conversations dealt with my progress as a student of Slavic and comparative literature, and my future prospects. It pleased him that I had followed him in pursuing the challenges of new languages and cultures. He read more languages than I did, but I learned three that he did not know: Polish, Spanish, and Portuguese. Actually, in the case of Spanish, my father had nothing but disdain for the language, and the culture, giving the Spanish cult of death as the main reason for his lack of interest.

In our conversations over the years, my father spoke little and selectively about his past life on Cape Cod, and elsewhere. He doubtless thought that I would later glean from his published journals all that he wanted the world to know about him. He did occasionally mention that we, his three children, would make lots of money from his journals' future royalties, and that they should not be published until all the major players in them were dead. It didn't quite turn out that way: Helen would inherit all his literary rights, while my mother, Rosalind, the Levins, and others who lived to find their portraits on the pages of his journals found them hurtful. Our father later spoke to us about the provisions of his will. Rosalind would inherit the Talcottville property, Helen and I would jointly inherit his Wellfleet house, I his library, and Helen the literary rights. When he died, he left his estate, represented by his widow Elena, burdened with a whopping $30,000 debt to his publisher. (Roger Straus had consistently lent him money interest-free, against future royalties.) Much of this had been borrowed to finance the trips to Jamaica and Naples, Florida. As mentioned, he responded negatively to these exotic locations. Jamaica did little for his health, for he succumbed there to a painful and frightening bout of seizure and nausea, which he attributed to a meal of ackee fruit prepared by their housekeeper. During the parts of spring and summer that he did spend in Wellfleet, his only outside recreation became the afternoon drives with Elena in her car—this in lieu of the nature walks he had enjoyed in better days. From his study window he could view an old apple tree, a few birds, and a row of lilac bushes. He died in Talcottville on June 12, 1972. A nurse was with him at the time, and Rosalind was living in a house just down the street. On his desk lay a codicil to his will, amending it so that I would lose my future interest in the Wellfleet property, all of which would go to Helen.

A few days before he died he had summoned Rosalind and Glen Morris, a friend from nearby Glens Falls, and insisted that they sign the codicil as witnesses. At the time he failed to sign the document, nor did he do so later. During the last telephone conversation I had with him, at the beginning of June, he mentioned a subject that we needed to discuss at our upcoming meeting in Wellfleet. I was then in Ontario, Canada, he in Talcottville. He must have been alluding to the codicil, drafted by a lawyer at Elena's urgent request. Anticipating the financial hardship that a debt-ridden estate would bring after her husband's imminent death, she wanted, I surmise, to reinforce her daughter Helen's future financial security by assuring her an eventual full ownership of the Wellfleet house. This would, however, occur only after Elena's own death, since she retained lifetime tenancy of the property. In addition, Elena resented the fact that our grandmother, Helen M. K. Wilson, had bequeathed a sizable trust fund to Rosalind and to me. According to the provisions of our grandmother's will, Rosalind would inherit two-thirds of the trust when she reached the age of thirty-five; the remaining one-third would be divided between me and Rosalind after our father's death. (During his lifetime he benefited from the income generated by the trust.) There was no mention in the will of Helen, who was two when her Wilson grandmother died. Faced with the legal invalidity of the unsigned codicil, Elena insistently demanded that I renounce my future interest in the Wellfleet house. I ended up negotiating a settlement with her: after her death Helen would inherit the house, while I would inherit the cottage next door, which belonged to Elena.

All of my father's three children, as well as my wife Marcia, were assembled in the Wellfleet house when Elena returned from Talcottville bearing her husband's ashes, the most recent installments of his diaries, and the unsigned codicil to his will. She had attended the ceremony held in his memory in Talcottville, presided over by Glen Morris, a former Presbyterian minister. Now we interred his ashes at the Rose Hill Cemetery in Wellfleet. The funeral was attended by a smallish group of friends, among them Charles and Adelaide Walker (Charley gave the oration), Arthur Schlesinger Jr., Harry and Elena Levin, Daniel Aaron, Stuart Hughes, Jason and Barbara Epstein, Roger Straus (Wilson's publisher), Morley and Barry Callaghan (the Canadian writer and his son), Penelope Gilliatt, and Lilian Hellman. The writer Renata Adler, who had once taken a graduate seminar with Wilson at Harvard—he later befriended her when she was writing for the *New Yorker*—made a surprise appearance, emerging from a clump of trees in the background. She disappeared after the service was over. (Perhaps this was to avoid meeting me; our two-year relationship had ended acrimoniously in 1962.) I, Rosalind, Helen, and Henry Thornton, our stepbrother, dug a hole and placed the modest urn with our father's ashes in it. We then covered it with sand. This impromptu, improvised scenario probably came from Helen, who for both emotional and financial reasons wanted to reduce the undertakers' participation. While all this was going on, Jason Epstein was noisily gunning his rental car up and down the cemetery dirt roads. Later he wrote a short piece about the funeral to which Rosalind took strong exception. In it he compared, perhaps insensitively, our behavior during the burial to that of "children playing at the beach." Actually Jason was deeply attached to our father, but seems to have had difficulty expressing his grief. Afterward we repaired to Money Hill for a modest reception, whose culinary high point was a fresh poached sea bass brought by Odette Walling, one of Elena's best year-round friends in Wellfleet.

I did not return to the Wellfleet house after my father's death. Some five years later I sold most of his library (with the exception of the French- and Russian-language books, which I kept) to the University of Tulsa. They repose there adjacent to the library of his old pal, the British critic Cyril Connolly. Elena would continue to occupy the house until her death in 1979, when I duly inherited the cottage. Her last years with my father were very difficult, through no fault of hers; some of the bitterness she felt toward him ended up tingeing her relations with me. Her overall record, though, as a stepparent to me and Rosalind was exemplary. Generous and nurturing, she made a habit of caring for others.

4 : EDMUND WILSON'S CAPE COD POETRY

**M**y father enjoyed writing poetry, and he practiced the art with great technical expertise. He can best be described as a gifted amateur who wrote poetry, mostly occasional, over the span of his lifetime. Much of his serious poetry was collected and published in *Night Thoughts* (1953, reissued 1961), where we find four short lyrics and two longish narrative poems dealing with Cape Cod themes. Here is the first lyric, "Provincetown," written during a visit to Provincetown in 1927:

PROVINCETOWN

We never from the barren down,
Beneath the silver lucent breast
Of drifting plume, gazed out to drown
Where daylight whitens to the west.

Here never in this place I knew
Such beauty by your side, such peace—
These skies that brightening imbue
With dawn's delight the day's release.

Only, upon the barren beach,
Beside the gray egg of a gull,
With that fixed look and fervent speech,
You stopped and called it beautiful.

Lone as the voice that sped the word!—
Gray-green as eyes that ate its round!—
The desert dropping of a bird,
Bare-bedded in the sandy ground.

To-night, where clouds like foam are blown,
I ride alone the surf of light—

As—even by my side, alone,
That stony beauty burned your sight.

The poem, the author informs us in his essay on Edna St. Vincent Millay (collected in *The Shores of Light*, 1952), evokes his memories of Millay, dating back to the summer of 1920, when he visited her in the rented cottage behind Longnook Beach in Truro. The first two stanzas suggest a Provincetown land/seascape; they imply a shared past experience that would never be repeated. Daybreak comes peacefully, and sensuously. In stanza three the viewpoint changes, from the sky with its "drifting plume" to ground level, the "barren beach," which echoes the "barren down" (dune) of line one. "You," here Millay's surrogate, has in the real event stopped to admire a seagull's gray egg lying in the sand. The poem's "I," Wilson's surrogate, has not shared his companion's ecstatic reaction to the egg, to him merely the "desert dropping of a bird." He takes note of her predatory nature: "Gray-green [the egg] as eyes that ate its round." The clouds return in the last stanza, while "I" remains alone with the woman's memory conjured up by "the surf of light." But, the last two lines suggest, she was "alone" even when they were together, when "[t]hat stony beauty burned your sight." The poem reflects Wilson's longing for, and frustration with, his elusive first lover.

"Cape Cod," a sonnet, appears in the "Poets, Farewell" (1929) section of *Night Thoughts*.

Here where your blue bay's hook is half begun,
I find you fled on those mad rounds you make—
As if with sleepless demons on your track
Yet lodging with the daughters of the sun—
Pursuing still that high romantic mood
Through flight from love to love, from friend to friend;
While she who dwells there sovereign to the end
Draws now her final strength from solitude.

—Yes, moored in a shadowy room I have seen that shape—
Who once by sleepless winds herself was sped—
She haunts me here in mind's and time's despite—
The last gray clouds and pale gold of the Cape—
The scent of sweet-fern crushed beneath my tread,
As once I smelt it through the smothered night.

The theme and tone closely resemble those of the preceding lyric. The subject could well be Millay again. The octave suggests that her persona has been tormented by "sleepless demons," while recklessly pursuing "that high romantic mood" in art and love. Lines seven and eight speak of her having finally achieved self-sufficiency and a "final strength from solitude." The sestet conjures up her presence and merges it with a Cape sunset, "The last gray clouds and pale gold of the Cape—" and the "scent of sweet-fern . . . As once I smelt it through the smothered night." Cape Cod's sights and smells serve as a frame for the image of a haunted and haunting woman.

The next lyric of interest, in the section "Elegies and Wakeful Nights" (1930s), evokes Provincetown and its outer shore, Peaked Hill, where Wilson spent the summer of 1930 with his second wife, Margaret Canby.

This blue world with its high wide sky of islands!
Pale cliffs, white cubes, the slender point, the little bay—
And over there, beyond the outer shore,
Its wildness and its silence,
Old kegs and beams of wrecks embedded in hot snows,
Will sink in awful lavender and rose
The red sea-faring sun—
This freedom of the sands, and summer new begun!

—But oh, my dear, among those dunes we lay,
And all the paths we left are drifted smooth
And we shall make no more!—
And death lies underneath
That cuts the world away.

The first stanza sketches Provincetown's "blue world" of sky and sea, with its cubelike white houses and fine view of "pale cliffs" in Truro to the south, the harbor, and Long Point, at the Cape's very tip. The "wild" ocean side, on the other hand, evokes danger (shipwreck), solitude, a rough "sea-faring" sun that sets "in awful lavender and rose," and the freedom of a summer vacation on a secluded beach. Stanza two records the couple's lovemaking on the beach, only to close the scene with the finality of her death (which occurred only two summers after the one alluded to in the poem).

Moving away from the theme of irretrievably lost women, "Provincetown, 1936" sounds almost a cynical note. It depicts the shoreline at low tide.

PROVINCETOWN, 1936

Fat-pronged starfish, oyster-fed,
That slow on spirit fingers slide;
Snails in plump blue folds that spread
Purple feet below the tide;

Crabs that, humped in stolen homes,
Fence from doors they cannot lock;
Polyps budded pink, like wombs,
Filamented to the rock;

Sand-dabs sandside up in pools,
That slip in bat-flights from the hand;
Tiny mackerel trapped in twinkling schools;
The little silver eels that dive into the sand—

Mussels with broken hinges, sea crabs lopped
Of legs, black razor-clams split double, dried
Sea-dollars, limpets chivied loose and dropped
Like stranded dories rolling on their side:

They lose their juice and stiffen in the sun:
The tide that shrinks has shed them like a scarf;
The tide that floods will stir with waves that stun
Frail shapes that crush before the faintest surf.

High and dry, exposed to the merciless sun, marine life, almost human in its wondrous diversity—and vulnerability—lies helplessly imprisoned. The tide, the sea's implacable agent, indifferently destroys life, without serving any "higher purpose." Whether ebbing or flowing, it brings death to its lowly subjects.

In writing "The Pickerel Pond: A Double Pastoral" (1948) Wilson set himself the formidable task of writing a modern English poem in elegiac meter, and with "amphisbaenics," or backward rhymes. For an explanation (that is perforce highly recondite) of exactly what the elegiac was in ancient Greek and Latin poetry, and how it was later adapted into European languages including English, the reader should consult Wilson's own "Note on the Elegiac Meter," the last entry in *Night Thoughts*. Backward rhyming involves reversing rather than echoing; for example, the first line of "The Pickerel Pond" ends in "ripple," which is paired with "leper" at the end of line two; "air" rhymes with "ray," "lissome" with "mussels," and so on. The rhyming word then shows the backward or mirror image of its predecessor—appropriately enough in a poem that unfolds on the edge of a still pond. The narrative, such as it is, describes a summer picnic. The motley participants—globe-trotting European émigrés to the New World, an American lady with an attractive protégée in tow, a college student with Stalinist views—give the narrator a sense of fatigue and déjà vu. Part 1 shows a satirical picture of the holiday makers and their dogs. In part 2 the narrator wanders away with his fishing rod in search of the elusive pickerel. Having cast his line, he is standing

> . . . on the slope
> That dips toward the densening shadow,
> Where lumps that loom turtlish or toadish,
> Vague fish-forms, a forest of stem
> And old leaf-mould and slime have met?
>
> To melt: the alert, the alive,
> Made one with the duller and viler . . .
> As I paused here, so long have I pored
> At the brink of the mind's dark drop. . . .

At this point he catches an iridescent sunfish, an unsubstantial, and inedible, prize. Having returned the fish to its element, he begins to "drop darkly" into a grotesque chain of "horrors forgotten." Just as the fish has been pulled from the murky depths, suppressed desires and memories swarm to the surface of his conscious mind. A struggle takes place "in this pond of the pan of my skull" to dominate raw images and give them form through language. As the words that occur to him become increasingly obstreperous and obscure ("boustrophédon," "dodecatonic," "cancrizans," "widdershins"), he loses his "last live bait." In the last stanza he admits that the "mutinous music as muttered / Between the bleak spring and mild autumn" has gotten the better of him. He has not succeeded in achieving creative harmony, just as he has failed to catch a pickerel. If, on the one hand, the poem has reflected the writer's own disillusionment with the summer rituals in Wellfleet, it also draws a parallel, like that already observed in his diaries, between the muddy, murky underside of the pond and his own dark, troubled, subconscious mind. The struggle to dominate the irrational and ugly also occurs in an earlier poem, to be discussed later, that served as the first version of the "Pickerel Pond" ending.

The last clearly identifiable Cape Cod poem in *Night Thoughts* is "The White Sand" (1950), also written in elegiac meter, but with an intricate rhyme scheme of the author's own invention. Here the Wellfleet pond-scape unites with the svelte figure of Elena Mumm Thornton, Wilson's fourth and last wife. We first glimpse her plunging into the pond's blue water and swimming effortlessly. Blue was the color of Elena's eyes, and she preferred it above all others. The poem is dominated by the Cape's salient colors—the blue of the sea, pond, and sky, the white of the sand, and Elena's fair skin, and the green of the abundant summer vegetation. All in all the poem sings Elena's praises as an ideal lover, and housekeeper. She has brought the richness of her German-Russian background to Wilson's corner of Cape Cod; she has embraced her new domain, and faithfully, though not slavishly, provided for its sovereign. Elena's enthusiastic assimilation into the Cape environment would, ironically, come to cause a rift between the couple. This all began only a year or two after he wrote the poem, when he decided to reopen the house he had inherited in Talcottville.

Nature in the "The White Sand" also has a dark and menacing aspect. In one episode that takes place in late fall, the narrator and Elena trek to a secluded little beach on a now-deserted pond. She lies down and "dozes" under the still-warm sun. Meanwhile, he follows an ominous shadow that seems to advance on him:

Drenched from the opposite bank, a shadow that, blank and opaque,
    lay
Deeper it seemed than the lake, daunting the mind with its blank,

Toward me, devouring but faceless, advanced till it darkly
    reflected—
Ochre-patched, pallid-streaked—headlong the humped pine-mass,

Marbling with objects seen that menace; then, mirror-wise
    spreading,
Painting cordovan-red, golden and tan and green.

Then, upon Elena's wakening, they make love, and everything changes: his alienation dissolves, replaced by a sense of pleasure and fulfillment. The poem's overall message is that her presence has given his verses "features and form." If the image of a loved and reciprocating woman has here brought a sense of well-being, and even meaning, to the narrator, we the readers may legitimately question his idealized view of her. One senses that this image of a perfect companion, wife, mother, and lover, all in one, contrives more than it artistically accomplishes. The Cape Cod landscape and the woman who has adopted it, however, give us a lyrical and even touching view of a world whose image Wilson would increasingly neglect in favor of a geographical space where Elena's presence would be lacking.

Among the Edmund Wilson papers at Yale's Beinecke Library is a portfolio titled "Wellfleet Poems" (the title is probably Wilson's own). This contains several full-length poems, a number of random jottings, and longer passages written in poetic prose (the longest of which runs seven handwritten pages). The entries were written in Wellfleet, beginning in 1941, the year he bought the house there. Among them is Wilson's undated note to himself about a five-part poem he would like to write about Provincetown, Truro, and Wellfleet. Part 5 would begin in the Truro cemetery, and there would be a scene at the Dos Passos house in Provincetown. Obviously Wilson was thinking of incorporating Katy Dos Passos' funeral (which took place on September 15, 1947, after the terrible car accident). Another, related, entry in the "Wellfleet Poems" under the rubric "V" reads: "Feeling at Katie's burial of the homelessness and impermanence of us all—brought together for that brief moment by the disappearance of one who had given an important center to our loose and uprooted community." Speaking of the projected poem, Wilson states that it would be "elegiac in the ordinary sense," and include Chauncey Hackett's silver hairbrushes.[1] Hackett, the former Washington lawyer who became a Provincetown year-rounder, was Wilson's chum and man in Provincetown over three decades. Although the long poem was never written, Wilson did write two Wellfleet elegies, as we have just seen.

Like the moving birthday poem to Mary McCarthy, discussed in the previous chapter, the other Wellfleet entries in this folder concern nature and reflect the writer's deep sensitivity to its changing aspects. Later, when he began to refocus his life on Upstate New York, Wilson would record the landscape of that region with equal virtuosity—but with one important distinction: Talcottville and its environs never betray the sinister underside he found in Wellfleet. Writing about Cape Cod nature in a purely descriptive vein, he shows it as enchanting. The journals of the twenties and thirties abound in spectacular views of sunsets and marine landscapes. When he is "connecting," however, he often finds nature to be replicating a "wild" abyss within himself. His jottings delineate a strange paradise outside, as well as a banal kind of interior hell. Here is a sampling.

—The deer at dawning leaves / Its cleft track in the sand.

—Pond, July 4, 1943:—The shallow fawn-colored water, in which the procession of herring, purplish above and yellowish below, slightly disassociated the fawn-color into a spectrum, seemed almost transparent, and seemed to repeat the patterns of the ripples on the surface.—the pollen from the pine buds across the pond gave the water a sulphurous rim.

— Pond:—the iris-blue rod of the dragonfly / with invisible wings / that does its levitation on a reed.

—little silvery transparent fish, little death / thread [NB: Wilson has juxtaposed here a pair of backward rhymes] of inside two big eyes,— the sinuous smooth and looping leech with its orange underbelly.

—Drunken Passage—the liquor consumed—which gets drunken and drunken—bad rhymes—ending with some kind of dim but deeply felt revelation.

> —Hot and unholy night
> The floorboards slip or a shade thuds,
> A bird is squawking in the night—
> Room, bedclothes, darkness, outside houses, trees
> and roads and inmost thought
> See all this sticky shredded decomposed
> material of a moist and umber,
> horrible murky world.

—Dark Sand
But how much was the reflection of my own darkness?

I Hades! Old Horrible Cape
—Writers who do not write, painters who do not paint.

Gull Pond, May 26, '47—pale dullish blue, as if unawakened yet with
summer (after long gray and raw spring)—smooth as metal with
only a few glistenings of light, few but intensely bright and far out in
the middle,—a loon (I thought) afloat, silhouetting its neck and its
long bill.—the trains in May—their bayings and shriekings—seem
already natural summer sounds, like the squawking of catbirds, the
peeping of frogs or the chirpings of katydids.

The last entry brings to my mind another unsettling Wellfleet sound that
my father fails to mention. Over the forties and fifties, every weekday at
exactly twelve noon, a siren sounded at the curtain factory in Wellfleet.
It was an ominous, piercing noise that one could never get used to. As
soon as our dog Reckie heard it, he never failed to mimic it with a long,
bloodcurdling howl of his own. With changing times the curtain factory
closed, and an outlet for tourist wares such as bayberry candles and
beach-plum jelly opened in the same building. This lasted through the
sixties and seventies, finally and mercifully to go out of business. In the
eighties the former factory was reconstituted as the new, improved Wellfleet Municipal Library.

One of the last entries in the "Wellfleet Poems" begins: "We are
older—Waves of July and August, just as cold and salt and stinging and
varied. . . ." It shows a domestic scene of supervising children who are
playing by the ocean; there is "no excitement." Alas, by the time he wrote
this, probably the early fifties, when my little sister Helen and I were regular beachgoers, my father was succumbing to a Wellfleet taedium vitae
that we have seen eloquently reflected in his journals.

Moving on from the short jottings, I would like to discuss the three
longer Wellfleet fragments, each of which represents a different facet of
the writer's creative sensibility. I begin with two variants of a "pond
poem," originally titled "Sunfish." The first version, written on a diagonal
across two sheets of the yellow legal-size paper Wilson favored, seems to
have been inspired by a fishing expedition he took with his wife Mary
McCarthy. It reads:

The pond at evening—water roughened by wind or clear but, deeper,
dim-dark shadows of mussels, mud turtles, plant-life, fish—the dregs

and deep deposit of the slime—then from the blurred uncertain floor where plants and sand and living things all in solution seem, you pull up, at its pull, a bright and solid little lacquered living thing: sunfish, perch, pickerel—a little eel that squirms and slips away and makes for the water again (like the one that got away from Mary's hook): dark striped yellow perch, sunfish blue-dappled orange or dark with radium-blue mottlings and red-jeweled gills, half-eclipsed with black-gold eyes—Like fishing up a solid live work through writing, suddenly, with a jerk at the right time, out of your mind, which that morning might have been blurred and swimming with hypnogogic images: faces that loom, grow sharp and fade, lacy patterns that cannot be all the reflection of phenomena of the retina, mere layers of consciousness where no shapes form—all is in solution, and all is shadowy and clear-opaque.—the bright and shining solid living thing pulled up into the evening light and landed in a pail—pulled up flapping and showing its colors in the evening light.—the orange-pink sun descending behind the pines with a color that is dry like a vin rosé.

The second version of this poem, written out neatly and legibly, unlike the first, is basically the same; only the reference to Mary losing the eel has been deleted, while some extra words, possible backward rhymes, are placed between the lines—for example, "might tire" written above "right time." Looking again at the later "Pickerel Pond," it becomes clear that the above-cited text served as a point of departure for the last section. Part 2, stanza six, shows "the sun a dry *vin rosé*, / Orange-pink, darkens the pines"; in stanzas eleven and twelve of part 2 we find: "Now my little line springs alive—pull:—it spills / a slim eel—a quick squirm and he slips / From the bank.—Is this sport? I might tire. / Have I brought the right bait at the right time." NB: the poet has transposed the "might tire"–"right time" backward rhyme from the earlier variant. More important, he has further developed the fishing-writing metaphor of the variant into a horrifying and grotesque vision of *angst*. The original "hypnogogic images, faces that loom, grow sharp and fade, lacy patterns that cannot all be the reflection of phenomena of the retina" become in stanzas twenty and twenty-one of "The Pickerel Pond" (part 2): "Unaccounted-for skims of the retina / From *bas-fonds* not barred by that janitor [the "retina"–"janitor" backward rhyme is also suggested in the earlier variant] / Who guards the true gate of dreams— / Where dreads with desires are smeared / Upon horrors forgotten since suffered, / Old foods now rejected refuse, / Out of which appear patterns of lace / That appall me, and faces assail / My consciousness. . . ." The same kind of imagery and themes continue until the long poem's gloomy end. The early short, contemplative prose lyric has given way to the grotesque climax of a narrative "elegiac" on the frustrations—social, psychological, and artistic—of summer life in Wellfleet. All in all, Wilson relished a good literary challenge—here it involved finding the right images and phrasing to express his alienation, while keeping his mental equilibrium. The artistic discipline imposed by his choice of a difficult meter and rhyme scheme only facilitated that task.

I shall now comment briefly on the "Woods near Miss Freeman's," written in late May 1947. Although this prose poem has a third-person narrator, it is clearly autobiographical. Miss Freeman, it will be remembered, was the agent who sold Wilson his house; her large property was in the woods on the other side of Route 6 from us. The text begins with the protagonist's late-afternoon awakening in a pine wood hollow where he has apparently stopped to rest during a walk. The sensitive description of a forest landscape recalls passages in Ivan Turgenev's *Sportsman's Sketches*, a landmark of Russian nineteenth-century literature that Wilson particularly admired. The stories in Turgenev's collection often show the first-person narrator glimpsing people and places of his home province in new ways. Wilson's character sees nature in a new way too:

This air was very clear and pure, and everything about the woodland was pleasant and light and fine.

The character notes the

. . . lady slippers, sandy path, turtle-egg nests, last year's pine cones embedded in the needles . . . a little [word illegible] white flower with a slightly unpleasant smell . . . tent worms had pitched their sordid speckled tents—pines budding with tiny fat pollen-stuffed cones—seven-petalled little white stars of anemones . . . the mild clear sun and cool air—places on the slope where the gray lichen-like moss mottled the sand—a signboard weathergray with no sign— a low white house half-hidden by an untrimmed hedge, against which an old oven door was resting, an old low woman's shoe in the path and beyond which he could see a rose-arbor-pagoda made of simple posts and slats and painted white—lavender wisteria that had climbed to the roof—a long shed of which the white paint was wearing off that prolonged the line of the hedge. . . .

As the description of the neglected house and its garden progresses, the reader gets the uneasy feeling that nature and man's work has been somehow perverted here. We see

> . . . a cucumber frame filled in with sand in which a colony of
> ants had built countless nests, a wooden birdhouse lying on the
> ground . . . a small sundial in which was resting a rusty pair of gar-
> den shears, a lawn-mower that had cut but one swathe in the dande-
> lion and clovergrass lawn . . . the big black dog that was bad, the
> white black-spotted setter mongrel that was sneaking and crawled
> sideways . . . irrelevant white and purple iris growing to a rather
> rank size.

Unlike a Turgenev landscape, which is invariably balanced by the unforgettable personalities of those who live in and around it, Wilson's spring-awakened forest frames a sinister void left behind by the house's absent owners. The narrator has wandered upon a Cape Cod travesty of the Garden of Eden, and here his tale ends, having never really begun. The manuscript itself seems to peter out toward the end, with its "irrelevant" irises "growing to rather a rank size." Nonetheless, the sketch itself suggests the writer's feelings of alienation from a haunting landscape that seems to have become overly familiar.

The "Wellfleet Poems" entry dated November 20, 1943, the "day after Thanksgiving and our Thanksgiving night party on Cape Cod," evokes many tonalities of his past experience on the Cape. The weather has been unseasonably warm, and Wilson has gone to Gull Pond for a picnic with Katy Dos Passos and Nina Chavchavadze. The piece makes no explicit mention of Mary McCarthy, although she was probably there for "our party" the day before. Judging by the increasingly rambling style of the narrative, it was written after the picnic and under the increasing influence of alcohol. The bucolic tone gradually fades, with the sunlight, into a dark and maudlin reverie. The text is consistently written on a diagonal slant.

> Gull Pond there with a slight astringency in the light, yet a slight
> dimness against the trees on the opposite shore, with the gulls lurk-

ing [?] tiny and white a decoration on the middle of the water—
Water terribly cold but bracing—air warm, this enchanted and endless Indian summer toward the end of November—incredible, the
Cape—we could float forever in the year like the white birds on the
water—it was as if the late autumn afternoon, just at the verge of
winter, was not even growing shorter.—Back in the quiet house,
while we drank the rest of the beer, yellow beer, while the sunlight
shimmered [?] like honey, the day, the never-ending enchanting day,
and in that quiet, the moderated moan-shout of the train, vibrated,
throbbed in the membrane of the honey-late afternoon that yet, almost like summer, never seemed to come to a close.—The sun on
the gourds, lemon yellow, frog-green-striped with yellow necks, with
the just-dry-pumpkin colored phallic ⌒⌒ squash behind them like
a nursing pig with its young—on the marble-topped old claw-footed
table against the three windows in the dining-room with the transparent old glass thermometer that still tells the weather outside. The
3rd window.—above the little ridge of hills behind our house, where
the austere radiance of the quiet sea still rises—those hills beyond
which I always mean to ride the light that is steady still, as if the sun
of summer remained still—lingers long with me in the library with
my writing—long for the afternoon play of love (though not that
afternoon)—but when we wake (this could have been true of
Margaret and me) we find ourselves benumbed in dark.

[Two parallel lines are drawn here below the text, and he continues:]

—Kissing a girl's wet and almost sticky mouth, and knowing that
that other little spot, that mouth, is growing moist and sticky too—
in which you will find delicious flowers.

[The next section recalls the twenties and thirties in Provincetown.]

Cape Cod light—dryness of the sand—great freedom of the ocean—
Gulf Stream that warms the fall, uniting us, beyond New England
and quite outside our consciousness, with the other half of the world
and other climate—the quiet hills and dunes in the middle of the sea
enjoying the late halcyon November light, incredible from [for?] the
countries of short summers—In that silence, aspirations did not
break, but prolonged themselves, and, left with the quiet or insistent
sea, poured out over the harbor, watched the clouds like vague

people coming into the port, sat on the long sea-bordering street, took to drink and talked, their talk dying out there—Floyd Clymer in his house on the wharf as I once saw him coming back from Chicago,—Provincetown is never provincial, whatever else it is—always new people you have never met, just come there for a month or having lived there in back streets for years with a whole circle—hopes and works, scandals, life and death, one never knew were there, nor did they ever bother you, or really know you were there—Pass on the back street, Bradford—just miss at Burch [the market on Commercial Street] or the liquor store—in Provincetown the streets are few but long, a long story that nobody ever knows, for nobody ever gets the parts together—the tide is always going in or out, the big rhythm that masters all, fishermen and others, that dominates our sleep, presses and lapses in our lives—when the tide goes out to sea, leaving us lonely, the lighthouse with its diamond lamp a watch-jewel in our hand, and comes slapping in, with growing but not humanly emphatic insistence, that brings our sleep to a climax of awakening before crisis or dawn—and then recedes before we can hold the pausing.—Still quiet, a few straight shredded lines of cloud, a very faintly orange-flavored pink or white against a pale blue.

[The next, and last, passage brings us back to the Wellfleet house and the present.]

—Buds on the horse chestnut—a buttercup by the roadside, denuded branches of shrubs and trees that look an anachronism of the season against that warm but pale winter sky . . .

Although the above text rapidly shifts focus—from Gull Pond, to the Wellfleet house, to thoughts of past sexual encounters, to the old days in Provincetown, back to the Wellfleet house—the tone remains constant. The unseasonably warm weather gives a sense of time having stopped, while the presence of the warm Gulf Stream out to sea leads Wilson to thoughts of unity with other human communities. The overwhelming nighttime silence of the outside world, only briefly interrupted by the moaning of a passing train, leads him into a nostalgic series of partly recovered memories. In the past, aspirations seemed to float with the clouds over Provincetown. The people he knew there, and those he didn't know, ebbed and flowed like the tide in the harbor. Life then, now remembered as clothed in silence and subject to constant flux, lacked consistency and coherent meaning. Cape Cod made its sensuous but "not human" presence felt, but gave no answers. He describes Provincetown as "a long story that nobody ever knows, for nobody ever gets the parts together." Eloquent as it may have been in its silences, the Cape ultimately lacked the kind of stable historical identity that would have sustained Wilson's omnivorous curiosity.

The last poem in the "Wellfleet" folder is a quasi sonnet (containing fifteen rather than the requisite fourteen lines). Its title is "Mary and the Minotaur," and it bears the date "1961" (not in Wilson's hand) at the bottom of the page. For reasons to be cited, I conclude that the addressee is the painter Mary Meigs, but the poem's exact context remains somewhat obscure.[2]

MARY AND THE MINOTAUR

O Minotaur of Brewster's mystic maze
Don't tempt so with your gin and tonic, dear
When nature catches your close listening ear
Fall not into the post-martini phase
Swinburnian, I smell your fragrant bays
And drop into my drink a tender tear,
That which will raise my uncombed hirsute fear
And leave my passions in a frenzied blaze.

But Mary murmurs how she'd love the world,
Which might be different if we'd paused and thought
But we pause not because we cannot pause;
Our torch is guttering and our banners furled,
We sit in stars and in sputniks caught
We grasp the silence with prehensile paws—
Here is the moment when we give applause!

The overall theme here is that of "Beauty and the Beast." The first stanza seems to be a dialogue between the minotaur and Mary, his demure interlocutor. She speaks the first six lines, urging him not to tempt her with liquor, not to lapse into a martini-induced facile Romanticism ("Swinburnian phase"). The minotaur is wearing the poet's traditional laurel wreath ("fragrant bays"), and this, his literary gift, causes her to drop a "tender tear" into her drink. The last two lines of stanza one must be spoken by the hirsute minotaur, whose "fear" and "passions" have been kindled by Mary's tear. Stanza two, in the first-person plural, except for the first line, recapitulates their conversation: she urges him to "pause and think," but he can not—he is too old and caught "in stars and sputniks." (The first Soviet Sputnik was launched in 1957.) With the rise of technology events have spun out of "our" control. The minotaur, who has been speaking since line three of this last stanza, concludes: "We grasp the silence with prehensile paws— / Here is the moment where we give applause!" Wilson is probably referring here to his ability to create art out of silence; the last line probably implies that the aging minotaur can only applaud his muse, rather than seduce her.

In 1961 Wilson's only close friend by the name of "Mary" in Wellfleet was Mary Meigs. The "real" context behind the poem may have been a trip to a restaurant in Brewster (about twenty miles south). When Elena was away, Meigs sometimes drove her elderly admirer to restaurants in neighboring towns. Brewster has several good restaurants located in large, former private houses. Possibly one of these had a garden with a maze or approximation thereof, which in turn might have suggested the minotaur theme to the poet. The "minotaur" designation for Wilson was originally Mary McCarthy's; Mary Meigs makes use of it in her autobiographical memoir, which discusses in some detail her separate friendships with both Wilson and McCarthy. David Chavchavadze, the son of Nina and Paul, referred to their long-standing family friend as "monstruo," while, as earlier noted, the Dos Passoses addressed the often-cantankerous Wilson as "Anti-Christ." Wilson, who had a surprisingly thick skin when it came to slighting remarks about his august person, doesn't seem to have objected to these—as the poem itself suggests.

Of all the women whom Wilson admired, and courted, in the sixties, Mary Meigs was the only one with whom he exchanged poetry on a regular basis. Meigs speaks of "lightening the winter cafard" in Wellfleet by exchanging valentines with him (*Briscoe*, 28). In his *Fifties* Wilson cites the sonnet Meigs wrote for a *bout-rimé* game with him. All the evidence, then, points to Meigs as the poem's addressee; the verses themselves constitute an eloquent tribute to her discreet charms.

Finally, it is worth mentioning another Wilson-Meigs collaboration, with an implicit "Beauty and the Beast" theme. In 1965 Wilson had published, at his own expense, a poem, illustrated by Mary Meigs, called "By

Dear Edmund,

"Full of bellicose cubs?"
"With refractory cubs?"
Is lion never thought of as
one syllable? Only accented?
I'm coming Christmas
Eve and going back on
the 27th & will bring
your mail — ..Barbara
is now in Washington
covering the HUAC
hearings on the W.I.S.P.
Do you know that
the Muganda
speak Luganda
and live in
Buganda, a
province of
Uganda?
Love,
Mary

WELLFLEETERA MELANCHOLATA

Sketch by Mary Meigs, with humorous note to Edmund Wilson, 1960s.
Mary was then living in the former McCarthy/Broadwater
house on Pamet Point Road in Wellfleet.

Dark Cocytus' Shore."[3] (The place of publication was Cambridge, Massachusetts.) Against a background of vegetation and gigantic flowers, Mary's black and white sketch shows an incongruous pair of lovers standing by a river. The man, dressed in black, is bald, oldish, and sinuously repulsive; the woman, in a low-cut dress, is young, blonde, and appealing. She was inspired not by Meigs but by Celia Carroll, a New York editor to whom Wilson was strongly attracted. He wrote the poem in Rome in 1964. (See *Sixties*, 330–331, 512.)

~~~~~~~~

To sum up, my father's Cape Cod poetry, whether written and edited for publication, or simply random jottings, tells us as much about himself as about the unique landscape that he sensitively describes. An animal lover and part-time naturalist, he enjoyed communing with nature. He was driven to write about this inseparable, and engaging, part of the world around him. Cape Cod was not, however, high on his list of literary priorities. A faithful recorder of lived experience, some of which he recycled into works of fiction, he channeled by far the largest and best part of his energy into the more disciplined and rational practice of journalism and literary criticism. Neither in his life nor in his work did he try to confront the inner demons that regularly possessed him, and caused him to torment others. His pursuit of the irrational was on the surface limited to a penchant for the grotesque: Max Beerbohm, Edward Lear, *The Ingoldsby Legends*, Punch and Judy, the Monsters of Bonmarzo, the world of bats (very late in life). His greatest writing, however, follows the lines of orderly, reasoned discourse and finds expression in a transparent style reinforced with periodic sentences. A total adept of his art, he gave most of his life to reading, research, and writing. When his demons surfaced, it usually happened during the night. Their destructive effects must have horrified him at times, but he seems to have felt few or no pangs of conscience for arbitrarily mistreating his wives. Like so many others of his generation who in the twenties embraced alcohol as a liberating force, he became addicted to it and, ironically, it ended up as a liberator of the darkest forces in him. These he refused to confront or even attempt to explain to others, or himself. For this reason, the above-cited texts are revealing: in some of them he tries, if only tentatively and through metaphor, to probe his irrational depths. The muddy bottom of a pond reflects his subconscious mind, which may be plumbed by rational thought, which ultimately, he implies, may lead to a creative synthesis. (We have already encountered a similar idea in a "Spectacle Ponds" entry in the diaries.) In practice, though, he achieved this only in a handful of poems, especially "The Pickerel Pond," which is perhaps more of an exercise in prosodial virtuosity than a work of lasting art. If Cape Cod nature sometimes held the mirror up to his troubled subconscious, that same nature remained as indifferent as the tide in "Provincetown, 1936." For him, nature was neither redemptive nor transcending; rather it was an infinitely self-renewing resource that he could mold through his writer's craft. Until the very end of his life he continued to be divided between the Apollonian and the Dionysian.

n January 1945 Mary McCarthy definitively left Wilson and the house he was renting at Henderson Place, off East Eighty-seventh Street, by the East River in Manhattan. She took me with her, and we led something of a gypsy life over the next few months in the city. The divorce would be finalized in October of the same year. In the meantime my mother rented Polly Boyden's house in Truro for the summer. My father spent that summer in Europe, covering the postwar scene for the *New Yorker*. Now my mother found the Cape highly stimulating, largely owing to the presence of a newfound mentor, Nicola Chiaromonte. In addition, Dwight Macdonald was there, as were other friends from her *Partisan Review* days in New York. She had seen little of this circle while married to Wilson, who viewed its members with condescension. Chiaromonte, a refugee from fascism in his native Italy, and his American wife Miriam were renting a cottage near Balston Beach in Truro. A philosopher by training and inclination, Chiaromonte had his own ideas on how postwar Europe should be reconstructed. He was both anticommunist and anti–U.S.-style capitalism. Dwight Macdonald, to whose magazine *Politics* (1943–1949) Chiaromonte contributed, described him as "a kind of Prudhonian anarchist" (Wreszin, *Moral Temper*, 122). Another Italian writer, Nicola Tucci, was also vacationing in Truro. (It was at the Tuccis' apartment in New York that McCarthy remembered meeting for the first time, her younger, future husband Bowden Broadwater.) Also on the scene were James T. Farrell; Lionel Abel (who wrote for *Partisan Review* and later became a university professor); Philip Rahv (for a visit); Robert Nathan, the poet and popular novelist; Charles Jackson, author of *The Lost Weekend*; and the sculptor Tino Nivola (Gelderman, 120). Next door to the Boyden house that my mother was renting lived Eben and Phyllis (née Duganne) Given. As mentioned earlier, Eben was a nonpracticing artist; Phyllis was a prolific writer of short fiction for popular journals. Their son, Eben Jr., was just my age, and we kept constant company. My mother and Phyllis commiserated with each other for spending much valuable writing time overseeing two very active seven-year-olds. Over the summer, my mother entertained a succession of houseguests. One of these was the art critic Clement Greenberg, with whom she had had a short affair a few months earlier. During the visit he volunteered to spank me, if it should become necessary—an offer that she deeply resented. Other guests included Hardwick Moseley, a courtly southerner who had replaced her former editor at Houghton Mifflin's New York office and with whom she was having "a transient love affair" (McCarthy quoted in Gelderman, 119), as well as Herbert Solow, an editor at *Fortune* magazine, and his consort Silvia Salmi, a professional photographer. (On several occasions, both during and after his marriage to McCarthy, Wilson hired Salmi to take pictures of him and his family.) McCarthy also invited Jack and Eunice Jessup and their child. Jack was an editorial writer for *Life* magazine; Eunice, née Clark, had been McCarthy's classmate at Vassar and is a likely prototype for Norine Schmidtlapp in her later novel *The Group*. It seems, however, that McCarthy ended up finding the Jessups a rental house in Wellfleet, while their renters came to stay with her as nonpaying guests in Truro (McCarthy to Bowden Broadwater, in a letter written around July 15, 1945, Vassar). Possibly my mother went to all this trouble because she wasn't keen on having another live-in child. An important repeat visitor that summer was Bowden Broadwater, a recent Harvard graduate whose poor eyesight had spared him induction into the army. At the time Bowden was working odd jobs, one of them at the *New Yorker*. During that summer, which McCarthy later felt had been the happiest of her life, she saw a lot of Dwight and Nancy Macdonald. They were living with their children Mike and Nicky in a house called "Four Winds" perched on a bluff in North Truro; next door was a small fish-packing operation called the "Ice House." Mike was just a few months older than I—we were to become lifelong friends. Ruth and Gardner Jencks, whom she had known while married to Wilson, also surfaced on McCarthy's radar. Unusually well-off by the then Cape Cod standard, the Jenckses had a large property on Bound Brook Island in Wellfleet. They were to play an important part in McCarthy's life when she returned to Wellfleet in 1953.

Although McCarthy's letters to Bowden during this period eloquently testify that she was in love with him, she was still juggling a romantic involvement, now on "hold," with Theodore (Ted) Spencer, a professor of

English at Harvard. He, it transpired, had been Bowden's Shakespeare professor. He was deeply shocked to learn from McCarthy of her friendship with his former student. Another, rather unlikely suitor whom McCarthy did not take seriously was Gardner Jencks. Gardner, a composer, had a winning personality and an omnivorous enthusiasm for intellectual subjects. Shortish, bespectacled, and balding, he cut a youthful figure, wearing jeans and an oxford white shirt. In a letter to Bowden, dated August 4, 1945, McCarthy writes:

> In Wellfleet met Gardner Jencks. Car ride to garage [where her car had been under repair], followed by declaration of love. (Secret.) "What I feel about you I can only express in music." Answer: "But I can't hear it; I'm tone deaf." Practical application of feelings fortunately seen as hopeless. I terribly embarrassed. Oh dear, isn't life awful, never felt such a dead lump of matter.

In another letter she informs Bowden that the poet John Berryman has kissed her after a party "with witnesses present." She has also found the time to translate Simone Weil's essay on the *Iliad*. Her friends reported that she took her typewriter to the beach and worked on the translation there.

Looming large on the Truro social horizon when McCarthy wrote to Bowden at the end of June was the impending visit of Charles Jackson to the house of his friend Robert Nathan. Jackson, a reformed alcoholic, had written a best-selling novel, *The Lost Weekend*, which was later made into a successful film. In a newsy letter dated June 25 she writes:

> The Robert Nathans (*Portrait of Jennie*) are entertaining the Charles Jacksons (*The Lost Weekend*) during the week of the 2nd to the 9th. Mr. Jackson does not like to meet more than seven or eight people at a time (he masochistically counts the drinks, I suppose, and higher multiplication or simple accumulation of envy unsettles him), so they are having two parties for him.[1] Mrs. Nathan, through lack of information, invited me to the inferior, non-intellectual one, and now Mr. Nathan is scrambling and desperately trying to repair the mistake and has finally floundered into asking me to both, but I shall accept Mrs. Nathan's category.

We have no way of knowing whether McCarthy attended one or both of the parties at the "Parsonage," Nathan's former house. Nestled in a rustic spot off North Pamet Road just below Truro Center, this graceful eighteenth-century house, then bounded by the owners' flower and vegetable gardens, represented an island of bucolic gentility amid Truro's generally sparse landscape. Actually, as will be shown, McCarthy was harboring the secret intention of using the Jacksons' visit as the starting point for a planned novella. Writing to Bowden in mid-July, she mentions that the recent visits of the Charlie Jacksons and Clem Greenberg have been "a sensation," and have become

> the subject of a witty novelette, now reaching page thirty-five, by a lady writer, M.M. The novelette is called "The Lost Week," and is the Middletown of the American literary life. It is going to make my fortune, so that I shall end by returning to Truro as the house guest of the Robert Nathans. I wish you could see it. Charlie Jackson is a Chaplinesque hero. The novelette has two practical effects: (a) it has got me into correspondence with Mr. Jackson, which is like getting into a chain letter, the return being so incommensurate with the original effect put forth—bulletins arrive here almost daily [McCarthy kept Jackson's voluble missives, and they are among her other papers at Vassar]; (b) it has produced some rather peculiar distortions in my relations with the Nathan family; on the theory that if you are going to write a satire about a man the least you can do is stop speaking to him, I have suddenly and from their point of view inexplicably begun to cut them (instead of the more normal vice versa); the other day, I crawled on my stomach into the ocean in order not to stand up and be seen by Bob Nathan, though of course I succeeded in directing his full attention to myself by the unusual means of locomotion. The trouble with the novelette (which is going to be a hundred pages long) is that it keeps getting very very John Marquand. This is not my fault, but the fault of the material—they *will* name their station-wagon "Hemlock Grange."

In view of the letter's overall facetious tone, we may discount the author's boast about the never-to-be-finished novelette's future success. The letter ends with a report on my bout with the mumps. The notorious contagiousness of the sickness has given my mother an opportunity to test the character of all the males who set foot in her house. Some, like Dos Passos and an unnamed friend of Conrad Aiken (whom the latter has called "a capon") have shunned me even outdoors. Other, younger men fraternized with me, getting a high score. And then, "a scientific young woman [Ruth Jencks] daughter of Raymond Pearl, the biologist, kept inviting Reuel over to spend the night at the height of his sickness (which was never serious), so that her child would get the mumps from him at a non-crucial period of his sexual life." The letter ends with the following short paragraph:

> Did I tell you that I'm going to teach at Bard College next year? One of my friends has the theory that Mr. W. [Edmund Wilson] has such a profound respect for academic institutions that he will withdraw all legal action against me as soon as the mortar-board is clapped on my head. Rumor has it that he will appear here around the middle of August. I keep expecting to come out in the morning and find a late symphony in browns sitting on the chintz sofa. So do come and get the measles.

McCarthy is referring here to Wilson's predilection for brown articles of attire; it was the color of his daily uniform, whether a dressing gown or three-piece suit. McCarthy's closing invitation to come and visit and get the measles (she means mumps) would ironically be fulfilled some sixteen years later. Recently divorced by McCarthy and living alone in New York, Bowden came down with a very serious case of the mumps, possibly contracted from one of the boys at Saint Bernard's School, where he worked. One of the female teachers at the school, a loyal friend, almost single-handedly tended to the incapacitated Bowden throughout the course of the debilitating illness.

We shall now turn to McCarthy's unfinished novella, which survives in a fifty-six-page manuscript that ends in midsentence. The subject for "The Lost Week or the Caged Lion" seems to have been suggested by friends in Truro. Later the author would mention it in a short article called "The Novels That Got Away" (*NYTBR*, Nov. 25, 1979). Her ambitious goal was to show that the desire for fame could be just as noxious to a writer as an addiction to alcohol. The first chapter, of only two, describes the community of Nottingham (based on Truro, whose year-round residents of nonlocal origin are mostly "has-been" or "would-be" writers). Like their real-life prototypes in Truro, Provincetown, and Wellfleet, these bohemians have chosen Cape Cod because life is inexpensive there and it does not subject them to the pressures of competition or public scrutiny. McCarthy shows some of the summer visitors as more successful: Herbert Harper (modeled on Charles Jackson) and James Theobald (Robert Nathan) have money, and they have a symbiotic link based on an attraction of opposites; rather than competing, they feed each other's egos. Harper has written a single self-lacerating and self-revealing autobiographical novel; Theobald churns out glib, pleasantly written fiction that reveals none of the inner man. The novella's main female character, a writer named Frani Farrar, whose viewpoint dominates chapter 2, is a stand-in for the author herself. Her friend Helen Staunton is an affectionate semiportrait of her real neighbor in Truro, Phyllis Duganne-Given. Some of the minor characters may be easily linked to real people— "William De Los Rios" = John Dos Passos; "David MacGregor" = Dwight Macdonald; "Laureato" = Chiaromonte, and so forth. The crude John Langley, on the other hand, is a composite portrait. A genuine proletarian by birth, and an ex-policeman, Langley is forced to work at odd jobs and other low-paying work in order to support his family. He does some creative writing in his free time and has overweening literary ambitions that exponentially exceed his meager gifts. He gives an excellent example of McCarthy's underlying thesis: that the desire for literary fame can become addictive. Frani feels uncomfortable in her relationship with Langley: out of pity or fear she can not tell him her real opinion about his self-indulgent scribblings. The narrative breaks off in the second chapter during a conversation in Frani's kitchen. The participants are Frani, John Langley, who has dropped in, and Martin Isaacs, a loutish New York intellectual (modeled on the real Clement Greenberg). The ostensible motivation for the plot, the double-barreled Fourth of July party, has been forgotten—although we are told that Langley wants to inveigle an invitation to it.

Perhaps the most interesting facet of this inchoate "novel that got away" is the revealing and perceptive analysis of the "Nottingham" community. The narrator describes it as:

> a rural Foreign Legion which incorporated a man into its ranks and asked no question about his past or indeed about his present. Most of these charming people, with their gardens, their domestic arts, their shelves full of pickles and jellies, their home-made bread, their coffee mills, their chickens, their beautiful old houses which they had modernized, often with their own hands, their water lily pools, their aquariums, had something to forget, sometimes a sexual scandal, sometimes a financial indiscretion, but most often a sadder

secret—the failure of talent. The salient feature of this community of writers and artists was that most of the writers did not write and most of the painters did not paint. ("Lost Week" MS, 22)

A good example of the above-mentioned unproductive artist was Eben Given, McCarthy's neighbor that summer of 1945. Of Welsh extraction, Eben's family had been in the circus business. He was courteous, well-read, a droll raconteur, and a generous host. His wife Phyllis was a petite, no-nonsense woman who served their guests impeccably cooked French dishes. They lived in an elegantly restored old Cape Cod house furnished with antiques. Eben, who had studied painting in Paris during the twenties, was nominally a portraitist. Although he had two well-appointed studios, one above the garage in Truro, another in the house he had inherited in Provincetown, he had long been neurotically incapable of painting. To the best of my memory, only two or three of his portraits hung in their Truro house. His son, Eben Jr., once showed me a couple of his father's portraits that were kept in a closet in Provincetown—the subjects' heads were missing. According to Eben Jr., their creator had excised and then burnt them.

All in all, Nottingham receives more sympathetic treatment than the equally dysfunctional community of New Leeds in McCarthy's later novel *A Charmed Life*. Her approach to the denizens of Nottingham is rather gentler that her scathing treatment of the bumbling New Leedsians. Readers of the unfinished draft of "Lost Week" may, however, well question whether the Nottinghamites' passion for wholesome activities, such as blueberrying, clamming, gardening, indeed the kind of labor that facilitates their physical survival, can overcloud their refusal to fight against, or even admit to, their own rampant mediocrity. Their indulgent egalitarianism, moreover, implies judgment suspended over themselves as well as their errant fellows.

As the summer of 1945 drew to a close, the world was shaken by the news of the atom bomb dropped on Hiroshima (August 6). McCarthy first learned of it from a newspaper headline she saw while buying a loaf of Portuguese bread in the Truro general store. The headline caused her to wonder "what I was taking the loaf home for" (*Seventeenth Degree*, 8). Writing to Bowden on August 22, she reports that, having realized that they could never see the world the same way again, she, Dwight Macdonald, Chiaromonte, and Gardner Jencks had been discussing retiring from civilization. The idea appeals to her, but she facetiously speculates that any kind of internal exile will deprive the world of her many talents. She would later return to the theme of utopian escape in *The Oasis* (1949), where the disciples of a European guru (loosely inspired by Chiaromonte) attempt communal living in a remote corner of New England. The protagonists, Macdougal Macdermott and Will Taub, who resemble the real Dwight Macdonald and Philip Rahv, end up at ideological loggerheads and abandon the high-minded experiment.

September 2, 1945, was "V-J Day." Even in little Truro the news of the Japanese surrender was feted by the populace. That night, people danced in the street of Truro Center while I watched from a vantage point just below the library that stood adjacent to the Given house. I beat a tattoo of accompaniment on my little replica of an Indian drum. A couple of days later my father materialized and took me back to Wellfleet. My mother then set off for Yarmouth, Nova Scotia, a destination she seems to have chosen almost at random. She intended to finish the novella there. She took an airplane from Boston to Moncton, New Brunswick, then a boat and a train to Yarmouth. Her sojourn in what she thought would be Evangeline country proved disappointing: she spoke to virtually no one and found nothing of interest in the town. After a week she returned to New York, and civilization, leaving the novella unfinished. We can only speculate that, after the Bomb, a satire centering on a Fourth of July party and the comings and goings of fatuous people may have seemed beside the point. The trip to Nova Scotia may well have been an attempt not just to finish a novella that was going nowhere but also to distance herself from some unresolved personal relationships.

McCarthy's letter to Bowden, sent September 6 and written en route to Canada, deserves citation in full because it shows the writer's tendency to play at life as though it were a game, something resembling the cold intrigues of Choderlos de Laclos' epistolary novel *Dangerous Liaisons*. Obviously she found it exhilarating rashly to tempt fate, with little regard for the possible consequences.

Bangor, Maine

En Route

Darling Bowden;

Eating a Howard Johnson brownie (purchased by T. Sp. [Ted Spencer, the Harvard professor with whom she recently had had an affair] in Boston Air Terminal), thinking of you. Last night not amusing, gruesomely prolonged pass, no proposal (did you know that fountain pens leak at high altitudes?)—the poor man only has $2500 a year now (secret). A really shocking moment of bad acting, details of which too painful to be furnished by me, but so bad that one could only dissolve one's embarrassment by getting in the play oneself. Emerged from the evening absolutely swathed in hypocrisy but knowing perhaps how it feels to be T. Sp. Examples of dialogue (Oh God!): "Please don't. I'm really not your thing, you know. And what if I should get so fascinated by you that I couldn't let you go? Please don't." He: "When I saw you in New York it was like an electric shock." All this utterly, utterly secret. A sonnet on an atom bomb is in composition. Suggested that another, slightly lower form, might be more appropriate to the subject-matter. Nicht war?—as Heidegger well says.

Depression felt by me so acute that the coarse leer of H. Solow across from me at breakfast was fresh and pleasant as a loaf of bread. Wonderful man, who if acting at all is somebody in a Marx brothers movie! He could pinch me all the way to Moncton if the fit was on him. . . .

However, today everything got quite funny. Theodore accepted the situation, though every once in a while he would remember and pretend not to. Called for me to take me to Mrs. Gardner's house [a museum]. Closed, we went on to Boston Museum, where I insisted on seeing the marble bench, between the statue of Laocoon and the Hermes of Praxiteles, where Bob Linscot used to —— the lady authors of Houghton Mifflin. Couldn't find it, found instead a Louis Quatorze bed. I said, I will yield, on condition it be here. Theodore not very tempted. Told him later on in garden in front of large orgiastic fountain that he should make it his endeavor to be as fraudulent as possible. Then taxi to Park St. where I went in to Houghton Mifflin to cash check and T. Sp. slipped into Athenaeum, where he found and consumed article on existentialism by A. Guerard. Introduced exis— to him night before, subject being hitherto unknown at Harvard. T. Sp. in marvelous position, owes it all to me—very stupid of him not to see what a fine wife he might be failing to get. Told him had friend who knew of definitive article on existentialism, would get reference from him [she is referring to Bowden], by wire if necessary, if Harry Levin and Mark Schorer seemed to [be] sniffing the air. Please oblige. Did not mention your name because felt I had already done so too often. What did you *do* to those Harvard professors? My intimation that I know you devastates their faces; they look like bombed villages. Après qu'il fût revenu de sa surprise [when he had recovered from his surprise], M. Spencer put me several searching questions, plainly did not believe a word I said in answer, hit mentally on Love as only possible explanation, rejected that hastily a second later, and simply floundered. Atmosphere not right for Travelling Fellowship question, so postponed it. Conveyed compliments, more disbelief. Began to think *I* was victim of practical joke. What *did* you do to him?

Asked about Boylston Chair: R. P. Warren, most likely. E.W. [Edmund Wilson], T.S.E. [Eliot], and W.H.A. [Auden], were sounded out on possibility and refused, E.W. saying no doubt, I can't spare the time from my hack work. T. Sp. plainly doesn't care for R.P.W. Jealousy? Found out about Nancy [Spencer's first wife, from whom he was now divorced]. It was Dr. Riggs, not Radcliffe girl who was at root of trouble. She did a term at Stockbridge [a mental institution] (Secret).

Have just crossed Canadian border. Bangor, Maine, very like frontier town in northern Washington, Minnesota, or Montana, and like my idea of Alaska. Air terminal has look of emergency structure, set down in wilderness, all beaver-board and rawness. However, raving tearing queer behind soda fountain struck metropolitan note. Imported perhaps by airline for that purpose.

Well-dear-Bowden, I am catching a frightful cold. I am glad—at least I think I am. One thing that I hold against Theodore is that he has shattered the fragile communion cup which I was still, at least subjectively, sharing with you. The cold will re-cement it. It is a delight to think about you. The Solows' apartment will never be the same to me—which is a positive blessing; perhaps they should hire you to come and sleep in it and leave behind an intimation, a gentle souvenir of romance.

We are in Moncton.

Good bye

So much love,

Mary

She has written on the outside fold of the envelope: "How is your cold?"

It would appear from the letter's last section that McCarthy and Bowden had an earlier love tryst at the Solows' Cambridge apartment. In any case, she set up the above-described meetings with Spencer (1) to elicit a marriage proposal from him, and (2) to secure his recommendation for a traveling fellowship. During that September, Spencer would write her three letters, one to Yarmouth, Nova Scotia, professing his continuing infatuation. At the end of the month she was still wondering whether he would propose to her. She says this in a letter to Bowden dated September 27. The potential triangle linking her to two men, Broadwater and Spencer, allows her to manipulate both. In Bowden's case she may be trying to seem more desirable by making known how much she is desired by another. She has intentionally provoked an atmosphere of ambiguity; the resulting emotional and intellectual posturing is eerily reminiscent of the fraught situations that often beset the characters of her fiction.

By the beginning of September my father had taken me to his mother's house in Red Bank, New Jersey. My mother called this a "kidnapping," since she had not been consulted and he was threatening to get full custody over me. According to the subsequent court order, however, I was to spend the school year with her and the main part of my vacations with him. She duly came to pick me up in Red Bank, and we then proceeded to Bard College in Red Hook, New York, where she had accepted a teaching job for the coming academic year.

The following summer, my mother traveled to Europe to join Bowden, while I remained in Wellfleet with my father, who was soon to wed Elena Mumm Thornton. I would continue to spend most of my summers in Wellfleet. I spent the school year of 1946 with my mother and Bowden, now a married couple; we lived in a tiny rent-controlled flat on East Fifty-seventh Street next to the Third Avenue "el." Bowden's sister Christie had been living there, and she stayed on for a while until she found another lodging. I attended Saint Bernard's School, a private boys' school founded and staffed by well-educated, no-nonsense Englishmen. In June 1949 the Broadwaters bought a house in rural Portsmouth, Rhode Island, and I went to school in nearby Middletown (Newport was just down the road); the last two years as a day student at Saint George's. Having sold the Portsmouth house in late fall 1952, the Broadwaters almost immediately bought another in, of all places, Wellfleet, Massachusetts. That same fall I was enrolled as a boarder at Brooks School in North Andover, Massachusetts, where I remained until I graduated in

1956. My father paid for my education and most of my support. Because of his ongoing financial woes, he occasionally fell into arrears. All in all, both parents contributed generously to my long, zigzagging course through schools (four) and universities (five, not counting the times I studied as a summer student or full-year stipend student at European universities).

My mother's return to Wellfleet, which many found surprising, did not interfere with the established pattern of my summering with my father. When he was in Europe during the summer of 1954, I spent a happy, though somewhat monotonous, time with my mother and Bowden in their house on Pamet Point Road. (I was then sixteen, and Wellfleet, with its circumscribed friends and activities, was beginning to pall; I would seek out work, study, and travel opportunities away from the Cape over subsequent vacations.) The Broadwaters seem to have bought the Wellfleet house on impulse. It was a red, wooden, eighteenth-century cottage with a detached studio and garage, nestling atop a gentle hill backed by many acres of uninhabited woodlands. The price was attractive, but the property was being sold as a "package" that included the yellow cottage next door. The Broadwaters quickly found in their friend, the artist Mary Meigs, a purchaser for the other half of the property.

We can only speculate as to exactly why my mother, who must have had some bad memories of her life on Money Hill with my father, chose to return to Wellfleet and a situation of close geographical proximity to him. She clearly delighted in the Cape Cod landscape: the alternately blue and steely ponds, the bracing Atlantic where she so intrepidly swam, the bay with its "white bluffs dropping to a strangely pebbled beach" (*Charmed Life* [hereafter *CL*], 16), and even the lowly mushrooms in the woods. Only a month before buying the house, she and Bowden had spent a glorious two weeks at the Macdonalds' Slough Pond cottage, located in Truro just over the Wellfleet border. From there she writes me at Brooks School, in early October 1952:

> It's very beautiful: we swim three times a day. The house is in pretty fair condition, except that Dwight, when he went away three weeks ago, forgot the half-eaten carcass of a roast chicken in the oven! . . . Did you hear Nixon on the air? Isn't it horrible? Like a dish of mush turned surly.

On September 11, 1953, she writes me at Brooks, from the house on Pamet Point Road:

It's marvelous here. John Biggs [a judge who had known my father and F. Scott Fitzgerald at Princeton] was down; your father said something to him about Cambridge and wondered where you got the idea. [I was thinking about applying to Cambridge University, but gave up the idea once I found out how radically different the British college system was from ours.] We went swimming with John and Anna at Slough Pond, without bathing suits; Judge Biggs thinks they can't arrest you for swimming nude on your own property. [Actually they were using the Macdonalds' little beach just below their house. Zealous nudists, the Macdonalds had their share of run-ins with the Truro constabulary on this very score.] Yesterday we went for a long walk with the Jencks to Great Island and gathered mushrooms and driftwood for the fireplace. We have a new variety—the boletus—that grows in woods among the bearberries and cranberry; it's not poisonous—we ate a large dish full last night. I also saw your father yesterday and had a long, very amusing talk about the Bible with him. I met Elena's uncle Walter. Who is very *jeune* for his age.

It's utterly deserted in Wellfleet; not a house on Slough Pond is open, not even the Chermayeffs'. The Walkers are gone. All the restaurants are closed up in Provincetown. Mary Meigs has never come back; we don't know why. We think her house may remain closed up and prim forever, like something in a novel or fairy tale. The only news is that Bowdie [Bowden] cut his hand trying to fix a window. [See John Sinnot's similar mishap at the beginning of McCarthy's *Charmed Life*.] We went to Dr. Callis, who seems pretty bad to me. Ruth Jencks is right; he only wants to give penicillin shots. Oh yes, Helvetia Perkins was here, on a lightning visit, which terminated almost before it started from sheer shyness. . . . And I've finished my story, for the nth time.[2]

Writing to me a month later (October 13, 1953) my mother reports that the social scene has picked up:

Dearest Reuel;

I'm so proud to hear that you're on first class; your letter was much appreciated. Ruth Jencks, seen on the streets of Wellfleet this morning, shook her black locks over the picture of a gaunt, pale Reuel, hitting the books and racked with diarrhea. "They seemed

happy," she shrugged, as if this *seeming* were the direst omen possible. Charlie, it seems, has lost all his healthy color, and is eating
nothing but a daily spoonful of peas while his innards writhe in peri-
stalsis. [Charlie had entered Brooks that fall; I was one class ahead
of him, having entered the previous year.] I assume none of this is
true. Pressed on whether you really had diarrhea, she confessed
that she didn't know but added brightly that Charlie and the rest
of the school had it. [In fact I had escaped this episode of mass
food poisoning—from tainted minced ham in the always dreaded
scrambled eggs, made from powder, that were often served for
Sunday dinner.] She really is Dickensian; Bowden says he can see
her in a Dickens illustration, wrapped in a black shawl, striding
down some wretched road with gnarled trees stretching their ten-
tacles in the distance. Mary Meigs says that when she came to dinner the other night she looked as if she were wearing a collection
of old cleaning cloths.

The Macdonalds were up last weekend and came to dinner Saturday with the Jencks. B. remarked that when Ruth and Nancy get in
the same room it looks like a fortune tellers' convention. The MacD's
were in very gay spirits, though; Dwight has gotten over his writing
block and is at the top of his form. Nancy seemed well too. . . . The
feud with the Jencks hasn't altogether subsided. All parties were
quite cold. The MacD's had the usual friend with them, also swathed
in a shawl, but rather nice actually—a girl painter named Madi Bloch
who does Bonwit Teller windows. She is a niece of Hans Sahl. [Sahl
had fled Nazi Germany; he would return in the fifties.]

The weather is still beautiful here but chilly. I went up to your
room the other morning about eight o'clock; it was the warmest
room in our house (because of the beaver-board insulation, I guess,
and the morning sun) and the tusk registered 48. [I had acquired a
phallic walrus tusk cum attached thermometer in an antique shop.]
I've taken it downstairs and we're getting a lot of use out of it; now,
with two fires going and an electric heater in the little front study,
the temperature had crawled up to 62. Mary Meigs borrowed it to
take a sounding of her house. She was going to put in a furnace but
decided not to, and instead bought a cord of wood, half a ton of
briquettes, and an electric blanket—she does everything in quantity.
She has also imported five hundred pounds of earth, peat moss,

dried cow manure, to grow three rose trees and six peony plants. But speaking of her electric blanket, the Macdonalds thought of an invention—an electric blanket you can wear around the house, like a coat, with a storage battery in the pocket. This conversation will give you a clue to the weather here. But we're still swimming, or were up to Saturday; we haven't gone since. Masses of people were up for Columbus Day; Vita [Petersen—she and her husband Peter were the Macdonalds' neighbors on Slough Pond], Alfred [Kazin], Chemayeffs and many strange women ordering gin and bitters in the liquor store.

We've been to tea at the Francis Biddles, also at the George Biddles. [The Biddles were brothers. Francis, an elegant man who made no concessions to Cape Cod informality, had been U.S. attorney general from 1941 to 1945 and a judge at the Nuremberg war crimes trials; George was an artist.] I talked French an hour with Léger [Saint-Jean-Perse, diplomat, poet, and Nobel Prize winner; he was quite a hit with the ladies in Wellfleet], the Biddles' guest, largely about mushrooms, which I'd been reading about fortunately in Larousse. It was a sweating ordeal; at the end of an hour my French instead of improving had deteriorated from the strain to the point where I couldn't remember simple words like "encore." But I was glorious with the subjunctive. Mr Léger looked at me finally in a courteous but stunned manner and asked where I had learned French. In the convent, I said, and he nodded thoughtfully. How is *your* French? . . .

The tusk has now hit 64½. Au revoir; mille baisers.

Mummy

The next year my mother brings me up to date on the Jenckses' most recent activities:

Ruth Jencks has got the mushroom craze in a big way. You should see her on the golf course, barefoot, in her shawls and petticoats, crouching over a patch of fairy-ring champignons, directly in the line of a foursome. Gardner says she has discovered that golf balls are "terrible poisonous." . . . Gardner, reading Kierkegaard, wonders whether he ought to kill his children (following Abraham's example in the sacrifice of Isaac). Ruth says Abraham did it to gain social prestige. (September 28, 1954)

The Wellfleet years, incomplete in that the Broadwaters never stayed there more than five months a year, directly inspired McCarthy to write her third novel, *A Charmed Life*. She wrote most of it in Wellfleet, over the summer of 1954. She finished it on Capri in April 1955; it was published in November of the same year. The novel met a generally unenthusiastic critical reception and won the author no new friends; in fact it antagonized, or wounded, some of the old ones. Although Cape Cod provided a needed backdrop, her primary objective was not realistically to portray Wellfleet or its inhabitants, many of whom were already familiar to her from the Wilson years. Rather, she wanted to write "a symbolic story" with a "fairy-tale element" about "doubt" (Gelderman, 190). The kind of doubt, we might add, that leads the main character to search for moral absolutes that even exceptional people can never attain in the course of everyday life.

The time frame of this novel-tragicomedy set in a New England seaside community is tightly constricted: it begins in September and ends in late November. The action begins in and around the charming red eighteenth-century house so impulsively bought by John and Martha Sinnot. John has badly cut his hand while trying to repair a broken window. The house, the initial incident, and the Sinnots' delicately balanced marriage reflect the Broadwaters' own circumstances and life on Pamet Point Road. The novel also reflects the problematic nature of McCarthy's decision to buy a house in easy proximity to her former husband, now remarried, with a new child. It seems hardly coincidental, moreover, that Miles Murphy, the novelistic ex-husband, has a very obliging wife by the name of Helen. Wilson's fourth and last wife, who adoringly pampered her famous, and very irascible, husband, was named Elena (the Russian version of Helen—her mother was Russian); in addition, they named their daughter Helen.

As already mentioned, the Cape's unspoiled setting appealed to McCarthy. Another reason for returning must have been the opportunity to see Dwight and Nancy Macdonald, who spent every summer at their Slough Pond cottage. Other old friends, Ruth and Gardner Jencks, enthusiastically welcomed the Broadwaters and often invited them to their house on Bound Brook Island.[3] The house—its location, architecture, interior arrangement—as well as its occupants find reflection in the novel. In real life, the Jenckses never invited the two former spouses to the same social event. In the novel, however, it is the fateful meeting of the two former spouses, Martha Sinnot and Miles Murphy, at the Coes' play-reading soirée, that prepares the way for the tragic ending. Mary Meigs, a newer friend (the model for the fictional Dolly Lamb), was ensconced in the yellow house next to the Broadwaters, and her company was much appreciated. The Broadwaters were also warmly received by Charles and Adelaide Walker. Adelaide had been a good friend and confidante to McCarthy during her marriage to Wilson.[4] She had written an affidavit supporting McCarthy at the divorce proceedings. When McCarthy left Wellfleet for good, she gave Adelaide the house washing machine. All this nearly cost the Walkers Wilson's friendship, but cordial relations were resumed after Wilson's remarriage. Using their considerable diplomatic skills, the Walkers remained on good terms with the Wilsons, while occasionally socializing with the Broadwaters. Wilson had known Walker since their college years (at Princeton and Yale respectively); both had been on the political left until the late thirties. The Wilson-Walker friendship ultimately lasted until the deaths of all four parties. Adelaide, who lived the longest, also kept up her friendship with McCarthy, although at long distance, until the latter's death.

Returning to Wellfleet in 1952, McCarthy renewed old ties; in addition the opportunity now presented itself to settle, through literary catharsis, accounts with her last failed marriage and, more broadly, to level her satirical guns at a bohemian way of life that she found intellectually dishonest and morally deficient. Whether consciously or subconsciously, she felt the need, through a novel, to exorcise inner, and outer, demons. I should stress, however, that drawing from real life, she transcends it. Like Tolstoy and Dostoevsky, her literary masters, she probed the ethical implications that result from the overzealous pursuit of rational thinking. Unfortunately she was lacking the Russians' ability to transpose ideas into lifelike characters. She chose for *A Charmed Life* an intentionally neutral New England setting. Although the dwellers of the fictitious New Leeds resemble some of those who really lived in mid-twentieth-century Wellfleet, the place merely gives the frame wherein the personae follow their own ethical, or unethical as the case may be, imperatives. The central conflict revolves around a series of dilemmas that confront the main protagonist, Martha Sinnot. "Sin not" represents an injunction she will be unable to follow; in fact it seems that the traditional notion of sin has little or no relevance to the world depicted here. Martha, a former actress who writes plays and studies philosophy, has elected to return to New Leeds with her new husband John. He is a tender soul who adores her, but his character is lacking in substance. The author has done little more than sketch in the main lines of his personality. We know only that he is a supportive though temperamental husband, and that he is a historian (underemployed) by vocation. Martha is hoping to become pregnant, and thereby strengthen a marriage that has begun to slip away. A woman of high standards in her everyday life, Martha dresses well, tries to drink in moderation, keeps a garden and a tidy house, and follows a rigorous work schedule. By setting a positive example, she is hoping to challenge the lazy and self-indulgent ethos that pervades the surrounding community. The New Leedsians have no fixed principles, and they justify their moral inertia by a "why not?" argument—an argument that parodies Rasolnikov's sinister creed in Dostoevsky's *Crime and Punishment*: "If God does not exist, then everything is permitted." Ethical relativists, the New Leedsians admit only to truths that can be painstakingly, and logically, demonstrated to them.

As though through the workings of some ineluctable fate, New Leeds will annihilate Martha Sinnot in punishment for the hubris motivating her decision to rejoin it. Symbolic of her imminent destruction is Warren Coe's six-by-eleven-foot painting of Martha. The artist, searching for a "fourth dimension," has entered into what he describes as a "fission" period. On the canvas he has exploded Martha's figure into almost unrecognizable component pieces. Ironically her ex-husband Miles Murphy buys the painting and hangs it in his house. Later, after a play-reading event at the Coes', which unforeseen circumstances have prevented their respective spouses from attending, Murphy lays claim to Martha as a live trophy. The drunken sexual encounter that unfolds on the horsehair couch in Martha's living room is of no lasting consequence to either of the participants, but its results are of critical importance to Martha when she learns she is pregnant a few weeks later. A manifestly rational person, she has accepted the "why not?" argument, if not the blind irrational, when she got drunk at the Coes' and then succumbed to her ex-husband's oafish advances. Because of the fact that she will never know for sure whether the child has been spawned by Murphy or her current husband, she decides to have a clandestine abortion. (The situation reflects McCarthy's own decision, early in 1942, to abort a child that could have been Wilson's or a lover's, possibly Ralph Manheim's. See Dabney, 282, 297.) In her own mind her decision stems from her uncompromising search for "the truth." Since the truth behind the child's paternity can never be known beyond any shadow of a doubt, bearing the child would engender ambiguity, in Martha's mind equivalent to a lie. Just when she has finally secured the necessary money from her only confidant and loyal friend, Warren Coe, Martha sets out in her car for an abortionist in Boston. Driving in the nighttime darkness of a country road in New Leeds, she is killed in a collision with an older, alcoholic, female writer who has been Martha's professional rival in the community. In a mental flash before dying, Martha realizes that she should have been driving on the wrong side of the road, since it is the other writer's established habit to drive on the left after imbibing.[5]

A Charmed Life features a grotesque cast of characters, only a fraction of whom are redeemed by sparks of humanity. The notable exceptions are Dolly Lamb, Warren Coe, and possibly John Sinnot.[6] Dolly feels compassion and even incipient love for the manipulative ne'er-do-well Sandy Gray. Gray, a transplanted Brit and former Communist, has been called a "typical backwoods blow-hard" by John Sinnot. Despite his boorish ways and arrogance, Dolly sees "something Christ-like" in Gray, whose fourth wife has just left him (CL, 124–129). During Sandy's divorce proceedings, in which he seeks custody of his children, Dolly testifies to his good character, only to realize that she has been bending the truth in his favor. The testimony of others, moreover, convinces her that Sandy's affectionate, though slatternly, wife is better suited than he for custody of their children. Dolly's weakness of will makes her seem human, in a way that the cold, egotistic Martha does not. Martha loves beauty and order in the abstract; humanity in the concrete with all its warts and foibles only exasperates her. The bumbling Warren Coe, who has consistently played the role of learned fool with his indiscriminate and omnivorous intellectual curiosity, almost becomes a positive hero at the end, when he conspires to help Martha get her abortion. Selflessly, and with a cunning foreign to his open nature, he procures her the money for it. No small feat, in view of the fact that he must conceal all from his inquisitive and domineering wife, Jane. Warren possesses a quality that McCarthy valued above all others in the people she knew: loyalty.

The New Leedsians are marked by weird idiosyncrasies that reflect their inner distortions. Willing slaves to their own weaknesses, these residents of seacoast bohemia lead contented lives. Miles Murphy, who lives in the neighboring community of Digby, stands somewhat apart from the rest. According to the omniscient narrator, Murphy is a self-styled Renaissance man who "truly loves the arts." Endowed with an incisive mind and formidable erudition, he makes sweeping pronouncements on philosophy, literature, art, and psychology. He is loosely modeled on Wilson, but his creator also endowed him with the physical characteristics of another man she knew. He was Robert (Bobby) Lawthers, a set designer in the theater, who was the companion of Virginia Chamberlin, a friend of the Macdonalds. Virginia called her hard-drinking lover "my wild Irishman." The Broadwaters met him in Wellfleet. All of Miles Murphy's bullying ways, his off-putting mannerisms, and his penchant for the lecturing, often brilliant monologue are, however, Wilson's own.

At the novel's center is a complex human drama that has really nothing to do with "real" prototypes. The action plays out as though onstage; the players enter, say their lines, and retire. Above the stage ticks a large clock, unnoticed by the players. It will determine Martha's fate. One of the novel's critics has pointed out that, unlike Martha, the other characters are not subject to time, because of their overall indifference to routine and normal conventions. Martha is, in contrast, "answerable to clocks" and "the measurable duration of things" (Hardy, 71–72). Reinforcing Martha's unique and tragic position—ironically she is the only one in this magic circle of dreamwalkers who does not lead a charmed life—is the discussion that follows the reading of Racine's tragedy *Bérénice* at the Coes' house. The only one of the discussants who believes in the notion of romantic love is Warren Coe. He therefore censures the Roman emperor Titus for rejecting his Jewish fiancée Bérénice. Reasons of state determine Titus' hard decision. The play's tragic outcome, that is, the lovers' permanent separation, shows their high moral character: neither would be worthy of the other if he/she had chosen the path of abdication and exile. Warren Coe, who condemns their decision, points out the example of King Edward VIII of England who, rightly in Coe's opinion, chose to follow his heart. The discussion then moves into comparisons: Racine versus Corneille (according to Miles, Corneille is more interested in psychology), Shakespeare and Sophocles, Racine versus Shakespeare and the ancient Greeks. According to Martha, Racine shows the inner passions, "the beast within"; if Shakespeare had written *Bérénice* he would have "shown up" Titus as he does Henry IV. She sees a "bitterness" in Shakespeare and Sophocles that is lacking in Racine. The discussion ends up as a scintillating exchange between Martha and Miles. The former implicitly identifies with Sophocles' Antigone and Orestes, both of whom act rightly and wrongly at the same time. Their divinely sanctioned actions, she asserts, cause death and suffering. Martha is now intoxicated. She has been more than keeping up with the bibulous Miles, to the consternation of Warren Coe, who despite his concern keeps bringing them drinks in order to keep them talking. Martha now voices a pessimistic belief in a "tragic perspective" that leads us all to overstep "by a kind of fatality." Unable, as she sees it, to be "wrong" or "right" in everyday life, and without the moral compass that religious belief (earlier rejected by all the discussants) might provide, Martha now seems to have relented to the pernicious New Leeds moral relativism. Some of her listeners think that she is alluding to her failed marriage to Miles, whose evil spell, we the readers sense, continues to enthrall her. The next moment the telephone rings. It is John saying that the car has broken down and that he will have to spend the night in Boston (*CL*, 180–195). Fate then has opened the door to Martha's future perdition. By some grotesque irony, Martha, who has explored the different kinds of truth that great writers pursue, will conflate the search for truth with her unshakable resolve to have an abortion. In the end, she disregards love, which she hardly believes in, to follow a duty to "the truth." In this she reproduces Racine's love/duty binary and chooses the latter, as do Titus and Bérénice. In doing so, she only proves what she has maintained in the postplay discussion: the inability to perform a completely wrong or right action. Her creator can resolve her hopeless situation only by killing her at the end; the other alternative McCarthy entertained for the ending was to have Martha die on the abortionist's table. One can speculate that this most pessimistic of all her novels reflects her preoccupation with a milieu that lacked high intellectual standards as well as moral scruples.

It is certainly true that, by late summer 1954, the Cape and its repetitive social rituals had palled on the Broadwaters. That August, I was staying with my father and stepmother in Talcottville, New York. My mother wrote to me on August 20 from Wellfleet:

We went to a cocktail party at Margaret De Silver's[7] yesterday—the usual gang, Ed Dickinson [the artist] in necktie and formal clothing, except for bare feet. Uncle Walter[8] was there talking to Edie Shay,

MARY McCARTHY ON CAPE COD : 135

and I, to make conversation with them, said I had just had a letter from you about your bicycle trip [through the Adirondacks, into Canada, and back to Talcottville]. He said, staring: "Ah, do you know Reuel?" And I said, "Yes, I'm his mother." He turned a sort of magenta; he had not realized, it seems, that the lady you brought into Lehmann Brothers was related to you, assuming, no doubt, on the Vita Petersen principle that it was the "older woman" in your life.[9]

Bowdie and I went beach-plumming this afternoon and then to swim in Long Pond, to vary the monotony. To tell the truth, I'm finding the Cape August rather boring: the same people (Dr. Rado, Joan Sinkler, the Petersens, various Biddles, the Levins), the same beach routine. One day last week, by ourselves, we walked from Phillips Beach to Ballston Beach and back, just for a change; it took a little over two hours, including swims. That night it seems there was a fairly wild beach picnic, graced by the presence of Jack Hall,[10] who is drinking again after fourteen years, since Jean Hall has left him and moved in with Mr. Lesser. Ruth [Jencks] is in a terrific state of alarm about this. The next day after the beach picnic (which we didn't attend, B. begging off because it was his birthday and he didn't want to celebrate it by having to see all those people), anyway, the next day there was a cocktail party at Janet Aaron's, which we did attend, and Ruth's eyes were bulging over Jack Hall. "Look," she kept whispering to Bowden, "he's helping himself to a drink!" This didn't seem so extraordinary to B., since all the other guests were helping themselves too, there being nobody to serve.

I wish I could tell you something high-minded and grave, but there isn't anything of the kind going on. You probably haven't missed much, even in your set. B. is getting very tough about guests. I protested this the other night, after Rhoda and her swain left, and said, "Heavens, what would you do if King Lear turned up?" "Get him out of the house by ten o'clock," he answered. But we've broken down and asked the Levins [Harry and Elena Levin, Harry the distinguished professor of comparative literature at Harvard] to tea tomorrow, with the Francis Biddles. The Levins had *us* to a cocktail party last Saturday, which was just the same as all the other cocktail parties. Oh, dear. Perhaps your generation will do better. But did you read about the teen-age killings in New York? As one reporter pointed out it's exactly the pattern of Raskolnikov in *Crime and*

Beside Elena's "Little House," now our cottage, May 1998.
Left to right: *the author, Bowden Broadwater, and James Parker.*
For more about Parker see note 6 to chapter 5.

Punishment. I'm disgusted with the Democrats, over the outlawing of the Communist Party bill; they seem completely irresponsible, almost worse than the Republicans. I think I will have to go back to voting for the Socialists, though B. is threatening to bolt to the Prohibition ticket. . . ."

Once *A Charmed Life* was published in November 1955, the Broadwaters decided to sell the Wellfleet house. My mother would later insist that the idea had been Bowden's. A buyer was quickly found: Mary Meigs, their next-door neighbor, who was relieved to see them go. In fact she had been deeply hurt by Dolly Lamb's portrait in the novel. She saw Dolly as a degrading caricature of herself. Years later Meigs would go on to write an autobiographical book, *Lily Briscoe* (1981), where she challenges what she perceived as McCarthy's heartless incorporation of living models into her fiction. Meigs told me that her book is an unusual example in literary history where the victim of a negative portrayal has fought back by writing another book. After reading *Lily Briscoe*, McCarthy wrote Meigs a letter of apology. Mary Meigs and the Jenckses kept up their friendships with McCarthy, although mostly at long distance. As for Wilson, neither he nor his wife Elena would admit to reading the novel. It is likely that he really didn't read it,[11] for he knew how to put an Olympian distance between himself and his detractors. During my school and college years he continued to see my mother from time to time, and their meetings, where I was the main subject of discussion, were cordial.

My mother's departure from Cape Cod was this time to be final. *A Charmed Life* marked a turning point in her life. Now she would set her sights on Europe, especially Italy. In 1955 she got a contract to write a book about Venice, published as *Venice Observed* in 1956. She went on to research and write *The Stones of Florence*, published in 1959. Her protracted stays abroad—while Bowden, now employed at Saint Bernard's School, remained in New York—were the symptom of a weakened marriage that left the way open for her to pursue other romantic involvements. The Broadwaters were divorced in 1961.

6 : REMEMBERING MY PARENTS AND CAPE COD

My earliest memories revolve around a handsome white house in Wellfleet, Massachusetts. Built around 1840 by Richard ("Rich") Freeman, it fronts on to Route 6, the main north-south artery of Cape Cod. Resting midway down a low-lying rise called Money Hill, it once boasted an English garden rooted in the rich soil brought as ballast in freightless ships returning to home port. Freeman was also the president of the Wellfleet Saving Bank. He and the bank's vice president built houses on the hill, which came to be known, appropriately enough, as "Money Hill." In contrast to his predecessor, Wilson never had enough money. This was due to financially irresponsible habits that included not paying income taxes, the lavish use of taxis (he never learned to drive), and copious long-distance telephone calls.

The ranging three-story house had six bedrooms, a front and back parlor, a functional kitchen with a small telephone room placed between it and the front hallway, an ample dining room, and my father's study, connected by a narrow stairway to an attic storeroom lined with bookshelves holding a red, multivolume Soviet edition of Lenin's writings; multiple copies, sent by the publisher, of my father's own work; old issues of *Life* and other magazines; and some materials that he seldom used. The storeroom connected to a little bedroom. Our elegant dining room had an air of formality; it was used only once a day, for supper. My father otherwise took meals in his study, while other family members ate at the kitchen table. The dining room's appointments are worth noting. The table was of solid mahogany with lion's paw "feet" supporting it, and on the walls hung two nautical pictures: one showed a clipper ship with all sails set (the medium was embroidered cloth rather than canvas or paper); the second was a Currier and Ives whaling print titled "THE WHALE FISHERY: Attacking a 'Right Whale' and 'Cutting In.'"[1] After my grandmother's death in Red Bank, New Jersey, in 1951, my father placed her imposing grandfather clock in the Wellfleet dining room. A few years later it acquired an odd companion in the shape of a large white Filipino straw chair whose back was shaped like an enormous fan. Elena had seen the chair in a hotel and found it irresistible. My father had succeeded in persuading the hotel's owner to sell it to him (see fig. 28). Although my mother, and later Elena, served elegant meals in the dining room, the atmosphere surrounding them was often tense, due to my father's alcohol-fueled outbursts of temper. (On one occasion my sister Rosalind exposed him for trying to pass off as water a large glass filled to the brim with gin.)

A midsize horse chestnut tree stood on the modest lawn in front of our house. It was the first tree I ever climbed. Every June, when its spiky, sticky green fruits fell to the ground, I broke them open with the same eager fascination—to find the same oily brown gleaming nuts with a white spot on the flat side. Our driveway led to a rotting barn behind the house, and then continued as a path though an overgrown clump of apple trees, out to a sandpit—the ideal spot for jumping and later war games. Beyond lay an impoverished farmstead belonging to the Roses (he was Portuguese and she, I think, Irish; I often played in the sandpit with their son Charlie) and a sparse landscape of marshland alternating with scrub pine–covered hillocks.

We had two dogs, both male: a big one, Rex (Reckie), half German shepherd and half English setter; and a little one, Bambi, a reddish brown cocker spaniel. Rex was my best friend in moments of loneliness or unhappiness. He was brave and independent. He sometimes disappeared for days and nights on end—to return, wounded, bedraggled, but fulfilled. He was very affectionate toward family members and overwhelmed them with a greeting ritual of jumping. He loved my mother, who was not particularly fond of animals. Long after the divorce he welcomed her affectionately when she once stopped at the house to pick me up. It was part of the summer ritual for my father to detick the dogs. He did this, as he did most of his daytime activities, within the confines of his study. As a young child, I watched attentively as he detached the blood-swollen white parasites from his willing subjects and deposited them in a can of gasoline. Only the female ticks, he pointed out, had the capacity to suck blood.

Almost every summer my father engaged a photographer to take a set of family pictures. Many of these show me with the dogs, in the vicinity of our front porch. I learned a fondness for animals from my father. In his case, this also seems to date from an early age—as witnessed by some photographs I have of him as a child of about four in Red Bank, New Jersey. They show him outdoors with a little menagerie: a large black and white kitten, two albino rabbits in cages, and an almost full-grown puppy, a mongrel with pointed ears and a long nose. In one of the photos his mother, a generously proportioned dame in a white muslin dress, kneels to play with the cat, perched atop the rabbits' cage. My father seems aware of the camera and looks away from it in all but one picture; he also averts his gaze from his mother and the pets. Two other photographs, taken when he was around seven, show him with a collie in the yard outside the Red Bank house. He is wearing a sailor suit and knickers.

Both my parents had bicycles, which were always kept on the front porch of the Wellfleet house. I remember riding balanced on my father's handlebars or perched in my mother's front basket. At least once she carried me thus to Truro, four miles away. Later, when I had a bike of my own, each day before sunset my father would dutifully admonish me to remove my "wheel" from the driveway, where it had been so carelessly abandoned, and place it on the porch where it belonged. During the war my mother acquired a car, a Plymouth, which was later succeeded by a Chevrolet sedan. I well remember our excursions in it to Provincetown, fourteen miles away. On the way, we passed a dark and uninviting body of water, "The Bottomless Pond," as my parents called it, probably following local usage. According to my mother, no instrument of measure had succeeded in plumbing its depth. As one approaches Provincetown along Route 6, a stunning view of the harbor and Long Point, the geographical end of Cape Cod, opens up on the left-hand side. My attention, however, always gravitated to the right, where a long weather-beaten wooden ruin lay, resembling the wasted corpse of a beached whale. The ruin had once, my parents asserted, been a plant to convert saltwater into fresh. (More likely, it had served to extract salt from seawater.) Another familiar landmark was the fish-processing building on Commercial Street, which declared its presence by an overwhelming stench. Today it has been converted into an upscale condominium, "The Ice House." Right on the water, at the far east end of Commercial Street (number 571), stood the graceful white house of John (Dos) and Katy Dos Passos. (As of the year 2000 a plaque now records the writer's tenancy there.) A tall man who liked to smoke cigars, Dos seemed imposing to me; nonetheless his demeanor was gentle, and he smiled often. Katy was kind and rather mysterious. Everything around her, the softly upholstered furniture, her ample attire, her fluffy dog, suggested languorous well-being. When he took the family out to dinner in Provincetown, my father always chose The Flagship, well known for its seafood and commanding view of the harbor. While we waited to be seated, I amused myself with a ship's wheel fastened to the wall of the lobby ("Growing Up," 235–238).

The only time I ever reached Provincetown by sea occurred later, when I was about fifteen. My father arranged for all of us including my stepmother Elena, her son Henry Thornton, my half sister Rosalind, and Lise Connolly, our very attractive house guest (just separated from her husband, the British writer Cyril Connolly), to embark on a commercial fishing boat in North Truro. It was well before dawn and the sea was very choppy when we put out in dories for the ship lying at anchor. The fishermen willingly partook of the bottle of whiskey furnished by my father. As the morning progressed, the wind abated and the sun beat unrelentingly down on the dark blue water. The fishermen steered methodically from one fixed net to another, and each net yielded a heavy cargo of flailing tuna fish. While still in the water the tuna were hacked to death with gaffs and then hauled on board. Clouds of their blood dyed the water crimson pink, and soon the flies descended on the mutilated corpses. Before replacing the nets, on which their livelihood depended, the fishermen patiently mended every tear and hole in them. Dazed by the sun and exhausted, we were met at the Provincetown pier by my father's loyal retainer Bill Peck, the Wellfleet taxi driver. The next day we all awoke with painful sunburns.

When I was a young child growing up in Wellfleet, the town had a tiny year-round population of several hundred, and one year-round major writer—Edmund Wilson. The inhabitants were for the most part poor, undereducated, and unenterprising. In those days there were three village idiots who functioned quite well within the community. One of them, Charlie Bean, was a short, good-natured man with somewhat mongoloid features. He had a job with the post office delivering special-delivery letters and telegrams. Wearing a black, short-visored cap, Charlie made his way slowly and surely in a duck waddle, saluting all comers with broken discourse punctuated by a raucous laugh. In those days there was no real restaurant in town, just a soda fountain at the drugstore and one at Newcomb's, known for its delicious frappes. There was a dry-goods store, Smith's; a hardware store, Atwood's (needless to say, named after their proprietors); and a grocery store, first an A&P, then the First

National, then Williams', later Lema's, and now the Wellfleet Market. When the town's dry laws were finally repealed in the fifties, Mr. Williams decided to open a liquor store adjacent to his market. Among his best customers were my father, Frank and Edie Shay (both writers; Frank wrote *The Best Men Are Cooks*, whose alcohol-laced recipes are worth sampling), and Paul and Nina Chavchavadze (the White Russian émigrés who introduced my father to his last wife, Elena). Elena, born into the wine-producing Mumm family in Germany, acted as Mr. Williams' unpaid wine consultant.

A few of the local characters inspired me with awe, even fear. One of these was the real estate agent, Elizabeth Freeman, a hard-drinking, heavy-smoking woman with a deeply creased face. Since buying his house from her in 1941, my father maintained a friendship with Miss Freeman. Hearing her gravelly voice emanating from our front sitting room, I knew that she had dropped by unannounced for an impromptu drink. Most intimidating of all were the local shell fishermen who hung out at the Higgins Shack by the waterfront. My parents took me along when they came here to buy fresh oysters. They exchanged pleasantries with Mr. Higgins and the regulars—all, like him, sinewy weather-beaten men in enormous water-resistant overalls. I could never understand their loud remarks, addressed to us in a thick local accent.

Another local character, Vinny Pierce, came weekly to our house to collect the garbage and take it to the dump in his truck. He was a small wiry man with sharp features, clad in faded gray work clothes and hip boots. Well versed in the town gossip, he always lingered a few minutes to chat with us. One September when I was about fifteen and set to return to boarding school, I had to abandon the chickens I had been keeping in the field by our house. We made an arrangement to "board" the chickens with Mr. Pierce over the winter. Needless to say, they ended up on his dinner table.

My father was interested in nature, and he was a keen observer of it. Unable to teach me handy skills that he had never acquired, he did introduce me to the outdoors. After finishing his work at around three o'clock, he often took me for walks in the woods. We hadn't far to go, since the wilderness began just on the other side of Route 6. (Today the same pine wood conceals a sordid housing complex.) As we walked through the bright blotches of light cast by the now-waning summer sun, my father initiated me into the ways of aromatic fern, and bread-

and-butter plants with their tender edible leaves. In June he liked to ferret out the elusive lady slipper, a delicate, fleshy, purple pink wild orchid. Having found a specimen hiding demurely among old leaves, pine needles, and green ground cover, he admired it, not forgetting to enjoin me never to pick one. During our walks we sometimes encountered a painted turtle. This timid creature, firmly suspended in my father's grasp, would retract its head and urinate copiously while we viewed its glossy orange and black underside. One day we saw some leeches wiggling around in the water at a pond's edge. Also marked with orange and black, they reminded him of his alma mater Princeton's colors. Today the painted turtles and leeches are very scarce, and so are the bobwhites, while the whip-poor-wills, whose haunting call once punctuated the night, have completely disappeared.

Up until I was about five, my father would tell me bedtime stories of his own invention. These spanned many installments; the main characters were animals including a rather fearsome bear. I went on to make up my own stories, peopled by gentle and consoling animal friends, which I told to myself. When I was older my father read to me every night after dinner—mostly fairy tales. I especially liked those in the Fairy Book Series edited by Andrew Lang (each volume is named for a color: *Blue, Green, Yellow, Pink,* etc.); later on I would read them by myself. Returning from a trip out west, where he had been researching the Southwest Indians, my father brought with him a volume of Zuñi folk tales. I found these stories enthralling, read as they were by candlelight after a storm in late summer 1948. He was now remarried, to Elena Mumm, who was in Europe at the time. During the forties, my mother read me most of *Grimm's Fairy Tales*; then we branched into Afanasyev's *Russian Fairy Tales*, the latter a gift from my father, now divorced. My mother and I agreed that the Russian stories were more brutal than their German counterparts. I doubt that my mother knew that Grimm's tales had been sanitized for their first publication (and so they remain today). When I inherited my father's library after his death in 1972, I discovered an 1878 edition of W. R. S. Ralston's *Russian Folk-Tales* and a French translation of the *Secret* (read "lewd") *Russian Folktales*. He read neither to me; the Ralston is too scholarly for a child's taste.

Over the years my father read aloud Poe's stories; Conan Doyle's Sherlock Holmes; Joel Chandler Harris' *Tar-Baby*, which we both found tedious although he had liked it as a child; Edward Lear, whose verse he rendered with real dramatic verve; E. Nesbitt; Lewis Caroll; Dickens (*Oliver Twist*), among others. We both found Harriet Beecher Stowe's *Uncle Tom's Cabin* gripping, but we panned her later novel *Dred: The Tale of the Great Dismal Swamp*. My father went on to finish this one on his own, since he was then getting up the literature of the Civil War. When I was around eleven, my mother read me *The Merry Adventures of Robin Hood* in Howard Pyle's version and *King Arthur*, also according to Pyle. Just as I once had replicated my father's bedtime improvisation with an imaginary world of animal friends, so now I took the elements of Arthurian romance and put myself in the company of knights and damsels in distress. The fantasy of rescuing these lovely women afforded me pre-adolescent erotic gratification. My favorite knight was Sir Tristram; my mother's was Sir Lancelot. She admired him most of all for his daring affair with Queen Guinevere. Later my mother read me *The Iliad*, *The Odyssey*, and Dickens' *Tale of Two Cities*, *David Copperfield*, and *Great Expectations*. The reading sessions with both parents ended when I was fifteen. Their willingness to read, and patiently to explain the hard parts, made literature, and later the teaching of it, an inseparable part of my life.

Although neither of my parents had any real gift for music, nor could they read it, my father loved listening to music, especially opera and other kinds of musical compositions that told a story. He initiated me into Paul Dukas' dramatic, and creepy, *Sorcerer's Apprentice*. As we listened to it on the phonograph, he narrated the story of a young boy's folly in invoking dark powers that he couldn't control. We had similar sessions with Prokofiev's *Peter and the Wolf*. Both parents liked to sing. My father had sung to entertain my older half sister Rosalind; he sang for me, and would do so for my younger half sister Helen, and finally for my two-year-old son Jay, the summer before his death. Enthroned on the settee in the inner room of his study complex and with a few drinks under his belt, my father held forth in a lusty baritone. His repertoire included "Pop Goes the Weasel" (for the very young), "A Bicycle Built for Two," and many Princeton songs from a book that dated back to his undergraduate days there. The performance always ended with a rather tipsy rendition of "Good Night Ladies." My mother sang mostly to while away the time on long-distance car trips. Her favorites were "The Battle Hymn of the Republic," "Men of Harwich," "Green Grow the Lilacs," and a song about a man-eating shark that would "touch neither woman nor child." Both my parents read and sang with dramatic feeling. My father rendered well the accents, dialects, and verbal idiosyncrasies of literary characters. Oddly enough, he never mastered the art of public lecturing, which he did poorly according to all accounts.

I started studying Latin early, around the age of eight, at Saint Bernard's School in New York. A few years later my father decided to teach me something about Latin prosody. During the Wellfleet summer sessions that I so dreaded we read Catullus, one of his favorite poets. I had to memorize the short poem that begins "Otium, Catulle, molestum est" (Idleness, Catullus, is bad for you—and by extension bad for me, too, although I didn't make the connection then). This line was to be recited with special attention to the elision whereby the "e" in "est" is swallowed up by the preceding "um." We also read Catullus' moving poem on his brother's death ("Multas per gentes . . .") and Tennyson's equally moving evocation of Catullus, inspired by the death of his own brother Charles. At my father's bidding, I memorized the following lines where the English poet's admiration for his great predecessor eloquently merges with a sense of personal loss:

> Row us out from Desenzano, to your Sirmione row!
> So they rowed, and there we landed—"O vetusta Sirmio!"
> There to me thro' all the groves of olive in the summer glow,
> There beneath the Roman ruin where the purple flowers grow,
> Came that "Ave atque Vale" of the Poet's hopeless woe,
> Tenderest of Roman poets nineteen hundred years ago,
> "Frater Ave atque Vale"—as we wandered to an fro,
> Gazing at the Lydian laughter of the Garda lake below
> Sweet Catullus' all-but-island, olive silvery Sirmio!

My father tried to show me the difference in Latin between long and short syllables, though he found the concept rather difficult himself. He often expressed disbelief that English boys in the public schools had been routinely caned for "false quantities" in their Latin verse recitations. He had his own theory as to how Latin should be taught. Caesar and Cicero, he maintained, were too dry for young people. How could students get involved in the details of the bridge that Caesar had built over the Rhine? (Interestingly enough, my mother remembered reading this same passage from Caesar's *Commentaries* with passionate involvement; in fact, she had enjoyed the challenge.) My father found it unacceptable that one could study Latin for two or three years without learning the word for "green." He thought, sensibly enough, that Latin should be taught as a living rather than a dead language.

All in all, my father was not a hard taskmaster; in his role as a teacher he never lost his temper. Actually these summer poetry lessons only took place over two of my long vacations. (On September 24, 1948, he reports in a letter to Elena that I have successfully "passed" the poetry examination he has made up for me.) I will, however, never forget the tedium of trying to memorize Ralph Waldo Emerson's "Concord Hymn," written in honor of those who died at the Battle of Concord during the Revolutionary War.

> By the rude bridge that arched the flood,
> Their flag to April's breeze unfurled,
> Here once the embattled farmers stood
> And fired the shot heard round the world. . . .

I have long forgotten the other two stanzas. In any event, the patriotic message was lost on me.

In the summer of 1953, when my father was in Talcottville, New York, I stayed with my mother and stepfather Bowden Broadwater in the house they had bought in Wellfleet, not far from Money Hill, on Pamet Point Road. I had no summer job and no structured activities; therefore it is not surprising that my mother undertook to teach me some ancient Greek, while renewing her own knowledge of that language, long ago acquired at Vassar College. I found the Greek very hard going; she only less so. The study sessions lasted less than a month.

The scene is Wellfleet, and I am somewhere between two and five. To amuse me, my father fashioned a mouse out of an old brown necktie (NB: almost all his clothes were brown, as were his eyes). The mouse seemed eerily lifelike, as he manipulated it in fits and starts. A Chinese lacquer box that stood on a shelf in my Wellfleet bedroom also has a large place in my early memories. Upon awakening each morning, I opened its drawers—sometimes to find a roll of Necco wafers or another sweet left for me by some benign spirit. In these ways, as well as through magic tricks and puppeteering, my father played a role that he clearly relished: that of a benevolent demon. His violent rages directed at my mother, however, showed him in a very different, and frightening, light.

During a particularly loud and ugly confrontation that took place on the study threshold I remember crawling over his hard brown cordovan shoes, in a vain attempt to bring my parents to their senses. In the years before their separation and divorce I often had nightmares. I dreamt, terrorized, that I was alone in the house and unable to leave my room. The starting point for these nightmares may have been my parents' early-hours departure to Hyannis Hospital, where my mother was treated for a miscarriage that had happened the night before in Provincetown, in the summer of 1942. It is unlikely that I would have been alone in the house that night or any other. I was often entrusted to the care of babysitters and part-time help. One of these women made a dessert I adored: brown tapioca in a little round dish with a happy face traced out in raisins. Sometimes I went to spend a day or afternoon at a sitter's house. One of these, in North Truro, held an impressive collection of locally found arrowheads. My own attempts to find some in the nearby woods were doomed to failure. On the whole, the time spent away from home was extremely boring. Today, on my way into Wellfleet Center from our cottage, I often take note of the sprawling house where I spent many tedious hours under someone's care. The family there referred to magazines as "books," which somewhat puzzled me; in any case I couldn't get interested in reading them.

Very few objects from those early days remain in my possession: a cheap little totem pole of wood, a miniature steel police dog, and an incomplete croquet set in the cottage attic together with a mound of decaying record albums. The only object of real interest is the "mungabowow," a mahogany oriental sculpture that once adorned the table in my father's study. Its odd figures once inspired me with awe. Viewing them today, I see four monkeys on top and two deer and a cock below. The monkeys have just opened a casket.

My parents often took me to the secluded beach on Gull Pond. Even today, and despite the presence of an ugly public landing (cut into the pondside in the 1950s), Gull Pond still retains much of its pristine beauty. The gulls are there, wheeling back and forth to their resting places in the middle; the ever-changing sky and clouds find a perfect mirror in the water, and a sweet pungent smell still wafts along the shoreline. Here I spent the happiest days of every summer, and here I learned to swim at the age of six under my mother's able tutelage. After I had mastered the "deadman's float," she got me a pair of inflatable water wings. Thanks to

The author in Gull Pond, summer 1950. Photo by Sylvia Salmi.
Special Collections, Vassar College Libraries.

these I quickly progressed to the dog paddle and real swimming. Each
trip to the pond invariably began with my father's cameo impersonation
of a water demon. His vigorous splashing and roaring made me, and assorted friends, run away, but his demeanor was just as comical as it was
scary. After this pantomime, he would describe a few circles in the water,
using an outmoded, flailing sidestroke called the "one-armed treadle"
("Growing Up," 241–242). After the pro forma swim, my father would
depart for a long nature walk around the pond. My mother, a strong
swimmer, liked to stay in the water. This caused me no little anxiety at
the ocean beach, where the restless Atlantic seemed threatening even on
a calm day. She and a friend, Anna Matson (who continued to swim in
the ocean when in her eighties), would range far from shore while en-
grossed in conversation. I meanwhile distracted myself by building sand
castles, a Sisyphean task when the tide was coming in. Once he reached
his midfifties, my father seldom went into the ocean, because it was too
rough, or too cold; it is often both. His appearance at Newcomb Hollow
Beach always attracted attention. Clad in a pair of baggy old bathing
trunks, a well-worn white short-sleeved Brooks Brothers shirt, and an
old brown fedora hat, he sat on the sand avidly chatting with friends and
acquaintances. One of these, the artist Edwin Dickinson, as slim and
wiry as my father was portly, cut an equally original figure with his wedge
beard, elegant shirt and slacks, and bare feet. He always carried a pair of
binoculars—more, it was speculated, the result of his interest in female
pulchritude than in Mother Nature. Ed Dickinson was the only person,

aside from my father's working-class lover Frances, to call my father "Ed."
Most called him "Edmund"; a few used his childhood nickname "Bunny."
The friends who called him "Bunny" had known him a long time, although some by doing so hoped to insinuate a greater intimacy than had actually existed. As a child I found it hard to call my father anything, but, as the result of my mother's gentle persuasion (long after their divorce), I learned to call him "Father," as he wished to be known.

As already mentioned, my father had two hobbies well suited to please children: conjuring and the puppet theater. One of his old Cape Cod friends, Eben Given, who himself believed in ghosts, explained my father's interest in magic as a counterbalance to his rationalist disbelief in religion and the supernatural. My father's brand of magic involved a lot of legerdemain. Because of his lapses of manual dexterity, however, he often inadvertently revealed the secret behind the "trick." In a sequence meant to turn white balls into red ones, he held up four white balls between the fingers of one hand. Just before the climax, the balls would pop out and crash to the floor, showing the red caps that had been concealed from the audience. Little daunted by failure, he would insist that the spectators remain in place while he repeated the sequence. He wasn't much better at card tricks, which he so often began with the solemn invitation: "Pick a card, any card." My father subscribed to a magicians' journal and had made contact with a couple of professionals whom he admired. He told me that magicians treat one another with respect and never reveal their shared secrets to outsiders. My father had read up on Houdini, a daring and flawless performer whose stunts mystified even his professional colleagues. (NB: While my father was a professional writer who dabbled in magic, the Great Houdini was the author of a few successful nonliterary books.) Houdini's premature demise was the result of hubris: having dared all comers to test his iron stomach with a hard punch, one day a college student hit him unawares, fatally injuring him.

In terms of professional skill, my father's mastery of the quirky puppeteering art far surpassed his mediocre attempts at conjuring. He owned a collection of hand puppets made by a German master craftsman. When after years of use the figures' attire gave out and their limbs began to fall off, my father went to great trouble and expense to have his troupe refurbished by another European. Each puppet's head was a highly individual caricature that represented one of the stock Punch and

Judy cast. I well remember Punch with his ruddy complexion and hooked nose; his penchant for mindless violence appealed as much to his manipulator as it did to his young audiences. Punch's ill-used spouse, Judy, was roundfaced and saccharine looking; the Judge solemn with his ruff and wig, the policeman undistinguished. A crocodile, and a black-faced devil in a red frock, had the role of chastising the unregenerate Punch.

The devil, who spoke in a high-pitched whine, was my father's mouthpiece of choice. One summer night when I was about eight, two of my friends, Christy Avery and Charlie Jencks, came over to spend the night. We were to share the large bed in the small attic bedroom above the study. (This bedroom served as the most private of my father's sleeping lairs in the house, and it was in the top drawer of the chest there that I found a cache of dried-out unused condoms. At the time I had no notion of what they were. I also found in the same drawer a hoard of outsized tarnished old coppers. Rechecking the drawer the following summer, I found that the condoms had disappeared, while the pennies remained. One day my father showed me the coins, explaining that they had been found at a grave site, having served to seal the corpses' eyes before burial.) On the sultry August evening in question, my father had been entertaining the three of us boys with puppets before we retired for the night (Elena was away at the time). After we had finally settled into bed, with the light still on, a demonic shape suddenly intruded from behind the door jamb and delivered a taunting oration in a rapid, high-pitched cackle. It was the Punch and Judy devil doing an encore. It disappeared, but not for long. Encouraged by our enthusiastic reception, it periodically resurfaced, even after we had extinguished the light, always with the same arrogant discourse. We were finally left alone, but not immediately to sleep, for the night was now punctuated by a violent thunderstorm whose distant growl soon reached a blazing, crashing crescendo above our heads. My father would subsequently complain in a letter to Elena that we had made a mess of the room and left the bed full of potato chips. He reports in the same letter that he has taken me and Charlie Jencks to a showing of *Anna and the King of Siam* in Provincetown.

In his theatrical productions my father acted as author/adapter, speaker, and *metteur en scène*. He usually engaged a child to help him behind the scene if the play involved several episodes. These performances had great success with children, whose joyful response was equaled only by my father's excitement at having achieved the desired effects. Over time, he accumulated several troupes of puppets, and he would set up a second theater in Talcottville, New York. An amateur, albeit gifted, puppeteer, my father spoke admiringly of the professionals' mastery of a little metal whistle called a swazzle. Air blown though a reed inside it gives the proper whining pitch to Punch's voice. Since no adept could practice this difficult art without swallowing the whistle occasionally, it was usually attached to a string. My father managed to procure a swazzle for himself, but he never succeeded in his attempts to produce a sound from it.

Although my mother was an accomplished cook, as was my stepmother Elena, my father's unpredictable and often churlish behavior at the dinner table could drive any of his wives to distraction—as could his habit of inviting cocktail guests to stay for dinner after the third round of drinks. My mother told the story of a dinner they gave in Wellfleet for which she had cooked a "broiler turkey." A friend, Jack Philips, had recently started a turkey farm on his property in the backwoods. (By doing so in time of war, he had qualified as a farmer and thus became draft-exempt.) One night an owl raided one of the turkey houses, killing several of its young occupants. Jack's friends got the unmangled dead birds— the owl ate only the heads. When my mother brought the cooked undersize turkey into the dining room her husband, whose latent paranoia had possibly been activated by the predinner drinks, eyed it suspiciously and queried: "What happened to the owl?" She later postulated that my father, expecting a large, festive bird, had imagined that the owl had somehow been substituted for its victim, with or without her connivance. Another possible interpretation might be that my father was making a not uncharacteristic nasty crack, to wit, "what kind of turkey is the size of an owl?" Less likely, he may have been merely curious as to the owl's ultimate fate.

Born on Christmas Day 1938, I was seven when my parents separated permanently. It was a great relief to see an end to their constant fighting. Each seems to have blamed the other for the failed marriage; my mother remained bitter, although she continued to respect my father as a writer.

After returning from a five-month trip to Europe in 1944 (sponsored by the *New Yorker*), my father had a rocky time with his hired help in Wellfleet. During this period before his remarriage in 1946, he acquired two outsize Cadillacs in succession. The second he inherited from his mother, who had had it custom built. These were driven by two black servants: Gus and then Bill, who came with his wife Joyce. Both men proved unreliable. While visiting my father in Wellfleet, the southern poet Allen Tate scrutinized Gus and later remarked: "Why Edmund, that's no house n——r, that's a field n——r." Then came Victorine, a large black lady who did some housework as well as driving. She had lived in Atlantic City. Seeing my Monopoly set (a game with which she was unfamiliar), she identified all the street names as belonging to that city. Victorine also prided herself on her ballroom dancing and gave me a memorable lesson therein. I put some music on the phonograph in the front room and off we went—in different directions, hopelessly out of sync with each other and the music. Elena, my future stepmother, witnessed this uninspiring scene and recounted it for the amusement of all those who had missed out on it. After Victorine's departure, my father took on a married couple of displaced persons from Russia. They didn't work out either, but he didn't have the heart to fire them himself; therefore he delegated this unpleasant task to his Russian friend Nina Chavchavadze.

I spent the summer of 1945 with my mother in Polly Boyden's house in Truro. It was a cheerful old house with a little-used tennis court, next to our friends the Givens. Bud and Polly Boyden were hard drinkers known for their communist sympathies. Polly's son, Archie, was in the air force and had been very baldly burned in combat over Germany. Just before he returned home my mother warned me not to show surprise at his scarred face. Although his disfigurement was worse, if anything, than expected, his sterling personality quickly drew me to him. As mentioned earlier, my mother saw a good deal of Nicola and Miriam Chiaromonte, who were renting a house in Truro for the second consecutive summer. His ideas and personality were to make a lasting impression on her. I remember Nicola as brooding and intense; Miriam, a New York schoolteacher, was outgoing and maternal. They had no children of their own. I often drove to the beach with my mother and the Chiaromontes. At this very time, my mother had devised an ingenious "game" to curb my loquaciousness in the car: the "winner" would be the one who spoke the least during any given trip; the "loser" would be he who most flagrantly defied the interdiction. When Nicola was a passenger, I insisted that the same rules apply—to my mother's discomfiture. The Italian, however, didn't seem to mind losing, for he spoke freely, although always sagaciously.

From the time of the divorce until I went away to boarding school at thirteen, I spent the school year with my mother and the summer with my father, as per the court's ruling. Under these circumstances I count myself lucky to have had the stepparents I did. My mother's third husband, Bowden Broadwater ("Bowdie"), often reminded me by word and deed that I was the only child that he had ever cared for. Never destined to become a parent himself—my mother had several miscarriages during their marriage—he took a keen and thoughtful interest in my development. Eccentric and sharp-witted, he was also patient and affectionate. While I was growing up, Bowden periodically struggled with a sense of failure, even self-hatred, for he could not live up to the literary promise he had shown at Harvard. The son of a doctor in rural Maryland, Bowden had overcome his role of outsider by "inventing himself" at Loomis, an eastern prep school, and later at Harvard, where he did a thesis on Henry James, who was not yet fashionable in academe. He was a contributing member of the *Harvard Advocate*, the college literary magazine. The man my mother met in 1945 was a dapper sophisticate who spoke somewhat affectedly but with no trace of a southern accent. As time passed, he had little luck in publishing his fiction; finally he resigned himself to an administrative job at Saint Bernard's School in New York (which I had once attended). But most of all he devoted himself to the three people closest to him: my mother, his sister Christie (struggling with mental illness), and me. Bowden first entered my life when he appeared as a houseguest in Truro, over the summer of 1945.[2] I should add that, in his role of considerate stepfather, Bowden stressed to me my father's positive achievements: he was first and foremost a "great man," for whom Bowden had nothing but admiration.

My new stepmother, Elena Mumm Thornton, had appealed to my father because of her beauty. Tall and willowy, she dwarfed his squat figure when they stood side by side. He was also impressed by her easy command of German, French, and English, as well as some basic Russian acquired from her aristocratic Russian mother. Elena was intuitive and practical, rather than intellectual, in her approach to life. Generous to the point of masochism, she gave all to those whom she loved. During twenty-five years of devoted service to my father, she afforded a passive target to his surliness and bouts of unprovoked anger. Seldom, and never in the early years of their marriage, did she allow herself to criticize him either directly or outside his presence. She possessed a whole gamut of homemaking skills, including frugality. It was her diligence behind the scenes that enabled him to write without interruption, and she learned

Bowden Broadwater, the author's stepfather, while married to Mary McCarthy, mid-1950s. Special Collections, Vassar College Libraries.

to drive in her fifties in order to chauffeur him around, once Bill Peck, the Wellfleet taxi man, had retired. Every noon she bore an exquisitely prepared lunch into the study ("Growing Up," 239–240). Later in the day she would cook a substantial dinner for family members and frequent guests. Even in the last decade before my father's death, when their relationship had somewhat soured, Elena graciously entertained the likes of Penelope Gilliatt, the younger English writer to whom he was romantically attached.

When I stayed in Wellfleet, Elena cared for me "like a second mother" (my father's phrase). In fact she did many things that biological mothers do but which didn't fall within my mother's purlieu. I still wear a heavy wool sweater with an Icelandic design that Elena knitted for me over a long Cape Cod winter. One summer, when I was in the throes of chess fever, she played games with me virtually on demand—until her son Henry (my senior by five years) firmly explained that I was curtailing her only hour of daytime respite. Elena sometimes took me swimming at Gull Pond after dinner, when my father was well in his cups. Moonlight bathing, au naturel, with my stepmother was an unforgettable experience. After the swim, droves of mosquitoes would swarm over us. At this point Elena would light up a Chesterfield to keep them at bay. She also taught me to speak French with a Parisian accent, something I couldn't have learned from my nonnative teachers at school. Elena herself had no formal education, although she had studied some drawing and taken a course at a European cooking school. She learned English, which she always spoke with a slight Anglo-German accent, from an English governess. The Mumm family had been in the wine business in Johannesburg for over two centuries, and they had owned Mumm Champagne. When Elena came into some money in 1949, from the sale of her family's interest in a false-tooth factory in Lichtenstein, she decided to invest it in a cottage that she would call "The Little House." Actually it was the ell wing of another nineteenth-century house, the one built by the local bank's vice president that stood across from ours on Route 6. When the state decided to widen the road, the neighbors who lived there chose to relocate by building a new house at the state's expense. By buying a piece of the old one from them, Elena created a new summer home for me and her son Henry Thornton. It was placed atop the incline overlooking our driveway, just opposite the main house. In our absences it was occupied by Rosalind Wilson, my older half sister, as well as frequent houseguests.

Champagne at the ocean, early 1950s.
Left to right: *the author's stepmother Elena Wilson and*
*half sisters Helen Miranda (*foreground*) and Rosalind Wilson (*behind*).*

Elena's thinking showed her usual consideration for others; her son and I gained much-needed privacy and were spared exposure to my father's late-night antics. Only occasionally, we heard the muffled swell of classical music emanating from the study during the early morning hours. Every summer evening, at my bedtime, our respective parents, in tandem or separately, would walk over from the main house to wish me and Henry an affectionate good night.

~~~~~

At one point, most likely in the spring of 1954, when I was sixteen, my father decided to hire a live-in secretary. He chose Anthony ("Tony") Whittier, an aspiring writer whom Rosalind had met in Boston through her job at Houghton Mifflin. Whittier came to Money Hill without his attractive wife—the job was for a limited term. He was a tall, clean-cut, soft-spoken young man. He didn't have much money and surely had to swallow some pride in choosing to become Wilson's humble amanuensis. In good weather he took his typewriter out to the sandpit behind our house, an odd place to work, I remember thinking. When I arrived home from Brooks School that June, Tony was in residence. He seemed to have ample free time when not copying my father's manuscripts, and we soon hit on the idea of going fishing together. One afternoon we rented a rowboat from old Mr. Eaton at the landing below his house on Gull Pond. Tony was wearing a turtleneck sweater and swimming trunks bearing what resembled a lifesaving insignia. I rowed us across Gull Pond and we headed through the narrow sluiceway into Higgins Pond, where the fish were more plentiful. Using worms as bait, we had scant luck: I caught one or two little yellow perch or sunfish; Tony nothing. He was kind enough, however, to remove my fish from the hook, a task I did not relish. Tony took the oars on the return trip across Gull Pond. By now it was getting late; the sky had become overcast, and a cold wind blew across the water. Tony was proving to be an unseasoned mariner—he rowed awkwardly, and then, when we had reached the middle of the pond, he abruptly let go of the oars. With some irritation, I told him to retrieve them. Little did I know that (1) the wind would quickly carry the oars away from our drifting rowboat and (2) Tony was a weak swimmer. He dutifully took off his sweater and plunged into the water. It soon became clear that there could be no question of his retrieving the fugitive oars, or even of regaining the boat; therefore I jumped into the water, in the shirt and long pants I was wearing. I accompanied him as he slowly and painfully side-stroked his way to the shore. The exhausted Tony and I, both shivering from the cold, walked around the pond to the Eaton house. (Mr. Eaton, a homespun Yankee whose family had lived on Gull Pond for many generations, took it all in stride; he would later recover the oars and boat after they swept ashore.) This sorry incident did little to boost my father and Elena's confidence in the feckless Tony, who was given his walking papers not long thereafter. He would return to that ill-fated afternoon in a short story he wrote later: "Gull Pond Is a Half-Mile Wide" (*Paris Review*, no. 13, Summer 1956, pp. 126–133). In it I am "Reuel," while the character based on the author is "Peter." Peter clearly feels ill-used by his heartless companion, ten years his junior, whose admiration he has hoped for. The story re-creates the place and the real events. Gull Pond, initially a "mineral turquoise blue," later seems "evil" to Peter. After he drops the oars and jumps from the boat, the water's "pale green-blue unconcern began to fill him with apprehension." While swimming, Peter feels tired and frightened; observing the clouds, he says to himself, "God, give me serenity!" After reaching the shore, he has the dry retches. The last line reads: "Peter didn't care what Reuel thought because now he knew what a man should fear." Whittier's story, as well as the events that inspired it, reflects the sinister aspect of Cape Cod nature that surfaces so persistently in Wilson's writing.

~~~~~~~~~

In 1952, not long after Adlai Stevenson's first defeat by Eisenhower, which my mother took very hard, she and Bowden, having sold their house in Portsmouth, Rhode Island, bought another one in Wellfleet. It was minutes by car from Money Hill, where my father was residing with his new wife. Adjacent to my mother's cranberry red main house stood a studio where we set up a Ping-Pong table in the main room. On the back side, facing an uninhabited stretch of forest, was a "secret" little room where she often did her writing in seclusion.[3] I enjoyed being able to shuttle back and forth between my parents' separate households. Although my parents did not see each other socially, my father would pay her an occasional visit to talk about me and my future. When I was staying with my mother and Bowden in the summer of 1955 (when my father was away), they would sometimes drive me up to Provincetown for an after-dinner drink at the Atlantic House or another bar with live music. Although underage, I never had trouble getting in. The Provincetown nightlife, with its all-female bands and transsexual performers, was quite an eye-opener. Only three years after buying it, the Broadwaters sold the red house in Wellfleet, and they moved to New York at the end of 1955. In April of the same year my mother finished *A Charmed Life* while staying on Capri in the Lorillards' villa (Louis and Elaine Lorillard were old friends from Newport, Rhode Island). It is clear from my mother's letters to me toward the end of the time in Wellfleet that she was tiring of the summer whirl: different party, same faces. Having gathered Wellfleet's flora and fauna for *A Charmed Life*, she clearly realized that it was time to move on.

Throughout my years in Wellfleet two families, the Macdonalds and the Jenckses, played an important role in my life. Dwight Macdonald and Gardner Jencks, and their respective spouses, Nancy and Ruth, had first met my parents during the 1930s. Their sons Michael (Mike) Macdonald and Charles (Charlie) Jencks were almost exactly my age, and we kept constant company during the long hot Cape Cod summers. Charlie would enroll in Brooks School the year after I did, and we both graduated from it, I one year earlier. All three of us would meet again at Harvard.

I remember the Macdonalds renting a lonely house with surrounding veranda called Four Winds. It was set next to a cold-storage plant for fish on a bluff in North Truro overlooking Cape Cod Bay. Dimly I see myself there with my mother at an evening gathering, while a violent windstorm raged in the background. The year was 1945. The following two summers the Macdonalds rented the Dickinsons' house on Cove Road next to the inner Wellfleet bayside. Edwin Dickinson was Wellfleet's most prestigious, and original, artist; he had moved there from Provincetown in the early forties. While the Macdonalds were renting their main house, the Dickinsons moved to their annex next door, where Ed had his studio. At low tide Dwight Macdonald would range over the mudflats, picking up oysters and consuming them on the spot. When invited to partake, I refused; I acquired a taste for oysters later. I remember many happy games of Famous Authors (the card game) and Monopoly there. Since then I have gradually made my way through some of the Famous Authors' fifty-two books, although I'm ashamed to admit that I still haven't gotten to Washington Irving, or John Greenleaf Whittier. The Monopoly sessions, often extended over days, were played with real passion. Toward the end of one epic contest, Dwight was reduced to one single dollar, so that he went bust when he landed on the Poor Tax square. There was no electricity at the Dickinsons'; lighting came from kerosene "Aladdin" lamps, which gave out an uncertain yellow light recalling the lighting effects in old movies. In the summer of 1947, a water heater in the kitchen ignited the curtains above it, causing a fire that almost completely destroyed the house. The Macdonalds were absent at the time. They would continue to rent elsewhere in Wellfleet over subsequent summers until they bought the house on Slough Pond in 1952. Jack Philips, the vendor, had fashioned it and others like it out of old army prefabs, which he had bought cheaply from the government. The house, slate gray with blue-trimmed windows, had its own discreet charm. The little beach below it used to abound in tiny gray frogs half an inch long; I once shot with my .22 rifle a large snake lurking in the water under the branches of a felled pine tree there, and the skeleton remained, a memento mori, for several years thereafter. The pond itself, whose velvet waters shine sparkling blue on a sunny day, gray or black under overcast or rainy skies, is surrounded by green, gently undulating hillocks. The Atlantic Ocean is only minutes away by foot, as are Herring, Horseleech, Higgins, and Gull Ponds. Access to these is almost exclusively by dirt roads. The Macdonalds usually bathed in the nude at their beach, as did their friends. One day, a neighbor who owned property on the other side of the pond—the same man who had been following Nancy Macdonald's swims through binoculars—called the police to complain about the Macdonalds' nudity. A policeman duly appeared. After hearing him out, Dwight invited him to take his clothes off and enjoy the water. As parents, Dwight and Nancy were ultrapermissive. Adepts of progressive education, they taught their children, Mike and Nicky, to call them by their first names. Their theory of parenting excluded structure and discipline; therefore the boys grew up unencumbered by bourgeois mealtimes and bedtimes. They were also spared the ministrations of sitters and had to accompany their parents to late-night parties sometimes far from home. It often happened that Mike would slip away and, guided by a sure homing instinct, return to his house in the early morning hours. One summer the boys subsisted for weeks on a diet of peanut butter and jelly sandwiches. My mother was scandalized by this.

My father was not at ease around Dwight Macdonald. He had much the same opinion about Dwight's good sense, or lack thereof, as did Leon Trotsky, who is alleged to have said: "Every man has a right to be stupid on occasion but Comrade Macdonald abuses it." (Although Trotsky did say that Dwight was "stupid," the actual quote cannot be documented. See the introduction to *MT*, xiv.) Unquestionably my father resented Dwight's close friendship with my mother. After the divorce, she sold Dwight her car, a Chevrolet sedan, for one dollar. This rankled with my father, since he had given her the money to buy it. Several different people remember him angrily shouting on chance encounters with Dwight: "You're driving my car!" My father also probably disapproved of what he saw as Dwight's verbal truculence and ideological extremism. I, on the other hand, found Dwight to be the most stimulating adult I knew. His willingness to listen to others, even children, his love of good-natured partisan debate, his egalitarian views and gentle disposition (the latter so consistent with his pacifist views), his bombastic hyperboles—all sharply distinguished him from my own uptight parents. In Nancy's case, a soft-spoken, deferent manner concealed inner strength. When I was in my middle teens, the Macdonald marriage fell apart—the result, said my mother, of a naïve pact they made to pursue sexual fulfillment with other partners. I would assume that my mother gleaned this information from one or both of the partners. Their decision was almost certainly ideologically motivated, free love being a tenet of some brands of non-Marxist socialism. Dwight would lead a less bohemian life with his second wife, Gloria. In any case he totally disappeared from the Wellfleet scene, leaving the house to Nancy, who never did remarry. Having sunk most of her own money into Dwight's magazine *Politics* (a noble experiment that folded after three years), Nancy devoted the rest of her life to the forgotten victims of the Spanish Civil War. Her Spanish Relief Committee, based in New York, brought help to hundreds of Republican refugees who were living under adverse conditions in France. Nancy showed by her own example that a single individual can make a difference—a fact that most of us disbelieve or choose to ignore.

Ruth and Gardner Jencks knew everyone who was anyone in Wellfleet, Truro, and Provincetown. Gardner, who had begun as a concert pianist and then moved on to composition, was financially independent and therefore able to follow his own inner drummer. He was much given to abstract thinking and had evolved his own ultramodern theory of composition that totally abolished harmony. During his life very little of his music was performed outside his studio on Bound Brook Island in Wellfleet. Despite his lack of worldly success, Gardner was upbeat and cheerful, although he could frown when confronted with an opinion that irritated his sense of moral rectitude or logic. For many years Gardner was the only serious musician who summered in Wellfleet (later on Truro had Arthur Burger); doubtless my father sought him out for that very reason. Ruth (née Pearl, originally a biologist) came from a distinguished medical family in Baltimore. She concentrated most of her zany energy on her two children, Charlie and Penny, her husband, and the numerous guests they entertained. She was tall and lanky with long, somewhat curly dark hair and a striking hatchet nose. She affected baggy peasant-style outfits, Mexican silver-ringed belts, and other bangles. Despite her (literally) bohemian appearance and casual approach to housekeeping, her underlying ethos was bourgeois. She and Gardner were two of the most stable adults I knew. They drank in moderation, provided well for their children, and appreciated the value of solid material property. In 1939 the Jenckses built a house and adjacent studio (later another studio was added to the garage) on the deserted, moor-like landscape of Bound Brook Island. The house, accessible only by dirt road, commands a stunning view of Cape Cod Bay. The beach is a fifteen-minute walk away, over a dirt road and then a path that works its way through a locust grove unexpectedly carpeted in lush grass; the path then emerges onto an exposed patch of sand, dotted with saw grass, and finally threads its way through a gauntlet of prickly red and white wild rosebushes. The beach itself, now rocky, was sandier when I was growing up, and the dunes, now eroded to almost nothing, made for exciting jumping. One vertiginous leap landed you close to the seaweed-marked high tide line. The Jenckses often held beach picnics here, which began about seven, well before sundown, and ended late, by the light of a driftwood fire.

With all of Ruth's daffy eccentricity and Gardner's so-serious pursuit of music and logical abstraction, the family operated smoothly according to a schedule of leisurely activity. Gardner, with his arsenal of Steinways, sought the single perfect atonal chord in his monastic studio. Ruth went about her more cheerful pursuits: shopping, cooking, ferrying children, her own and other people's, to and from ocean, pond, and bay. (Actually she had some talent for painting, as can be seen from the evocative landscapes that she produced after her children left home.)

From a very early age I was a frequent guest in the Jencks house. Penny Jencks recalls an amusing incident that happened when she, age six, was designated to babysit me, age two, and her brother Charlie, slightly younger. We were given a kind of picnic in Penny's upstairs bedroom while our parents were having drinks outside, in front of the house. Penny describes me as "a very sensitive boy who would cry at the drop of a hat." On those days when I was left at the Jenckses' to "play" with Charlie, I seem to have spent much time in Ruth's arms, crying for my mother. During the late afternoon in question, Penny took the job of keeping me entertained "VERY seriously." She writes:

> Each time you would go to the window and call out to your mother,
> I had to lead you back to the "picnic" and try to persuade you that
> we were having fun. So, I hit upon the idea of doing a somersault,
> which I had only recently learned to do, to amuse you. You were not
> amused at all, in fact you looked quite startled and on the verge of
> tears by it. So Charlie, who must have been barely 2 decided that HE

would do one too . . . to stave off the tears, but unfortunately he went plop into your applesauce, which splattered all about, got you covered with it and just made a huge mess. You took one look at the chaos and totally lost it . . . ran to the window and screamed for your mother, who came running up the stairs to rescue you.

(Letter from Penny Jencks to the author, July 6, 2005)

In a pine copse near the dirt road Charlie and I later built some quite weatherproof "forts" out of branches, whence we would repair in time of rain. We also played the role of Israeli (or was it Polish?) motorcycle troops while ranging over Bound Brook on our bikes. Sometimes Penny, her best friend (another tomboy called Jenny), Charlie, and I would shut ourselves into the upstairs bathroom and tell ghost stories in the dark. Keeping us in taut suspense, Penny did most of the telling. Because she was a few years older than we boys she exercised a certain moral authority. As a result of her suasions, we too grew to scorn "dainty ladies" and their affectations.

Before dinner Gardner prepared hors d'oeuvres, usually sliced salami and cheese on Triscuits, and drinks would be served. During the day, we young people snacked on a liberal supply of Fig Newtons. The Jenckses liked children and treated them as equals in conversation. They were sometimes critical of my behavior, but with justification. I had the habit of moving unpredictably, leaving in my wake an overturned lamp, a broken toy, or a shattered glass. By early adolescence I had become such a menace to the Jenckses' household that they gave me a series of lectures on the evils of clumsiness. I believe the word was passed on to my father. The lesson was salutary in that it taught me to think before acting. The Jenckses later found their portraits in Jane and Warren Coe, two central characters in my mother's novel *A Charmed Life.* Their daughter Penny thinks they were depressed by the book and "felt betrayed, though they would not admit it, having too great an admiration for 'ART.'" In fact Dwight Macdonald, who had not been amused to find himself in an earlier novel, *The Oasis*, complained to my mother that Gardner came off in the novel as *better* than he really was. I should point out that my mother strenuously denied that her characters were mere copies of real-life originals. They were, she asserted, fictitious personae who spoke and thought as the real models *might have*. After finishing *A Charmed Life*, she showed me a list that she had compiled enumerating expressions and idioms suitable for Warren Coe but not to be found in Gardner Jencks' equally quirky discourse.

Although they seemed not to envy others' worldly successes, the Jenckses were very proud of their large circle of friends, some of whom were famous. This, along with their generosity of spirit, may account for the sustained close relations with both of my parents. After their divorce, my parents and their new spouses were frequent guests (although never at the same time) of the Jenckses: for swimming, drinks, and dinner parties. In the early days of their marriage, my mother and Bowden visited the Jenckses on weekends at their winter house in Westport, Connecticut, and I remember spending a school vacation there when both sets of my parents were abroad. Penny also remembers that I stayed with them at the time of my parents' divorce. Later the Jenckses would move to Washington, D.C., in order to breathe the zeitgeist of the new Kennedy administration. Arthur Schlesinger Jr., the American historian and Wellfleet summer dweller, had been named one of President Kennedy's advisers. My mother and her last husband, James West, would stay with both the Jenckses and the Schlesingers when on various trips to Washington.

The Jenckses' admiration for my father led to their being, albeit willingly, exploited by him. Gardner was a useful source of information on music, as well as modern philosophy. Penny remembers them having passionate discussions "about Wittgenstein, Russell, Whitehead, Boas, & all the rest, on the beach or taking walks or even over drinks" (letter cited above, July 6, 2005). During the last two decades of his life my father found in the Jenckses a receptive audience on summer afternoons. After finishing work, he would ring them up and invite himself over for a swim and, inevitably, drinks afterward. Another variant: my father would ask them to arrange for us to swim at a pond beach belonging to the Hustons, relatives of the Jenckses who lived in Wellfleet but whom my father never saw socially. My friend Charlie Jencks was a frequent visitor at the Money Hill house. One day when he was about sixteen he stopped by while I was absent. My father saw him and invited him into his study, where he came right to the point: what was Charlie's future calling to be? Charlie answered confidently, "a writer." This response surprised my father and those who heard about it later. Charlie was then known as an athletic, happy-go-lucky guy with an irresistible appeal for girls his own age and younger. Today Charles is a well-known writer on postmodern art and architecture.

During the four years I spent at Harvard I often made the drive from Cambridge to Wellfleet for weekends or a week or two in the summer. By this time my father had found the Cape holiday-time rituals both tedious and distracting. He loved Upstate New York for its unspoiled green landscape, broad horizons, and natural curiosities, such as Tug Hill and the Dry Sugar River. He also respected its unsophisticated inhabitants for being "real" people living "real" lives. As he told me more than once, the people who had settled New York State had come west to escape the confined spaces of New England. As mentioned earlier, Elena, who had finally cast anchor on Cape Cod after a long gypsy life on two continents, did not share her husband's passion for Talcottville, nor did I. Therefore she and I (to a lesser degree) and sundry other volunteer chauffeurs relayed my father back and forth between Wellfleet and Talcottville. Without his daunting presence, the Wellfleet house filled up with young people, friends of mine, and my half sisters, Rosalind and Helen. Elena's kitchen became a haven for impromptu visitors. Here the burning issues of the sixties were debated in a spirit of good fellowship induced by Elena's moderating presence. The carousing, if it became that, ended quickly enough, for Elena retired early. One summer, while my father and Elena were both absent and the house was rented to Jason and Barbara Epstein, I arranged for a friend of mine from Harvard, Lowell Edmunds, and his girlfriend to stay in the cottage. Lowell wrote in a note to me in Cambridge (where I was working part-time in the Widener Library and taking a summer course on modern French theater) that he couldn't decide whether Wellfleet was "the Slough of Bliss" or "the Bower of Despond." He had a point: I have seen Wellfleet bring out the best, and the worst, in my parents, myself, and others. Perhaps the Cape's sights, smells, and dolce far niente appeal too exclusively to the senses.

As I grew older, my relationship with my father improved. He got me interested in learning Russian—if only, initially, to read Tolstoy in the original. I grew to share with him a keen interest in acquiring new languages and experiencing new cultures. He made sure to be in Wellfleet when I stopped there, as I always did, on trips back and forth to Brooks School; Cambridge, Massachusetts; Europe; California; the Midwest; and finally Canada. Before I left we would speak of my interests and plans, he would give me a check, and then, the morning of my departure, he would come out onto the front porch clad in his pajamas and dress-

Family portrait in Wellfleet, circa 1958. Left to right: *the author, Helen Miranda, Elena Wilson, Henry Thornton (her son), his wife Daphne (Sellars), Edmund Wilson. Photo by Rollie McKenna.*

ing gown to say good-bye. On one occasion the trip to California ended two miles up the road when the wheels fell off the gray, beat-up, tail-finned Chevrolet that Elena had bought when she was learning to drive and had now passed on to me. The notoriously unreliable Wellfleet mechanics had forgotten to machine-tighten the wheels after taking them off for a brake check.

Over the years I had many tête-à-tête conversations (invariably one-sided) with my father, usually in his study or while I was driving him on long-distance trips. He usually spoke about his own work in progress. By doing this with family members and friends he refined his ideas before he actually began writing. Sometimes he would deliver an admonitory lecture on behavior. For example, he warned me that if I cut a professor's classes at college I would probably incur his enmity (such indeed is often the case, as I have found from my own experience teaching). On the subject of sex he took a decidedly Victorian stance, hardly consistent with the licentiousness of *his* behavior as detailed in his journals. He spoke of sexually promiscuous women as "having led a long life of crime." Nonetheless he idealized a few such women with whom he had fallen in love. In brief, his was a double standard. The idealization of women, he emphatically stated, was exclusive to Western culture and quite foreign to the Orient, for example, whose languages have no word that corresponds to our "love." He was on shaky ground here, but he was referring specifically to the tradition of courtly love that goes back to the Middle Ages in Europe. To me, an adolescent boy, his view of sex was as simplistic as it was dogmatic. The sole purpose of love, he pontificated, was marriage and children. Like his Puritan ancestors, and his idol Leo Tolstoy, my father maintained that the aim of sex was procreation, not recreation. When I was seventeen and on my way to Paris for a summer session at the Sorbonne, he gave me a short lecture in his Wellfleet study about the dangers of unguarded sex. The gist of it was (1) that I should never "knock a girl up" and (2) that I should under no circumstances get a venereal disease. He clearly apprehended, not without foundation, that I might succumb to the sexpots of Paris. All in all, he preferred writing about sex to talking about it. Interestingly enough, he talked very little about his earlier life, and when he did it was strictly anecdotal: a trip in an air force plane in Europe (in 1945) when one of the two engines failed and the pilot had to land in the English Channel; Ernest Hemingway getting himself outboxed by a boy in a Paris gym; swimming in a little river in Russia (in 1935) to the amazement of his Russian companions, none of whom knew how to swim at all. When I once told my father that I would like to take a trip to Saint-Pierre and Miquelon, the French islands off the south coast of Newfoundland, he remembered Harry Kemp, years before, speaking of his desire to go there. Harry had heard that wine was delivered to one's doorstep there along with the morning milk, an idea he found very appealing. My father put the best of himself into his writing, but his correspondence with me shows him to have been an involved parent.

Coming back to Wellfleet, as I do each spring, I return to a past that is fairly well preserved. Our white wooden cottage, Elena's Little House, still looks out on Route 6 from atop Money Hill. Supported underneath

The author prepares to clear tall grass from around the Wellfleet cottage, late 1990s.

by only three longitudinal beams, now sagging from the wear and tear of over 150 years, the floor inside is gradually sinking. Someday the house will need an expensive face-lift. In the meantime, its plain exterior remains graceful: hinted Doric columns rise at each corner; an elegant bay window looks out of the blue room so lovingly created by my stepmother. The ancient wooden eaves troughs, which were causing leaks on the inside, have both been torn away and not replaced. Maple and poplar trees (the latter reduced by old age and windstorms) tower overhead; wild rosebushes, wild blackberries, along with profuse honeysuckle and other rampant vines trained on a now invisible rotten fence, encircle the backyard. The hardy daylilies, planted by Elena so long ago, bloom a vibrant orange in late June and July. The interior configuration of the house is just as it was: two rooms downstairs, a tiny kitchen, a bathroom; an attic, and a "studio" with three beds upstairs. Just before writing this, I got an anxious telephone call from some of our tenants, who, shortly after their arrival at the cottage, found a large snake curled up in the attic.

I surmise that it was a rat snake attracted by our mice; its access route has now been blocked.

Since my father's death, our part of the Cape has been experiencing a construction boom caused by an influx of city people, yuppies and old folks alike. If the Cape's unique landscape has been largely preserved up until now, it is thanks to the National Park and Seashore. Created by then-senator John F. Kennedy, and now underfunded, it has stood against a rising tide of greedy developers and rampant commercialism. Even within the park's limits, however, property owners have been building new houses (expressly forbidden) disguised as "studios." Outside the park, almost every paved turnoff from a tarred road hides a new subdivision. Like a juggernaut, the Cape building boom sweeps over the land, leaving in its wake an ever-expanding leisure infrastructure. Route 6, where our dog slept on sunny days, grudgingly to move for the occasional oncoming car, is now a scene of summer gridlock.

Nonetheless, roaming the same backwoods dirt road where my father took me for nature walks, I even make a few discoveries of my own: a quite tame dainty-legged fox, a Baltimore oriole asleep on a branch looking like a gleaming orange feather duster. My childhood friends Mike Macdonald and Charlie Jencks have inherited their parents' houses and return, as do I, for brief summer visits before or in between tenants. When we meet, it is both gratifying and comfortable to re-create the past. Most of the familiar faces have either died or left the Cape for good.

CONCLUSION

When Helen Wilson, my half sister and neighbor in the big house next door, and I, and those who still remember Edmund Wilson are gone, I wonder how much of him will remain here. Not much, I suspect. The only literary tourists who come to Wellfleet these days are writers who seek not a nostalgic communion with the past but a chic downscale resort. To be sure, the old Cape will remain, immutably fixed on the pages of my father's journals, where it shimmers ghostly and remote, throwing into relief the writer's own conflicted personality. The diary seascapes of Provincetown and the pondscapes of Wellfleet, sensually impressionistic yet coldly realistic, show his power as a descriptive artist. These telling glimpses fix isolated moments of perceived experience seen against the continuum of ever-renewing nature. In *The Forties* entry commemorating Katy Dos Passos my father speaks of a sense of community with Cape Cod locals and old friends who still live there. He writes:

> All the parties, the days at the beach, the picnics, the flirtations, the drinking spells, the interims of work between trips, the moldy days of winter by stoves, the days of keeping going on a thin drip or trickle of income, stories and articles, bursts of prosperity, local property and cars, bibelots from Mexico or elsewhere, pictures and figures by local artists accumulated in P'town front rooms, walled in against the street—that was what our life had been when we had dedicated ourselves to the Cape, to the life of the silver harbor—and all the love and work that had gone with it, that we had come there to keep alive. (*Forties*, 221)

Looking back at my father's past on Cape Cod, about which I knew relatively little (aside from my own firsthand recollections) when I undertook this project, he and the other participants appear like black-and-white figures against a slightly faded background of harbor, sea, weather-beaten houses, and endless sand dunes. In his later journals my father evokes Provincetown in the twenties and thirties with nostalgia, but that nostalgia came with retrospect. Recording his experience, he framed the place and its restless bands of artists and writers with critical aplomb. When he moved to Wellfleet with his third wife, Mary Mc-Carthy, he already had a long-standing attachment to Cape Cod. The place was a familiar quantity—and when it was a matter of long-term residency he always preferred the known to the unknown. The Wellfleet house gave him ample working space, and the tiny local community, three or four hundred permanent residents in those days, made no demands on him. After his remarriage to Elena, he became gradually disenchanted with the rapidly changing Cape, while his enthusiasm for upper New York State and its tradition-directed way of life exponentially increased.

From the time of childhood and adolescence, when she had spent so many happy summer days in Provincetown, his daughter, my half sister Rosalind, had a special affection for Cape Cod. An indefatigable swimmer, she prized its beaches, while the summertime whirl appealed to her extroverted and boisterously ebullient nature. In 1968, however, Rosalind made a decision to live permanently in Talcottville. She ended up buying a charming old wooden house there that belonged to the Loomis sisters, old family friends who were related to the Talcotts. She named it "Villa Rosalinda." Living just down the street from her father's stone house, she began a new life near her "magician" father, but not necessarily in his shadow. When he died, she inherited his house, which she found too large to live in. (Rosalind never married and always lived alone, albeit surrounded by a large menagerie of dogs and cats.) A well-to-do family from Washington, D.C., bought the stone house from her, and they have treated it well. Rosalind's choice to cast last anchor in Talcottville was judicious. There was little reason to go back to Wellfleet—Elena and her daughter had become the mistresses of Money Hill, while Rosalind's oldest Cape friends, the Chavchavadzes and the Givens, were rapidly succumbing to sickness and old age. I, for my part, occasionally returned to Wellfleet in the summer, but rented accommodations there. After Elena's death I and my family took occupancy of the Money Hill cottage.

As already mentioned, my mother, Mary McCarthy, had two sojourns on Cape Cod: the four years of on-and-off residency with my father, and the seasonal time spent there with Bowden Broadwater from 1952 to

1955. Once close to Adelaide Walker, and friendly with Anna Matson, she saw little of them when she returned in the fifties. She had a desire for acceptance that Cape Cod society could not completely satisfy. Some of Wilson's friends there, particularly the Chavchavadzes and the Givens, showed little enthusiasm for her when she returned with a new husband. The Jenckses welcomed her back, only later to discover their likenesses in *A Charmed Life*, and the friendship subsequently dwindled. With her fourth and last husband, James West, my mother took up summertime residency on the Maine coast. In 1967 West, a Mainer, bought a grand house in Castine, a well-manicured historical town that overlooks Penobscot Bay. Although Maine's rocky seascape and rolling hillsides doubtless appealed to her eye, it is unlikely that my mother would have settled in Maine, or earlier on Cape Cod for that matter, had her partners, first my father and then West, not taken the initiative. To be sure, she chose to return to Cape Cod in the early fifties, but she soon realized that natural beauty could not substitute for a monotonous and uninviting social scene. Curiously enough, both of my parents ended up alienated by the déjà vu quality of the Cape's predictable social patterns. My mother was a cosmopolitan intellectual who craved the vitality and excitement of a major city—New York up until 1960, and Paris from 1962 until her death in 1989. Wilson, on the other hand, with the onset of middle age, increasingly saw himself in the role of a country squire—first in Wellfleet, then in Talcottville. It is ironic that McCarthy would end up spending the summers in Castine, Maine, where the bucolic meets suburban gentility, with a husband who also had squirish aspirations.

For me, the Cape Cod landscape remains inseparably linked to my parents. It always conjures up their presence, reminding me that my life with them has so often been filtered through its changing prism. My re-exploration of this, their world, has brought me closer to them. By writing this, I have renewed my own memories, while, I hope, doing something to perpetuate theirs.

NOTES

CHAPTER 1. THE BACKGROUND

1. A new coast guard (to use the newer terminology) station was built down the beach from the old one. Both the old and the new figure in Susan Glaspell's play *The Outside*, first done by the Provincetown Players in 1917.

CHAPTER 2. EDMUND WILSON'S PROVINCETOWN
IN THE TWENTIES AND THIRTIES

1. The most interesting of these is the unjustly forgotten *Love Among the Cape Enders* (1931). Its broad canvas surveys Provincetown in its halcyon days. Many of the quirky characters are modeled on real people, the most famous of whom is Eugene O'Neill (Bill Travis in the novel). All in all, Kemp creates a mock-epic, teeming with literary allusions as well as references to historical events (the visit of a Portuguese naval flotilla bearing wine to the Prohibition-deprived residents, the ugly confrontation between the local Ku Klux Klan and Catholics). All this plays out against a powerfully rendered natural background. Bathos turns to tragedy. Human passions, as intense as they are often misplaced, bring fulfillment to some, death to others. Sexual desire coexists with mystical philosophy. The "liberation" sought by the Cape Enders (read "Dead-Enders" for some), natives and bohemians alike, hardly makes them happy, but it affords us, the readers, an unforgettable view into a crazy exuberant world whose bubble was soon going to burst.

2. Susan Glaspell (1882–1948) came to Provincetown from the Midwest with her husband George Cram Cook in 1912; in 1914 they bought a house at 564 Commercial Street. The couple would also buy a farmhouse on Higgins Hollow Road in Truro (near the Millay rental of 1920). Glaspell then built on the property a tiny studio among the pines. Here, away from the Provincetown seasonal mayhem, she could concentrate on her writing. Cook, whom everyone called "Jig," was older than Susan and had left his previous wife and two children to begin a new life with Glaspell. A dynamo of manic energy, Cook wrote poetry, fiction, philosophical-political tracts; most important for posterity, he founded the Provincetown Players and then established it in New York. He spent his last years in Greece, whose culture, ancient and modern, irresistibly attracted him. He was accepted and revered by the local people around Delphi, where he settled. After his death in Greece in 1924, Glaspell wrote a romantic memoir, mostly about him, *Road to the Temple*. By far the better writer of the two, Glaspell is today best remembered for her hard-hitting plays. (The advice to turn to playwriting from fiction came from her hus-

band.) *The Outside* (1917) presents a haunting evocation of Provincetown's outer reaches. The one-act play's setting is a former lifesaving station modeled on the O'Neill house (which Wilson later rented). Its occupants are two unhappy women: Mrs. Patrick, a rich cosmopolitan whose husband has left her, and Allie Mayo (played by Glaspell in the first Provincetown Players production), the local woman she employs as a servant. Allie has lost her husband, a fisherman, at sea many years earlier. When the coastguardsmen bring the body of a drowned man into the house, both women are forced to confront the dead inertia of their lives. Their attitude contrasts with that of the homespun coastguardsmen, who must face death often, while having accepted the mission to save lives wherever possible. Face-to-face with the corpse on the floor, the women overcome the silence that has stifled their communication with each other and the world outside. They speak of the trees that sustain the land in its ongoing struggle with the ever-encroaching sea. Allie senses the oncoming spring, which promises hope to this desolate, hurtful place. At the end, when the coastguardsmen remove the dead man, even Mrs. Patrick acknowledges the Outside (i.e., the Atlantic), not just as a taker of life, but as a challenge to the living.

One of Glaspell's best novels, *Fugitive's Return* (1929), also shows a lonely, heartbroken woman against a Cape Cod landscape. The overall moral is similar to the play's: it involves transcending self-centered suffering in favor of an active commitment to lived life. By advocating female solidarity and mutual assistance over heterosexual love, the novel bears a distinct feminist message. It traces the odyssey of Irma-Lee Shroeder, an Iowan, who moves with her architect husband to a Cape Cod community like Truro (where Cook and Glaspell had bought an old farmhouse). After the heroine's husband leaves her, their young daughter dies. The story begins with Irma-Lee in a catatonic state of grief and planning suicide. She is saved by her sister, who sends her off to Greece with the passage and papers of another woman. The Grecian interlude helps to restore her faith in life. While in Greece, she remembers her Cape Cod house, looking out on "The Wellfleet Woods." By restoring the old former parsonage, its vineyard, and the garden with "white and purple iris, lilacs," she has felt part of "an older pre-war way of life." She will ultimately return to Cape Cod, bringing with her Constantina, a Greek country girl who once succumbed to the advances of a shepherd boy. Rejected by her lover, she has become the object of community scorn. The American woman rescues Constantina from a mob of locals who are threatening to lynch her. Both landscapes, Cape Cod and Delphi, orchestrate Irma-Lee's alienation from herself and the outside world. For a while she has felt happy in Greece as the result of her romantic friendship with John Knight, an enthusiast of Greek culture and history. In the end, however, the future will center around Irma-Lee's and Constantina's lives together on Cape Cod. Glaspell's last published work, the novel Judd Rankin's *Daughter* (1945) moves along an Iowa–Provincetown axis. In his politics, one of the characters (Steve) strongly ressembles Dos Passos. After the novel's publication, Katy Dos Passos stopped speaking to Glaspell (Ben Zvi, 390).

3. Hawthorne was the author of *Salt House* (New York: Frederick Stokes Co., 1934), an unjustly forgotten novel that records the ebb and flow of life on Provincetown's outer edges. Although it revolves around a city (here New York)–country (the Lower Cape) axis, the novel focuses mostly on a duneside house whose location recalls Peaked Hill, where the author herself lived. The nearby town of "Blackwell" is modeled on Provincetown. Judith, the first-person narrator, a young divorced woman who follows her instincts and lives life to the fullest, records her experience over the course of a single summer and early fall. The fast-paced narrative relates the dilemma of a woman in love with two men: Philip Hatfield, a narcissistic painter who returns to her after a long absence, and Rake Basque, a nineteen-year-old aspiring writer and pacifistic rebel to whom she is irresistibly attracted. (Both lovers ultimately prove to be ambivalent in their sexual orientation.) On two occasions the narrator and Rake take an "on the road" journey to New York in sequences uncannily reminiscent of Jack Kerouac's later novel. Because of the rambling narrative and the nonconformist attitudes of the protagonists, Hawthorne's writing evokes a beat generation avant la lettre. At the time, however, Harry Kemp and other freewheeling Provincetonians had no difficulty in finding themselves on the novel's pages. By the finale, the narrator has separated from both lovers after alternately breaking and renewing her intimacy with each. Before saying a last good-bye she and Philip venture out to observe a forest fire that is ravaging the countryside around the town. They encounter "burning stumps concealed beneath the charred moss and fine hot powder of the holocaust" (275). The "Salt House," which has sheltered the narrator, now stands undermined by the storm tides and ready to fall into the sea "at once abandoned and vivid." The ending contains a feminist message of newly discovered inner resources. The narrator feels not abandoned but "powerful and content," though "the day behind lay unfulfilled and lonely"; "yet somehow it had been like music" (294). Because of its evocative description of landscape and the human drama in the narrator's emotional progress, *Salt House* has a freshness and scope that makes the story appealing to contemporary readers.

4. Robert Nathan (1894–1985), popular writer of fiction and poetry, was a part-time Truro resident in the forties and fifties. Cape Cod, which he renders in vivid and sensitive detail, appears in two of his novels, *Portrait of Jennie* (1940) and *The Seagull Cry* (1942). *Journal for Josephine* (1943) is a beautifully written semi-autobiographical diary of a summer the writer spent with his family in wartime Truro.

5. Anna Matson (1915–2003) would occupy the same house in the Wellfleet Woods until her death. It is idyllically located in a clearing just off a dirt road still called the King's Highway. After Norman Matson's death Anna married the *New*

Yorker writer Philip Hamburger. Anna never lost her good looks, gentle disposition, and an intrepid love of bathing in the Atlantic Ocean near her house.

6. The L'Engles' daughter, Camille ("Cammy"), was marrying Jack Hall, a young would-be bohemian from an affluent Long Island family. The marriage began with an inauspicious honeymoon that took place on a sailboat, whose crew the bride found irresistible, and vice versa. Jack's third wife, Jean Shay, was the daughter of Frank and Edie Shay. During Jack's long life as a full-time resident of Bound Brook Island in Wellfleet, he married four times. He was a reformed alcoholic—one episode of backsliding cost him his third marriage. He painted abstract pictures, designed a modern house, and worked as a handyman. He had a stable income of inherited money. Always faithful to his early left-wing ideals, Jack became a kind of genial patriarch in the company of his loving fourth wife, Martha (Marty), his daughter, and grandchildren.

7. Joris Ivans was a Dutch filmmaker who, with Hemingway as the scriptwriter and narrator, had made a documentary-style film, *The Spanish Earth*, in Civil War Spain. Archibald MacLeish, Lillian Hellman, and Dos Passos were listed as scenarists.

8. Thomas Blakeman, a painter, was to become president of the Provincetown Art Association in 1939.

9. Niles Spencer, the modernist painter, and his wife Betty. Within two years Niles would die and Betty would take up with a man called Ernest from one of the Portuguese fishing families. He worked as a janitor at the Atlantic House bar. Wilson and other old friends were horrified by this sleazy individual (see *Thirties*, 714).

10. Robert Morss Lovett, professor of English at Chicago, critic, fiction writer; he became editor of the *Dial* in 1919 and was later associate editor of the *New Republic*.

11. John Peale Bishop (1892–1944) was a fine poet who never quite realized the potential that other writers like Wilson and Alan Tate saw in him. Bishop spent the last six years of his life on Cape Cod. Echoes of its sea- and dunescape find resonance in his late poetry. "A Subject of Sea Change" (1942) affirms human dignity and love against the ever-changing give-and-take of the sea. Amidst destruction and disorder, the storms of history merge with the dropping bombs of World War II. The sea is linked with ancient Greek legend and art, but speaks with the voices of the dead, whose warnings will not be heard by the living. Only the poet, a Ulysses figure, may give order to the sea's ambiguous voice. The last stanza reads:

Death greets us all without civility
And every color of the sea is cold,
Even as now, when sensual greens advance
Under the contrary waves' propensity
Toward desirable blues. The sea is old,

Severe and cold, secret as antiquity
Under the scud of time. And the sea rants,
Storm-crossed, thunder-tossed,
Yet has a poetry so profound
That none but the unwaxed ear to the mast bound
Should hear it, or it may be the lost
Long-listening bodies of the drowned.

In another, short poem, "Colloquy with a King-Crab," Bishop finds his double on the bay shore. Framing the shore are "Dwarf pines: the wild plum on the wind-grassed shore / Shaken by autumn to its naked fruit; / Visions of bright winds across the bay. . . ." The "hideous," carapaced, black horseshoe crab, which has doggedly survived millennia in unchanged form, has crept into the poet's imagination:

. . . Though voiceless yet he says
That any monster may remain forever
If he but keep eyes, mind and claw intent
On the main chance, but not afraid to skulk.
This proletarian of the sea is not,
But scuttles, noble as the crocodile,
As ancient in his lineage. His name
Is not unknown to heaven. But his shell
Affords no edifice where I can creep
Though I consent like him to go on claws.

In *The Forties* Wilson describes the mating practices of horseshoe crabs observed on the bay beach in Wellfleet. The odd (to us) ritual involves the female depositing her eggs in a hole she digs at the surf line; subsequently she drags the smaller male to the hole so that he can fertilize them. All this reminds Wilson of Bishop's poem: "It was extraordinary to think of the creatures perpetuating themselves in their present form through all those thousands of years. It inspired one with a certain respect for them. He [John Bishop] seems to have found in them a symbol for his own later life: crawling about but never destroyed. I thought rather of the superficial differences, but underlying identity, between their sexual life and ours—driven on to carry on the species, resisting any attempt to interfere with it" (Forties, 271).

CHAPTER 3. EDMUND WILSON'S WELLFLEET, 1941–1972

1. Frank Rounds had already spent time in Moscow when Rosalind met him, through Houghton Mifflin, which had published his book *Window on Red Square*. The engagement soon fell through, however, torpedoed by the prospective groom's

tie-up with his mother. Rosalind was often attracted to men who were "light on their feet." She would never marry.

2. Edwin (Ed) O'Connor, a Boston radio broadcaster and newspaperman, originally met Wilson through his daughter Rosalind, who was working in Boston at Houghton Mifflin. From total obscurity, the impecunious O'Connor became famous, and rich, overnight with the publication of *The Last Hurrah* (1956), a novel loosely inspired by the life of Boston's rascal mayor James Curly. O'Connor got a lot of mileage out of his friendship with Wilson and Wilson's endorsements of his writing. Usually wary of opportunists, the latter was impressed by O'Connor's skills (which surpassed his own) as an amateur magician.

3. Gilbert Seldes (1893–1970) was a journalist, drama critic, editor, fiction writer, and social analyst, today best remembered for his writings on movies, television, and other forms of popular culture. A short, voluble, mercurial man, he had known Wilson since the twenties. The Seldeses had been coming to Truro in the summer since the forties. Marian was Gilbert's daughter.

CHAPTER 4. EDMUND WILSON'S CAPE COD POETRY

1. A reference to Chauncey's "monogrammed," "silver," "military" brushes also occurs in Wilson's notes for a novel he never wrote, one section of which was to take place in Provincetown. See *Forties*, 10–24, especially 21. Curiously, the Hacketts' daughter Wendy, who still lives in Provincetown, has no memory of these brushes, which seem to have left an indelible mark on Wilson's imagination.

2. Lewis Dabney's recent study *Edmund Wilson* refers to an unpublished limerick by the poet Conrad Aitkin. Its title is "The Minotaur and Mary." Aitkin had a house in Brewster on Cape Cod and knew the Wilsons. The limerick, written at the time of their marriage, pokes fun at the contentious couple:

But as for the Minotaur's doxy
Although you'd mix gin with her moxy
I'm afraid she's too subtle
For mortal rebuttal.

Dabney, regrettably, only paraphrases the last two lines: "Her 'maze' was 'beyond orthodoxy,' and she'd 'have to be done in by proxy'" (Dabney, 288). Wilson was clearly familiar with Aitkin's verses, since the title and the first two lines of his poem echo the original. The idea of re-creating Aitkin's minotaur with a new "Mary" must have appealed to Wilson's ludic imagination. The reference in his poem to Brewster gives a further link to the limerick's author.

3. The Cocytus, a real river in Greece, was associated with the Styx, the mythical boundary of the Underworld. Wilson probably saw his flirtation with Carroll as overshadowed by his own approaching death.

1. McCarthy's supposition concerning Jackson's agoraphobia, based on a reluctance to see alcohol, the forbidden fruit, consumed in large quantities, was probably mistaken. Nathan's stepson, Barry Bingham Jr. (who lives on Cape Cod), told me that Jackson often volunteered to serve as a bartender at his friends' parties. Bingham's mother, who was married to Nathan at the time McCarthy knew him in Truro, was the model for the narrator's wife in Nathan's semifictionalized diary, *Journal for Josephine* (1943), about his life in Truro during the war.

2. Perkins was a would-be backer for the new magazine, to be named *Critic*, that McCarthy wanted to found that year, 1953. The project never materialized, owing to a shortfall in funding. That summer Perkins had invited the Broadwaters to stay in her Vermont house in the foothills of the Green Mountains. They accepted, and rented their newly acquired Wellfleet house to the actor Montgomery Clift, a close friend of my mother's brother, the actor Kevin McCarthy. They tactfully thought it best to stay away from Wellfleet that first summer, while I was staying with my father and Elena. The story my mother alludes to is "The Appalachian Revolution," based on her experiences in Vermont that summer. Although she only spent a month there, she responded to its unspoiled landscape with its waterfalls, quarries, lakes, and wild animals. The story, one of her best, evokes nature with great sensitivity. It shows the incursion of crass, rich city folk into a pristine swimming place, heretofore used only by respectful locals. If she here shows the Vermont landscape in masterfully rendered detail, her next work of fiction, the novel *A Charmed Life*, barely sketches in the contours of a Cape-like setting.

3. The Jenckses were hospitable and generous to a fault, although Ruth's housekeeping was not her strong suit. On June 26, 1951, my mother wrote her sister-in-law Augusta McCarthy (Dabney) about a recent visit she and Bowden had had with the Jenckses in Wellfleet:

> We went to the Cape from Portsmouth Rhode Island last weekend, stayed with the Jenckses and had something of a gruesome experience gastronomically. The icebox was broken when we arrived, Ruth studying it rather pensively. We were offered a martini made with cold water; the cream was sour; there were no napkins, Kleenex, paper towels, or toilet paper. By the end of the visit I should have appreciated the archaic sight of a saucer under a cup. But there was a great deal of brilliant sun and serious conversation.

A few years later, a similar description of an erratically functioning household (The Coes') would surface in *A Charmed Life*.

4. Adelaide later recalled their times together when they were neighbors in Wellfleet. On September 12, 1963, she wrote McCarthy, now Mrs. James West:

I have been thinking of you these last days because I have been reading *The Group* [just published] and picking beach plums. Not many beach plums. I've grown lazy about such things, but it was so nostalgic up on the old dump road, I could positively see your neat and careful basket and mine full of leaves and twigs—a difference in our housekeeping characters that I fear was reflected in more important things. (Vassar)

5. The real model for this literary deus ex machina was Polly Boyden, Wilson and McCarthy's old Truro friend and occasional landlady. Polly had written a few slim volumes of poetry and an obscure allegorical novel (self-published), *The Pink Egg*. She claimed that George Orwell had plagiarized from her novel when he wrote *Animal Farm*. Actually she was best known not for her writing but for her flamboyant character, drinking, and far-left political ideas. It was said that her driving habits while under the influence mirrored her politics, that is, she kept to the left.

6. John Sinnot was inspired not only by McCarthy's current husband, Bowden Broadwater, but also by a family friend, James Parker. Charming and quirky, Parker was the upright scion of a landowning Rhode Island family. Serving in World War II as an army officer, he carried on the long-standing military tradition of his family, which numbered high-ranking officers over many successive generations. The younger Parker had something of a "crush" on McCarthy, and she was well aware of it. After the Broadwaters' divorce in 1961 Bowden and Jim Parker would maintain a close and staunch friendship that lasted until Jim's death in 2002. Despite some admirable traits (boyish good looks, shy diffidence, sensitivity, and devotion to his more purposive wife), the John Sinnot of the novel lacks vitality and psychological depth. Having read the novel—McCarthy showed him her work in progress, chapter by chapter—Bowden intuited that the days of their marriage were numbered. McCarthy did not draw on people with whom she was deeply in love when she sketched the portraits of her fictitious characters.

7. Margaret De Silver was a rich widow, to whom Wilson may once have proposed marriage. She had lived with the Italian anarchist exile Carlo Tresca, the editor of an anti-Fascist paper called the *Hammer*. He was assassinated in New York in the early forties, probably by the Mafia, contracted by the Mussolini regime. I remember Margaret as a very gracious, overweight woman. She spent several summers on the Cape in rented houses during the fifties.

8. Walther Mumm, Elena's German uncle, was a frequent visitor at the Wellfleet house. A charming, well-bred bachelor, Walther had been very popular with the ladies. Although at this point he was still working in New York as a wine salesman at Lehmann Brothers on Madison Avenue, his mental capacities had begun to deteriorate as a result of chronic ill health.

9. Vita was a beautiful, flirtatious Berliner who painted semiabstract landscapes; her husband Peter was in the import-export business. The couple had come to the

United States to escape Nazism. They shared ownership of a cottage on Slough Pond with Arthur Schlesinger Jr. and his family.

10. A reformed alcoholic, Jack Hall had recently ruined his third marriage by hitting the bottle again. His wife, the daughter of Frank and Edie Shay, had taken up with Bob Lessor, a plumber. Luckily Jack soon stopped drinking again and went on to marry, very happily, Marty Hall, whose previous husband's name was Rody (Monro) Hall (no relation to Jack).

11. In a letter he wrote to McCarthy on December 7, 1955, Wilson disavows having been "annoyed" by *A Charmed Life*; in fact he hasn't even seen a copy of it.

CHAPTER 6. REMEMBERING MY PARENTS AND CAPE COD

1. The print had been a wedding gift to my parents from Adelaide and Charles Walker. My father often spoke of its high monetary value. He gave it to me as a wedding present in 1963. Years later, when I had to have it restored, I found that it was a copy—one of several hundred sold by subscription to readers of the *Saturday Evening Post* in 1937. I recently discovered a better-preserved duplicate (same subscription) hanging in Moby Dick, a fast-food restaurant just down the road from us on Route 6. When asked about the picture a few years before her death, Adelaide Walker remembered that she and Charlie were very impecunious in the late thirties.

2. My mother asserted that she first met Broadwater at the New York apartment of the writer Niccolò Tucci, the very same day that she definitively left my father. Bowden, however, remembered meeting my mother (and father) at a New York party a few months earlier. The hostess was Jeanie Connolly (née Bakewell), who was separated from her husband, the British critic Cyril Connolly. Bowden seems to have commanded my mother's temporary attention by some bold conversational ploys.

3. She also wrote in the little front room in the main house, which once served as a sleeping place for visiting clergymen. Arthur Schlesinger Jr. wrote much of his *Age of Roosevelt*, part 1, in the studio's hidden room. My mother had offered it to him as a retreat from his cottage, packed with his large family, on Slough Pond (Gelderman, 182–183).

SELECTED BIBLIOGRAPHY

Ben-Zvi, Linda. *Susan Glaspell: Her Life and Times.* New York: Oxford University Press, 2005.

Bishop, John Peale. *Selected Poems.* Intro. Alan Tate. London: Chatto and Windus, 1960.

Blais, Marie-Claire. *American Notebooks: A Writer's Journey.* Trans. Linda Gaboriau. Burnaby, B.C., Canada: Talonbooks, 1996.

Brightman, Carol. *Writing Dangerously: Mary McCarthy and Her World.* New York: Clarkson Potter, 1992.

Carr, Virginia Spencer. *Dos Passos: A Life.* New York: Doubleday & Co., 1984.

Castronovo, David. *Edmund Wilson.* New York: Fredrick Ungar Publishing Co., 1984.

Castronovo, David, and Janet Groth. *Critic in Love: A Romantic Biography of Edmund Wilson.* Berkeley, Calif.: Shoemaker Hoard, 2005.

Dabney, Lewis. *Edmund Wilson: A Life in Literature.* New York: Farrar Straus and Giroux, 2005.

Edwards, Agnes. *Cape Cod Old and New.* Boston: Houghton Mifflin Company, 1918.

Egan, Leona Rust. *Provincetown as a Stage: Provincetown, The Provincetown Players and the Discovery of Eugene O'Neill.* Orleans, Mass.: Parnassus Imprints, 1994.

Engel, Monroe. "An Exemplary Edmund Wilson." *Yale Review* 76.3 (1987): 323–333.

Finch, Robert, ed. *A Place Apart: A Cape Cod Reader.* New York: W. W. Norton and Co., 1993.

Gelderman, Carol. *Mary McCarthy: A Life.* New York: St. Martin's Press, 1988.

Glaspell, Susan. *Fugitive's Return.* New York: Frederick A. Stokes Co., 1929.

———. *Judd Rankin's Daughter.* Philadelphia and New York: J. B. Lippincott Company, 1945.

———. *Plays.* Ed. C.W.E. Bigsby. Cambridge: Cambridge University Press, 1987.

———. *The Road to the Temple.* New York: F .A. Stokes Co., 1927.

Hapgood, Hutchins. *A Victorian in the Modern World.* Seattle: University of Washington Press, 1972.

Hardy, Willene S. *Mary McCarthy.* New York: Fredrick Ungar Pub. Co, 1981.

Kazin, Alfred. "The Great Anachronism: A View from the Sixties." In *An Edmund Wilson Celebration*, ed. John Wain. Oxford: Phaidon Press, 1978.

Kemp, Harry. *Love Among the Cape Enders.* New York: The Macaulay Co., 1931.

Kiernan, Frances. *Seeing Mary Plain: A Life of Mary McCarthy.* New York: W. W. Norton and Co., 2000.

Macdonald, Michael C. D. "The Admirable Minotaur of Money Hill." In *Edmund Wilson: Centennial Reflections.* Princeton, N.J.: Princeton University Press, 1997. 154–168.

McCarthy, Mary. *A Charmed Life.* New York: Harcourt Brace Jovanovich, 1955, 1982.

———. *The Seventeenth Degree.* New York: Harcourt Brace Jovanovich, 1967.

Meigs, Mary. *Lily Briscoe: A Self Portrait.* Vancouver: Talonbooks, 1981.

Meyers, Jeffrey. *Edmund Wilson: A Biography.* Boston: Houghton Mifflin Company, 1995.

Moffett, Ross. *Art in the Narrow Streets: The First Thirty-Three Years of the Provincetown Art Association.* Provincetown: Cape Cod Pilgrim Memorial Association, 1989.

Nathan, Robert. *Journal for Josephine.* New York: Alfred A. Knopf, 1943.

Shay, Edith, and Frank Shay, eds. *Sand in Their Shoes: A Cape Cod Reader.* Boston: Houghton Mifflin Company, 1951.

Thoreau, Henry David. *Cape Cod.* New York: W. W. Norton and Company, 1951.

Vorse, Mary Heaton. *Time and the Town: A Provincetown Chronicle* Provincetown: The Cape Cod Pilgrim Memorial Association, 1942 (reissued 1990). 1990.

Whalen, Richard. *Truro: The Story of a Cape Cod Town.* XLibris Corporation, 2002.

White, Robert L. *John Peale Bishop.* New York: Twayne Publishers, 1966.

Wilson, Edmund. *The American Earthquake: A Documentary of the Twenties and Thirties.* Garden City, N.Y.: Anchor, 1958.

———. *Edmund Wilson: The Man in Letters.* Ed. and intro. David Castronovo and Janet Groth. Athens, Ohio: Ohio University Press, 2001.

———. *The Fifties: From Notebooks and Diaries of the Period.* Ed. and intro. Leon Edel. New York: Farrar Straus and Giroux, 1986.

———. *Five Plays.* London: W. H. Allen, 1954.

———. *The Forties: From Notebooks and Diaries of the Period.* Ed. and intro. Leon Edel. New York: Farrar Straus and Giroux, 1983.

———. *Letters on Literature and Politics, 1912–1972.* Ed. Elena Wilson. Intro. Daniel Aaron. Foreword by Leon Edel. New York: Farrar Straus and Giroux, 1977.

———. *Night Thoughts.* New York: Farrar Straus and Cudahy, 1953.

———. *The Shores of Light: A Literary Chronicle of the Twenties and Thirties.* New York: Farrar Straus and Young, 1952.

———. *The Sixties: The Last Journal, 1960–1972.* Ed. and intro. Lewis Dabney. New York: Farrar Straus and Giroux, 1993.

———. *The Thirties: From the Notebooks and Diaries of the Period.* Ed. and intro. Leon Edel. New York: Farrar Straus and Giroux, 1980.

———. *The Twenties: From Notebooks and Diaries of the Period.* Ed. and intro. Leon Edel. New York: Farrar Straus and Giroux, 1975.

Wilson, Reuel K. "Edmund Wilson's Cape Cod Landscape." *Virginia Quarterly Review* 80.1 (2004): 100–113.

———. "Growing Up with Edmund Wilson and Mary McCarthy." *Paris Review* 153 (Winter 1999–2000): 237–251.

Wilson, Rosalind B. *Near the Magician: A Memoir of My Father.* New York: Grove Weidenfeld, 1989.

Wreszin, Michael, ed. *A Moral Temper: The Letters of Dwight Macdonald.* Chicago: Ivan R. Dee, 2001.

———. *A Rebel in Defense of Tradition: The Life and Politics of Dwight Macdonald.* New York: Basic Books, 1994.

INDEX

Page numbers in **bold** indicate illustrations.